STUDIES IN RELIGIOUS FUNDAMENTALISM

Also by Lionel Caplan

LAND AND SOCIAL CHANGE IN EAST NEPAL
ADMINISTRATION AND POLITICS IN A NEPALESE TOWN
CLASS AND CULTURE IN URBAN INDIA

Studies in Religious Fundamentalism

Edited by
Lionel Caplan

Reader in Anthropology
School of Oriental and African Studies
University of London

MACMILLAN

First edition 1987
Reprinted 1990

Published by
MACMILLAN ACADEMIC AND PROFESSIONAL LTD
Houndmills, Basingstoke, Hampshire RG21 2XS
and London
Companies and representatives
throughout the world

Printed in Great Britain by
Antony Rowe Ltd
Chippenham, Wiltshire

British Library Cataloguing in Publication Data
Studies in religious fundamentalism.
1. Religion
I. Caplan, Lionel
306'.6   GN470
ISBN 0–333–41974–X

Contents

Preface

Fundamentalism has become an evocative notion in our time. But while those concerned with religious studies have considered fundamentalist tendencies in specific religious traditions, there has, to date, been little attempt to examine the phenomenon comparatively. The participants in this volume, though insistent on the importance of understanding the particular socio-cultural conditions in which fundamentalist ideas and behaviours emerge are, at the same time, inclined to explore the possibilities for more general insights. Two kinds of question, therefore, underlie our studies. First, what, in the complex historical context(s) discussed by each author, may be said to constitute 'religious fundamentalism'? Second, can we identify certain kinds of beliefs, discourses and activities which, though occurring in disparate cultural circumstances, enable us to speak of 'religious fundamentalism' as a viable category for cross-cultural analysis?

The origins of this book lie in an inter-collegiate seminar series organised by the Department of Anthropology at the School of Oriental and African Studies (University of London), which was held during the spring term, 1985. Six of the original participants appear in this volume, while three additional contributions were sought to provide a better regional and religious balance. The disciplinary emphasis is predominantly anthropological, though several of the participants identify themselves as sociologists. The chapters were all written for this symposium, with the exception of that by Jean-Loup Amselle, which appeared in a slightly different form, in French, in the *Revue canadienne des études africaines*, to which we are grateful for permission to reproduce the article.

It is hoped that readers who are regional specialists will excuse our decision, made in the interests both of consistency and of appealing to a wider readership, to omit all but the most basic diacritical marks when rendering foreign terms in the vernacular.

I am much indebted to the participants in this volume (as well as to those who are not in the collection but contributed to the original series) for their enthusiasm, perseverance and support in respect both of the initial seminars and the preparation of this publication. My greatest obligation is to Donald Taylor, who encouraged the idea of a collective exploration of religious fundamentalism, helped to recruit several of the participants, offered a chapter on his own research, translated Amselle's article from the French, and in every way played a full and active part in the project.

LIONEL CAPLAN

Notes on the Contributors

Jean-Loup Amselle is Maître de Conférences at the Centre D'Études Africaines, École des Hautes Études en Sciences Sociales, Paris, where he teaches anthropology. He has conducted fieldwork in Mali, and is the author of *Les Négociants de la Savanne*, and other works.

Steve Bruce is Lecturer in Sociology in the Department of Social Studies, Queen's University, Belfast. He has studied conservative Protestantism in Ulster, Scotland and the USA, and has written several books, including *Firm in the Faith: the Survival of Conservative Protestantism*.

Lionel Caplan is Reader in Anthropology with reference to South Asia at the School of Oriental and African Studies, London. His previous research in the Himalayas gave rise to several monographs, including *Land and Social Change in East Nepal*. He has also produced a number of essays on his recent research among South Indian Christians.

Angela Dietrich completed her MA in Ethnology, Sociology and Indian History at the University of Heidelberg. She is currently a PhD student at Konstanz University, specialising in the sociology of Sikhism, in connection with which she recently spent 14 months in the Punjab, and published a paper on Sikh demands for autonomy.

Nancy Tapper is part-time Lecturer in the Department of the History and Philosophy of Religion at King's College, London, where she teaches the anthropology of religion. She has done fieldwork in Iran, Afghanistan and, most recently, Turkey, and has written numerous articles on the anthropology of women and religion in the Muslim Middle East.

Richard Tapper is Reader in Anthropology with reference to the Middle East at the School of Oriental and African Studies. The primary focus of his research has been on ritual and tribalism in Afghanistan, Iran and Turkey. He is the author of *Pasture and Politics*, and has edited *The Conflict of Tribe and State in Iran and Afghanistan*.

Donald Taylor is Senior Lecturer in Religious Studies at Middlesex Polytechnic, London. He holds a doctorate in theology from Oxford, and is currently completing a thesis on the anthropology of religion at the School of Oriental and African Studies, based on research among Sri Lankan Tamil Hindu migrants in Britain. He has published several papers on this work.

Andrew Walker is Honorary Research Fellow at King's College, London, and Director of the C. S. Lewis Centre for the Study of Religion and Modernity. His main research interests are in the sociology of charismatic movements and in philosophical and theological anthropology. He is the author of *Restoring the Kingdom: the Radical Christianity of the House Church Movement* and other publications.

Jonathan Webber is Junior Research Fellow at Linacre College, Oxford, and Fellow in Social Studies at the Oxford Centre for Postgraduate Hebrew Studies. He is senior editor of JASO, the *Journal of the Anthropological Society of Oxford*. He has done research in Jerusalem and has written a number of articles on modern Jewish society.

Sami Zubaida is Senior Lecturer in Sociology at Birkbeck College, London. He has recently completed a research project on the Islamicisation of government in Iran, and has published several papers on religion and Islamic movements in that country as well as in the Arab world.

1 Introduction
Lionel Caplan

POPULAR CONCEPTIONS OF FUNDAMENTALISM

There can be few terms which have, of late, obtruded on popular consciousness in the West as persistently as 'fundamentalism'. During the past several years the label has been employed prodigiously by the mass media to describe and explain a host of apparently disparate religious and political developments in various parts of the world.

In Western Christianity, where the expression was first mooted, fundamentalism has come to identify conservative evangelicals inside the mainline Protestant denominations, as well as the charismatic sects which comprise what is now the fastest-moving current within the Christian world. In the American setting, it no longer exemplifies the hill-billy element in rural or small-town Protestantism, as it did half a century ago. Today, it denotes an aggressive and confident religious movement which, in coalition with conservative political forces, seeks to combat what is regarded as the liberal takeover of the state, family and church since the days of Roosevelt's New Deal (Whitfield, 1982).

The term 'fundamentalist', however, is not applied only to groups and activities within the Christian fold. Nowadays, it may refer equally to militantly orthodox sections within the Jewish population in Israel, separatist and nationalist elements in the Sikh community, Tamil 'liberation' movements in Sri Lanka, or Hindu groups opposed to foreign missionary influences in India. The most prolific rhetoric of fundamentalism, however, is reserved for Islam, and especially for the depiction of contemporary events in the Middle East. Said (1981) has documented how, for the West especially, the Islamic world has become an obsession. The reasons for this preoccupation seem obvious enough: the dependence of the industrialised nations on Middle Eastern energy resources, and the threat Islamic revival is thought to pose to the stability of this strategically vital area.

More to the point, fundamentalism has become a prominent focus of the imagery through which Islam is presented to the Western public. Thus, the overthrow of the Shah and the emergence of Khomeini's Iran, Sadat's assassination in Egypt, the assertiveness of Lebanon's Shi'ite community, even various forms of 'terrorism' have alike been reported as manifestations of the fundamentalist resurgence within Islam.

1

To the extent that Islamic fundamentalism is portrayed as radical and extremist, and so as menacing Western interests, it is, as the Tappers suggest in Chapter 3, a 'problem' for the West. But while the media have obviously helped to constitute it, the notion of fundamentalism is by no means entirely of their making. This interest reflects a widespread popular view that such tendencies are on the increase if not in the ascendant, and parallels a growing scholarly curiosity in the phenomenon. An issue which not only enters the arena of public discourse in this way, but affects the very regions and disciplines in which many of us live and work, and touches directly on themes which have traditionally engaged academic interest is, to say the least, worthy of serious attention.

Fundamentalism is unquestionably an evocative image *in* our time, but it is important to counter what seems to be a popular assumption that it is uniquely *of* our time. Recent historians of Protestantism in the USA, anxious to dispel an earlier idea that American fundamentalism was entirely a product of the 1920s (which witnessed the controversy over evolution, leading to the infamous Scopes 'monkey' trial) have shown how it existed as a religious movement before, during and after the events of that decade (see Sandeen, 1970). Marsden has traced its roots back to the Holiness and Pre-Millenial movements of the nineteenth century, and argued that fundamentalism in this century has 'emphasized doctrinal tendencies already strong in American culture and religious traditions' (1980, p. 224).

In south Asia, there are also strong links between revivalism and fundamentalism (Frykenberg, forthcoming). In this volume Dietrich (Chapter 6) stresses that present-day Sikh fundamentalism has direct antecedents in religious renewals at the turn of the century, the most significant of which sought to resurrect the sacred *khalsa*, or traditional religio-military brotherhood. This was established at the end of the seventeenth century by Guru Gobind Singh to abolish the authority of intermediary spiritual representatives and invest the community itself with ultimate power and responsibility (Shackle, forthcoming). Writers on Islamic communities similarly draw attention to the recurrent pattern of religious revivals. Zubaida and Amselle (Chapters 2 and 4) link contemporary fundamentalism in Egypt and Mali to earlier movements, both reformist and fundamentalist. Baharuddin, referring to Malaysian Islam, suggests that Islamic revivalism is a 'misnomer', since it 'occurs at such regular intervals', and adds that the only revival is in 'foreign scholars' interest in studying Islam' (1983, p. 400).

I leave the particular issue of how much contemporary Islamic resurgence is a creation of Western scholarship to the consideration of those better qualified than I am. However, in this connection it is worth reminding ourselves that the very people whom outside observers – whether media or academic – designate as fundamentalists (often with pejorative intent) may appropriate these same idioms to describe their own religious beliefs and behaviours or those of others within the same social and cultural contexts. Fundamentalism is no less an emic (insiders') category than an etic (observers') one.

Indeed, the changing significance of its deployment in Protestant circles provides a piquant illustration of the 'tyranny' of language. Walker (Chaper 10) recalls that fundamentalism was initially a self-advertising label, a proud epithet used by and of those who saw themselves as defending the fundamentals of their faith. Because of the unsavoury connotations it has acquired of late, however, it is increasingly being abandoned by those to whom it was once a 'badge of pride'. Leaders of the new Restoration movement in Britain refuse the label because they see it as imposed upon them by disapproving outsiders and opponents.

We have also to note the importance of what Zubaida in Chapter 2 calls the 'demonstration effect' of fundamentalist effervescence today. Nagata observes that the 'upsurge of Middle Eastern prosperity and power and the increasing Islamic fervour in that region have had profound effects elsewhere', and she reports how Muslim fundamentalists in Malaysia 'see themselves as part of an international fundamentalist resurgence' (1979, pp. 412–13; 1980, p. 129). The rapid spread of Wahabi fundamentalism in West Africa from its source in Saudi Arabia involves a similar dynamic, while within Christianity we witness the spread of such forms of religiosity throughout Europe and especially the USA, and from there to the Third World. The close ties between fundamentalist groups in such indigenous settings as the Punjab, Israel, and Sri Lanka and their diasporas in the West provide further evidence for a global diffusion of this tendency. This should not surprise us, given technologies which allow near instantaneous communication of ideologies around the planet, and where vast sums are deployed for the very purpose.

The contributors to this volume, therefore, profess two complementary aims. On the one hand, they are concerned to investigate the historical and cultural specificity of fundamentalist manifestations in diverse ethnographic settings, each author seeking to understand what constitutes fundamentalism in the particular context examined. On the other hand, while insisting on the integrity of a plurality of ethnographic depictions and analytical approaches, the collective intent is to interrogate the possibilities for comparative insights into the notion of fundamentalism.

We approach a cross-cultural examination of fundamentalism with an equal measure of curiosity and wariness. The latter is called for on two main counts, both of them already familiar to anthropologists concerned with comparative studies. The first touches on the sometimes glib employment of concepts whose roots lie in the Western tradition to make sense of data lying outside that tradition. Crick has criticised anthropologists for applying the seventeenth-century English notion of witchcraft to certain beliefs and behaviours in twentieth-century African societies which are superficially similar but semantically distinct. He suggests that 'great violence must be done to the conceptual structures of another culture in speaking of witchcraft if it lacks the environing categories which defined it in our own' (1976, p. 112). A similar note is sounded by Dumont when he questions the usefulness of studies which fail to consider the wider configuration of societal values in which are situated the religious ideologies and institutions being compared (1971, p. 32). These are salutary reminders of the difficulties attending the cross-cultural employment of a term like fundamentalism, with its particular Protestant origins and history.

A second, related issue concerns the diverse phenomena which, as already pointed out, are conflated in the notion of fundamentalism even within the English-speaking West. As Needham has remarked about kinship, 'it has an immense variety of uses, in that all sorts of institutions, practices and ideas can be referred to by it' (1971, p. 5). As a general term, therefore, it can at best identify 'family resemblances' among the disparate phenomena it is intended to describe. The recognition of such polythetic categories, moreover, can have serious implications for comparative studies, rendering them 'more daunting and perhaps even unfeasible' (1975, p. 358). However, the designation and subsequent deconstruction of a host of similar 'odd-job' words (as Wittgenstein called them) should not be an end in itself, nor indeed lead to the abandonment of comparative exercises. Rather, we are encouraged to pursue more appropriate abstractions or frames of reference, as Lévi-Strauss (1962) did for totemism, Crick (1976) for witchcraft, Rivière (1971) for marriage, and Needham himself for kinship (1971). Parkin has recently noted, in respect of another polysemic term – 'evil' – how, in seeking to identify equivalent concepts in diverse cultural circumstances, we may be led to re-cast them in new terms (1985, p. 23). The challenge of fundamentalism as our object of investigation, therefore, lies precisely in its ambiguity and equivocality, in the realisation that it is not a self-evident category, as Webber (Chapter 5) observes, nor a unifying paradigm that can encapsulate the diverse phenomena under consideration (Walker, Chapter 10). To what modes of religious discourse and behaviour in the modern world, then, does 'fundamentalism' refer?

FUNDAMENTALISM AND THE MODERN WORLD

The fundamentalist engagement with the modern world is complex. Those labelled fundamentalists are sometimes portrayed as fossilised relics, insulated from and oblivious to their surroundings, living perpetually in a bygone age. As Marsden puts it, their detractors see them as clinging to the past in 'stubborn and irrational resistance to changing culture...' (1980, p. 185). The ethnographic accounts in this volume belie such a portrayal. They demonstrate, rather, that fundamentalism must be seen as quintessentially *modern* in the sense that it constitutes a response to events and conditions in the *present*. It is not an inexplicable resurgence or revival, but a symptom of perceived threat or crisis. As such, it is frequently deeply involved in contemporary political processes, and so cannot be divorced from the operation and implications of power. The incidence and character of fundamentalist ideologies, moreover, as the Tappers stress in Chapter 3, depend on the nature of the polities in which and in relation to which they emerge.

The fundamentalism sweeping much of the Muslim world today is frequently interpreted as a reaction to Western imperialism and its predatory economies and ideologies (see Firth, 1981, p. 581; Vatikiotis, 1982, p. 69). Zubaida (Chapter 2), while lending support to this general view, also demonstrates how important it is to examine institutional settings and historical conjunctures for an understanding of the disparate relations obtaining between Islamic fundamentalist movements and the modern states in which they are located. He records how the Muslim Brotherhood in Egypt was antagonistic not only to the European colonialists and their cultural influence, but to Nasser's nationalist regime, which the Brotherhood pilloried as a secularist, ungodly tyranny (and for which hostility it paid dearly). He also shows how Khomeini's opposition to the Shah in Iran arose not only from the latter's association with American power in the region, and the oppressive nature of the Western-backed monarchy, but Khomeini's own novel convictions about the need for an Islamic republic led by benign jurists to replace the rule of princes. Though presented in the terms of Shi'ite discourses, the idea assumes the existence of the modern state and nation.

Considering a different Islamic context, the Tappers (Chapter 3) suggest that the character of the fundamentalism associated with the dominant ideology of republicanism in Turkey relates directly to the degree of perceived threat to the stability and prosperity of the state. In the circumstances, those who are thought to pose such a threat are members of clandestine Islamic sects ('fanatics'), and political dissidents of both left and right, as well as members of minority communities, seen as agents of outside powers. The reaction to this threat is the adoption of a hard line nationalist stance, paralleling the move to an exclusivist and oppositional fundamentalism, which the Tappers regard as akin to the ideological structure of evangelical Protestantism as described by Barr (1977).[1]

Non-Islamic fundamentalisms are no less implicated in contemporary social and political currents. In the Protestant milieu of the USA, fundamentalism crystallised in response to the liberals' eagerness to bring Christianity into the post-Darwinian world by questioning the scientific and historical accuracy of scripture. Subsequently, the scourge of evolution was linked with socialism, and during the Cold War period, with communism. This unholy trinity came to be regarded as a sinister, atheistic threat to Christian America (Marsden, 1980, pp. 209–10). Bruce (Chapter 9) suggests that to understand the recent success of the Moral Majority, an alliance between the conservative forces of the New Right and the fundamentalist wings of the mainly Southern Baptist churches, we have to appreciate these fears, as well as the impact of a host of unwelcome changes – in attitudes to 'morality', family, civil and women's rights, and so on – which have, in the wake of economic transformations since the Second World War, penetrated especially the previously insular social and cultural world of the American South.

Of late, with the support of the New Right, fundamentalist organisations have moved outside America's borders, not merely to join in spreading the Christian gospel, but to challenge the traditional hegemony of the orthodox churches already established abroad. The growing popularity of such sects in Latin America, for example, where they are encouraged by a number of regimes favoured by the present

American administration, may be interpreted, on one level, as an attempt to undermine the Catholic Church, many of whose priests now openly call for political and social reform. In south India, fundamentalist groups overtly challenge the liberal and ecumenical 'social gospel' favoured by the dominant sectors within the orthodox Protestant church and community. In the context of local power structures they provide an alternative to the latter's authoritative theology, and thus a means whereby 'ordinary' Christians can resist their social and cultural subordination (Caplan, Chapter 8).

Considering recent developments in a different part of the Indian sub-continent, Dietrich (Chapter 6) traces the rapid rise to prominence of a Sikh fundamentalist movement, led by the charismatic Sant Bhindranwale, and its sudden demise in the tragic events of June 1984. She situates these developments against the backdrop of (among other things) inadequate access by Sikh peasants to the Punjab's ample water resources (partly because these are treated as a national resource), unequal distribution of the benefits of the region's 'green revolution', and declining employment opportunities for Sikh youth. These conditions are attributed by the fundamentalists to what they see as an oppressive, alien (that is, non-Sikh) power in Delhi, and its secularist and Westernised allies within the Sikh community itself, who support the 'moderate' Akali Dal party which has singularly failed to alter these conditions, or to persuade the central government to do so.

Similarly, the emergence in Britain of a fundamentalist strain among Tamil Hindu migrants from Sri Lanka only becomes comprehensible in the context of that country's recent troubled history. Taylor (Chapter 7) relates the background to Tamil demands for a separate state to the complex struggles for power in the post-independence period. In the course of these events there arose (and was encouraged) an increased self-awareness among Buddhists, and a sense of being a threatened minority in south Asia, despite their numerical predominance in Sri Lanka itself. The ensuing ethnic conflict gave rise to divergent views within the Tamil population concerning the appropriate response, and these differences are represented within the migrant community in Britain.

What emerges clearly from the narratives in this volume is that fundamentalists interact dynamically with their contemporary social and cultural surroundings. The nature and extent of this engagement is of course variable, but nowhere do they seem to remain unaffected by or immune to local, national or global tides. What is also clear is that fundamentalists do not assume, nor can they be allocated in any a priori way, a consistent stance in political affairs. In some contexts they seek to subvert the existing regime, in others they are its most fervent supporters, in still others they are compelled to adopt a neutral position. A fundamentalist ideology may contain within itself elements which lend themselves to interpretations in diametrically opposed ways. Zubaida (Chapter 2) notes how the Muslim Brotherhood in Egypt contained some elements claiming to be 'Islamic socialists', although their 'socialist' opponents branded them as 'fascists'. Furthermore, even within the same setting the political posture of fundamentalism may alter over time. Barr, referring to Protestant fundamentalism in the USA, remarks that the 'claim of the evangelical gospel to be a radical questioning of the inner bases of human self-certainty is suddenly reversed, when the religion becomes the ideological guarantor of the rightness of the existing social order' (1977, p. 110). According to Carter (1968) prior to the First World War American fundamentalists were as apt to be political liberals as conservatives. Of late, however, fundamentalists have seldom failed to take a strong right-wing position on most issues (Barr, 1977, p. 110; Bruce, Chapter 9).

Nor is it possible to identify a universal constituency of support for fundamentalism. In the USA, Ruth suggests, fundamentalism was once the 'social and spiritual preoccupation of a minor segment of the ignorant and poor', but it has of late become associated with a much larger 'economically pinched and hostile middle class' (1983, p. 345). In Britain, too, according to Walker (Chapter 10), while fundamentalism was, at one time, identified with 'working-class enthusiasms', nowadays a number of movements, like Restorationism, attract primarily the middle class.

Although there seems to be a widespread consensus that Islamic fundamentalism appeals primarily to the educated classes (Dessouki, 1981, p. 108), this provides only a crude indication of the population from which an active following is actually drawn in diverse ethnographic situations. In Bamako, although Wahabism now draws recruits increasingly from the urban youth, Amselle (Chapter 4) reports that its mainstay has for some time been the commercial bourgeoisie, who find it a conducive and supportive ideology. The main activists in the Egyptian and Iranian fundamentalist movements discussed by Zubaida in Chapter 2, however, are drawn from a much wider social base. They include not only what he calls 'the intellectual proletariat' (students, teachers, minor functionaries), but elements of the urban working class, petty shopkeepers and artisans who, he notes, tend invariably to become involved in oppositional politics, of whatever hue. But the peasantry and uneducated urban poor seem to be excluded from participation in these movements, although they may, of course, be mobilised sporadically to support their activities.

This contrasts with the Sikh fundamentalist movement considered in Chapter 6. According to Dietrich, it suggests a form of populism which not only seeks to re-establish the rights of ordinary people against those of the dominant economic and political interests in the society, but also involves the peasantry in a direct way.

If a comparison of disparate fundamentalisms does not offer the possibility of generalisation in terms of the substantive social locations or political tendencies of those to whom such religiosity appeals, it does expose clearly its oppositional character. Fundamentalism requires to be defined 'idiomatically', as Webber phrases it (Chapter 5), in terms of a significant 'other', to which it is antithetical and with which it constantly engages. In attempting to identify the cultural space within which to situate the phenomenon, therefore, we are impelled to seek its conceptual adversary.

FUNDAMENTALISM AND MODERNISM

Several contributors address the question of the relation between fundamentalism and modernism. Although, as Ardener reflects, there are as many versions of modernism as persons attempting to define it (1985, p. 46), in the religious field, it has come to imply, among other things, innovation in scriptural interpretation, a less stringent application of religious codes, secularism, liberalism and rationality: in short, the adaptation of religious ideas and practices to modern culture. In the Protestant West, as already noted, fundamentalism arose as a self-conscious movement to proclaim and defend the 'essentials' of the faith in reaction to what were regarded as the compromising tendencies of modernist theologies. Indeed, without modernism, Carter remarks, 'there could have been no fundamentalism' (1968, p. 188). Walker (Chapter 10) suggests that modernism, and the strategies developed to guard against its effects and implications, is the focal problem to be addressed in any consideration of fundamentalism. In this connection, he comprehends the emergence of the Restoration movement in Britain as a strategic resistance to the social and moral climate of 'permissiveness' pervading the 1960s, and as a

particular response to the extreme liberal position represented by
Robinson's *Honest to God* (1963), as well as to the recent debates
within certain Protestant circles regarding the interpretation of
Christ's incarnation and resurrection.

Both Dietrich and Taylor (Chapters 6 and 7) employ Eric Sharpe's
formal model which identifies fundamentalism as the last in a
three-phase dialectical process. This features *rejection* (of existing
ultimate authority), *adaptation* (of the old to the new, hence the
emergence of the liberal position), and *reaction* (on the part of those
– fundamentalists – who reject the modernist position and seek to
re-establish traditional 'ultimacies'). Thus, Taylor attributes the
emergence of 'incipient fundamentalism' among Sri Lankan Tamil
migrants in Britain to the influences of liberalism and permissiveness
in the host society, and to the plural beliefs of other Hindu settlers.
This has led some members of the community to perceive a challenge
to the traditional authority of Saiva Siddhanta precepts, but their
attempts to reassert the fundamentals threatens to lead to isolation
from other Hindus as well as from more 'moderate' Saivites.

Sharpe's model underlines clearly the oppositional nature of the
fundamentalist–modernist link, but the suggestion that it provides a
universal paradigm for religious processes must be met with some
reserve. Taylor, for one, suggests a need to separate the notion of
secularism from that of modernity, though the two tend to be
conflated willy-nilly in much Western sociological thinking. (Walker
in Chapter 10 suggests that the secularisation thesis has generally
been somewhat overplayed). Another caveat must be entered in
respect of the sequencing of Sharpe's three phases. Webber's
explication of the Jewish experience of modernity (Chapter 5)
indicates the possibility for alternative histories of fundamentalism.
In this situation, modernity has meant, on the one hand, an
increasing assimilation into the cultural mainstream of those predominantly Western nations in which Jews have settled during the past
century and, on the other, the emergence of a range of social and
cultural associations which preserve group solidarity and define
Jewish identity ethnically rather than in terms of traditional religious
beliefs and institutions. The modern synagogue has become more a
community centre than a place of worship. Those who appear to
resist assimilation, and remain committed to non-modernist formulations of Judaism, attract the label 'fundamentalist'. Here, then,
fundamentalism has not arisen in response to the challenge of
modernity, but remains, for the modernists, a crucial residual

category. The tension between the two lies at the very root of contemporary Jewish society.

The fundamentalists' engagement with modernity is often alleged to involve a Luddite-like rejection of new technologies, consonant with their assumed disavowal of modern science. This view is refuted by the evidence from contributors which indicates that fundamentalists have not been slow to appreciate the advantages of these technologies and to adopt or adapt them to advantage. This may simply mean devising a special refrigerator motor to circumvent ritual prohibitions on the use of electricity during the Jewish sabbath (Chapter 5), or, more seriously, where fundamentalist groups are engaged in armed conflict, using up-to-date weaponry (Chapter 6). The acceptance of modern technologies and economic changes required by growing industrialisation is encouraged, according to the Tappers (Chapter 3), by the fundamentalist ideology of Turkish nationalism/republicanism, with its 'Protestant ethic'. This seems to accord with Humphreys's refusal to see any inherent contradiction between a commitment to fundamentalist ideals and a modernising, technocratic regime – such as that in Saudi Arabia (1979, p. 4). Amselle (Chapter 4) makes a similar observation in respect to the Wahabi community in Bamako.

Fundamentalists have also been quick to enter the field of modern mass communications in propagating their views. In the USA there are scores of television channels and hundreds of radio stations devoted exclusively to religious programmes, and dozens of gospel shows utilising secular commercial networks and stations. They are, for the most part, funded by and serve the interests of fundamentalist organisations, and Crawford (1980, p. 161) estimates that they reach close to 100 million Americans each week (see also Bruce, Chapter 9). In south India, several of the most popular local fundamentalist personalities also utilise the latest sound recording and broadcasting techniques (based on Western counterparts) to attract and retain their followings (Caplan, Chapter 8).

A refusal or inability to accommodate science in their world-view is often singled out by observers as evidence of fundamentalists' retreat from the modern world, yet such an assertion is also challenged by ethnography. The post-First World War controversy over the teaching of evolution in American state schools is increasingly regarded by historians of the period as a 'typical expression of the America of the 1920s', which actually discouraged various forms of dissent, rather than as the peculiar concern of Protestant fundamentalists (Sandeen, 1970, p. 267). Moreover, hostility to the spread of Darwinian ideas does not in itself constitute antipathy to science. The recent emergence of 'scientific creationism' within Protestant fundamentalism in the USA suggests precisely the opposite. What is posited is that 'science is knowledge, and the Bible is a book of true and factual knowledge throughout'. The Bible is said to 'contain all the basic principles upon which true science is built' and 'those who say the Bible is not a book of science have not read it very attentively' (H. M. Morris, quoted in Williams (1983, p. 98)). While it is possible to challenge creationist theory in a number of ways (as Williams does), what is relevant to note for our present purposes is that this knowledge is intended to be validated not on religious but on scientific grounds; on the grounds, that is, of the dominant explanatory paradigm in the most 'modernised' Western society. The fact that Morris, the major exponent of this theory, and many of his colleagues at the Institute for Creation Research are professional scientists (who 'know the difference between religion and science') adds to the authority of their claims: it is an 'argument by credentials', as Williams observes (1983, p. 101).

A tendency to read sacred texts in the light of contemporary scientific knowledge is also found among fundamentalists outside the Christian fold. Jewish and Muslim fundamentalists see no inherent difficulty in asserting that scripture can be made to fit within the framework of our scientific knowledge of the world today. In Mali, part of the appeal of Wahabism to young Bamakois is its favourable attitude towards science (Amselle, Chapter 4). Followers speak of the 'complementarity' of Islam and science, of how the former provides the latter with a 'soul', and of how Islam has in so many ways anticipated modern science, a recurrent theme among Muslims in Turkey as well. The Tappers (Chapter 3) report how fasting during Ramazan is said to be healthy and in accord with up-to-date ideas about what is good for the body. Hence the legitimacy of modern science is acknowledged within what is purported (by opponents) to be an anti-modern world-view.

Fundamentalists, by refusing to accept many of the cultural assertions and social implications of their contemporary world, are assumed by modernist protagonists – as by many academic and literary observers – to have excluded themselves from the mainstream of intelligent, rational discourse. In its mild form, this assessment may simply note an absence of theological sophistication (see Hollenweger, 1972, p. 186) or, as V. S. Naipaul has written of Islamic fundamentalism, the lack of any 'intellectual substance' (see Said, 1981, p. 7). In its more severe form, fundamentalism is represented as the very antithesis of science and reason: 'rationalism and fundamentalism are two different ways of thought' (Amin, 1983, p. 24).

Any discussion of fundamentalism is bound, at some point, to confront the difficulties inherent in the notion of rationality. Both fundamentalists and modernists would claim rationality for their own beliefs and practices, though modernists – many of whom, as we have seen, tend to nominate others as fundamentalists in the first place – are also inclined to regard the beliefs and practices of the latter as less than rational. While this may tell us something about the construction of hierarchies of knowledge, it reveals little about the observances themselves. Perhaps Webber (Chapter 5) is right to complain that there is altogether too much stress on rationalism in current notions of modernism. But then Barr (and the Tappers in Chapter 3) regards rationalism as a crucial characteristic of fundamentalism. Walker (Chapter 10), for his part, criticises Barr for his refusal to see 'reason and rationality' in those modern forms of Protestant fundamentalism (such as Restorationism) which emphasise emotion, the supernatural and the miraculous. Caplan's discussion of a charismatic form of fundamentalism in south India (Chapter 8) certainly does not suggest that it implies an absence of reason or rationality. If anything, this particular brand of fundamentalism offers what most Protestants believe to be both a more satisfactory (reasonable? rational?) explanation for, and a more adequate (reasonable? rational?) means of coping with evil and misfortune in their everyday world. Further, given the threat of cultural and social absorption or annihilation, whether real or imagined, which confronts minorities like the Jews, Sikhs or Sri Lankan Tamils (Chapters 5, 6 and 7), a desire to defend the irreducible principles of their faith is in no sense an unreasonable or irrational project.

Instead of incorporating the notion of rationality as a defining ingredient of either modernism or fundamentalism, we might more usefully acknowledge its discursive potential, its capacity for proposing or constituting others as inferior, superstitious, or otherwise deviant, because they are seen to operate with a different 'mode of thought'. The notion of rationality, after all, assumes meaning only in the context of the kinds of knowledge or truth it seeks to reveal (Overing, 1985, p. 5).

We are therefore led away from seeking to understand either fundamentalism or modernism in terms of peremptory, essential qualities, or as categories which can be known by their objective characteristics. Each varies ethnographically, and so requires to be approached in the context of interaction with its conceptual 'other'. This relationship, moreover, is too subtle and complex to be denoted by a crude and emphatic binary distinction which, as Webber suggests (Chapter 5), fails to convey adequately the manner in which fundamentalists and modernists contend, oppose, qualify and affect one another.

The abandonment of a rigid dualism also compels us to recognise that boundaries are permeable, so that particular religious ideologies can and do in fact incorporate elements of both fundamentalism and modernism. This is most evident in the Turkish and Malian studies by the Tappers and Amselle (Chapters 3 and 4). In both cases the predominant opposition is not between fundamentalism and modernism, but between a puritanical and conservative ('Barr type') fundamentalism – which includes many modernist elements – and those kinds of Islam organised around Sufi brotherhoods which feature mystical beliefs and practices. In Bamako, the Wahabis consider these activities as semi-pagan, and their leaders (the marabouts) as charlatans and 'mixers', who contaminate the purity of (Sunni) Islam. Here, those who would regard themselves as fundamentalists appoint others as deviant, and the latters' religious behaviours are rendered heterodox, superstitious, fanatic and the like. In different circumstances, they might be labelled 'fundamentalist'.

FUNDAMENTALISM, TEXT AND TRUTH

The tendency to seek authority in scriptures on the basis of their infallibility touches on what is widely held to constitute one of the most significant features of the fundamentalist stance, though most contributors to this volume, as we shall see presently, suggest a more complex relation between fundamentalism and text. In the most general sense, however, any particular fundamentalism legitimates its existence and world-view by reference, among other things, to a corpus of sacred writings, the belief in whose veracity constitutes a prime test of faith. Protestant fundamentalism places a 'very strong emphasis' on Biblical literalism (Barr, 1977, p 1; see also Sandeen, 1970, p. 103). For Jewish fundamentalists, it is the rabbinic law (*halacha*) which is regarded as the authentic and inerrant amplification of the Torah; for Sikhs the Guru Granth Sahib is the Holy Book which symbolises and carries the authority of the 'living Guru'; for Sri Lankan Tamil worshippers of Siva, the Agamic canons are as sacred as the Vedas; while for Muslims, it is the Quran and the Sunna (the traditions and example of the Prophet and his companions) which provide the irreducible written sources, and upon which the *shari'a* (the body of Quranic laws established over time by eminent theologians and jurists) is theoretically based. In Turkey, the Tappers (Chapter 3) note the emergence of parallels between Muhammad and Ataturk, whose texts are considered equally inerrant. The sayings and biographical highlights of both are beyond critical comment, and presented without wider social context.

The sacred texts are not simply the expression of timeless verities, but may constitute prime symbols of religious identity. A shared commitment to particular canons encourages a sense of exclusivity among believers. The more distinctive the beliefs, moreover, the clearer the dividing line between the faithful and those excluded. The growing 'fundamentalisation' of Islam in urban Malaysia and south India, for example, serves as an important means of distinguishing Muslims from the rest of the population (Nagata, 1980, p. 129; Mines, 1981, pp. 65–6). Walker (Chapter 10) stresses the point that doctrinal exclusivity need not be absolute to be effective. Restoration-ists in Britain subscribe to a range of beliefs and practices in common with a variety of other fundamentalist groups, as well as with some Protestants who might not normally attract such a label. They are distinguished and distinguish themselves primarily in respect of their observances relating to 'shepherding'. Based on a reading of several verses from St Paul's epistle to the Ephesians, this entails a hierarchy of ritual offices, whereby each member submits to a spiritual overseer.

Likewise, fundamentalist Sikhs are not alone in observing the tenets of their faith, and Dietrich (Chapter 6) suggests that they become differentiated from the generality of co-religionists by assuming a total commitment to a particular charismatic leader who is pledged to uphold the honour, integrity and equality of the community of believers. His followers demonstrate loyalty by a readiness to sacrifice their very beings to re-create the spiritually sanctified order of the *khalsa*.

The distinction may be expressed spatially as well as doctrinally. Zubaida (Chapter 2) reports on how one recently formed fundamen-talist group which regards Egypt (indeed, most contemporary Middle Eastern societies) as not truly Islamic, encourages its members to live and pray apart from the mass of unbelievers, likening their separation to the *hijra*, the Prophet's flight from the corrupt society of Mecca. The 'Kingdom people', as Restorationists in Britain are sometimes called, also foster a sense of exclusiveness by living close together – even taking over whole city streets – and providing various practical and professional services for one another (Walker, Chapter 10). A similar tendency is evident among certain Jewish groups who erect spatial and cultural boundaries which mark them off from the wider society, as indeed from the rest of the Jewish community (Webber, Chapter 5).

Such attempts at removal from constant exposure to the influences of the outside world underline the tendency for fundamentalist ideologies to address and appropriate the faithful as whole persons. The modernist dichotomy between the secular and religious realms is refused: the domain of the true believer is indivisible. In a paper at the original seminar series, to be published elsewhere as part of a larger work, Epstein (1986) considered the case of the Watchtower movement on the Copperbelt during the late 1950s (in what is now Zambia), and especially its implications for individual members. What he found striking was the 'new sense of self' it engendered, encouraged and moulded in the context of regular assemblies where the individual was made the focus of attention, given scope for personal expression, and offered suitable support in every endeavour by the entire congregation. The resulting commitment of such appeals to the self is often total. In the West, especially, this kind of attachment often leads to accusations of 'brain-washing' by the popular press (see Walker, Chapter 10), or is regarded as a form of addictive illness. There is now a Fundamentalists Anonymous in the USA to deal with the 'problem' (*Guardian*, 1 March 1986). One common Western diagnosis for similar 'afflictions' in Muslim societies is the 'martyrdom complex', or simply a primordial inclination for such religious activities, a view which Zubaida (Chapter 2) is anxious to dispel.

The advocacy of an exclusive doctrine unites its proponents against the mass of non-believers, but is also self-limiting. This becomes especially evident where a fundamentalist group, seeking to acquire wider political influence in a pluralist setting, is compelled to compromise with some of the very elements in society against which it has defined itself. Nagata reports how one particular Islamic fundamentalist leader in Malaysia speaks with conviction on a host of universal social issues when appearing before secular audiences in national and international contexts, but adjusts his oratory when among fellow believers. Here, she notes, the focus is on Islam and its identification with Malay interests, and 'the idea of *jihad* [holy war] is heard' (1980, p. 137).

Such compartmentalisation, as Bruce (Chapter 9) calls this kind of discursive alternation, is also practised by Jerry Falwell, leader of the Moral Majority. Falwell must constantly negotiate the thin line between an accommodative, inclusive rhetoric required of a national political figure, and the more exclusive rhetoric demanded by his fundamentalist constituents. The latter, Bruce notes, increasingly resent the invitation to join forces with Jews, Catholics and other Protestants who may share certain of their political views, but few, if any, of their religious beliefs. This fuels their growing suspicion of having been used as 'vote fodder' by the politicians.

Most of the texts which are held to be infallible can be located in history, and tend to be situated in this way by modernist theologians and believers. Scriptures are viewed principally in the context of conditions obtaining during the periods in which they were produced or to which they refer, and new exegeses are constantly offered to reinterpret doctrines and reflect their moral relevance in a changing milieu. Islamic modernists, for example, argue that the *shari'a* was 'shaped by scholars who were concerned to deduce an Islamic way of life which would fit the conditions of their time... [it] thus cannot be understood as a fixed repository of commands and prohibitions but... the end result of a long process of jurisprudence' (Humphreys, 1979, p. 5). A reformist like Mohammad Abdu in Egypt, therefore, would not insist on the strict application of Islamic law, particularly elements of the penal code and restrictions on women (Zubaida, Chapter 2). Similarly, Jewish modernists suggest that the *halacha* only codified (and should continue to codify) Jewish social and cultural realities existing at a particular moment in historical time (Webber, Chapter 5).

Fundamentalism, however, tends to represent these texts as timeless, out-of-time, and so valid for all time (Tappers, Chapter 3). By asserting the eternal verities of scripture, fundamentalism implies an ahistorical world-view (as Barr indicates), or perhaps we should say an altogether different conception of history, arising from a view of knowledge at variance with that of modernism. Rather than a discovery of the unknown, or an expansion of frontiers, the acquisition of knowledge is seen, in effect, as an archaeological process, an uncovering of truths already revealed in the texts, and only hidden from us by our own refusal or inability to apprehend them. This is 'an old Islamic view of knowledge', according to Cudsi and Dessouki (1981, p. 10), while such a notion is also 'central to Indian thinking through the ages' (Van Buitenen, 1968, p. 35; see also Parry, 1985, p.

205). It is the fundamentalists who nowadays defend this view of knowledge against the modernist conception.

In as much as fundamentalists desire a return to the pristine moral condition elucidated in the *vade mecum*, history itself comes to be perceived as a process of decline from an original ideal state, hardly more than a catalogue of the betrayal of fundamental principles. Thus, fundamentalist ideologues like Qutb in Egypt assert that the holy realm inaugurated by the Prophet and his followers in Medina – which exemplified all the principles of Islamic perfection – lasted for only a brief period, and degenerated after their death into *jahiliyya*, the chaos and corruption which attends the 'rule of man' and not the 'rule of God'. The perceived inferiority of Middle Eastern nations *vis-à-vis* European powers is thus attributed not to Islam as such, but to its defilement and decline (Zubaida, Chapter 2; see also Amin, 1983, p. 17). This view has echoes in the portrayal by the fundamentalist New Christian Right in the United States of a formerly 'great' America which obeyed God's commands but which has gradually been undermined by the secular humanists who control its government and institutions (Bruce, Chapter 9). Here too, the original state of perfection is recoverable only by a return to the essential principles contained in the holy scriptures.

In this connection, one of the most obvious concerns of the fundamentalists is to reverse the trend of contemporary gender relations which are seen as symptomatic of a declining moral order. In America today, one of the Moral Majority's principal anxieties is what it perceives as the undermining of the father's authority, which it attributes to women's growing role in the economy. This fading authority can only be re-established, it is argued, by the removal of wage-earning women from the labour market and their return to the home, and Falwell calls for the provision of an adequate and inflation-proof income for the sole (male) breadwinner. This wish to revive what it sees as the traditionally sanctioned sexual division of labour in the home leads, among other things, to the Moral Majority's vigorous opposition to the Equal Rights Amendment. In its view, women should be reinstated in their rightful domestic place, under the benign control of men (Eisenstein, 1982, pp. 576–7; see also Walker in Chapter 10 on the patriarchal character of Restorationism in Britain).

In the Islamic *shari'a*, as in the Jewish *halacha*, women are allocated a restricted and inferior ritual position. While modernists seek to ameliorate the effects of these codes, fundamentalists are more likely to insist on their strict application. Women thus appear to assume a symbolic poignancy in fundamentalism – their dress, demeanour and socio-ritual containment providing eloquent testimony to what is regarded as the correct order of things.

Within both Christian and Islamic fundamentalisms this vision of a return to perfection is sometimes conveyed in starkly dyadic terms, so that history is seen to involve a cosmic struggle between good and evil, the former deriving from adherence to the essential principles propounded in scripture, the latter attributable to countless human digressions from them (Amin, 1983, p. 14; also Marsden, 1980, p. 211). Wahabis in Bamako are convinced that those who do not travel the Sunni path are followers of Satan (Amselle, Chapter 4), and similar sentiments characterise Protestant fundamentalist discourse (Bruce, Chapter 9). For this reason, Hofstadter describes the 'fundamentalist mentality' in America as essentially 'Manichean' (1964, p. 135).

Whether such texts are regarded as revelational or authoritative in some other ultimate sense, they are clearly the provenance in which fundamentalists seek a definitive blueprint for their contemporary beliefs and lifeways. But the proposition that a religious tradition is an integrated unity whose essentials are readily apparent and discernible is challenged from a number of sides. In the early part of this century there was, in fact, a collective effort within the Protestant fold to agree the basic principles of the faith. But the 'essentials' which emerged with each successive attempt expanded or contracted in number, or were differently stressed (Sandeen, 1970, p. xiv). Within Islam, even this degree of consensus is absent. Ahmad tells us that while Muslims in India subscribe to the fundamental Islamic precepts, there is 'no unified definition of what is truly orthodox or truly "Islamic"' (1981, p. 18).

Thus a return to the text, though presented as a rediscovery or reiteration of the fundamentals, involves of necessity a process of reformulation. Dessouki observes that innumerable groups each present their teachings as the real Islam (1981, p. 107). Fundamentalist movements in both Egypt and Iran, which equally regard the Quran as their 'constitution' and insist on the strict application of the *shari'a* none the less offer distinctive versions of the 'sacred history' of Islam (Zubaida, Chapter 2).

The degree of 'creativity' tolerated will depend on a number of factors, not least of which resides in the authority of the ideologues themselves, and so their capacity to win acceptance for their particular constructions. Taylor (Chapter 7) records a somewhat audacious (and not entirely successful) attempt by the leader of a fundamentalist circle within the Sri Lankan Tamil community in Britain to insist on a public declaration of devotion to Siva as a sign of faith and loyalty, a practice which has no sanction in either scripture or custom.

The possibility of multiple constructions of the sacred history reminds us again that fundamentalist ideologies may be related oppositionally not only to modernist but to alternative fundamentalist discourses as well. Thus, the three pillars of Religious Zionism – the People of Israel, the Land of Israel and the Torah of Israel – were given a new priority of emphasis by the fundamentalist and politically expansionist Gush Emunim movement, with its stress on the Land of Israel. Aronoff reports that its political activities, which at times embarrassed even the sympathetic Likud Government, led at least one prominent minister and member of one of the strongly orthodox (fundamentalist) religious parties to regret the Gush's 'nationalist emphasis on the Land of Israel' at the expense of the 'religious emphasis on the Torah' (1983, pp. 74–8).

Similarly, writing about the Protestant community in Madras, Caplan (Chapter 8) describes how a stress on different aspects of the Bible produces two quite distinctive forms of fundamentalism. One is the legacy of the 'Evangelical Awakening' which concentrates on the salvation of the individual through a personal relationship with Christ, enjoins prayer and stipulated exercises of piety, and in general displays the attributes of conservative evangelicalism which Barr identifies as fundamentalism. It differs starkly from another variety of fundamentalism which has become popular during the past two decades. This stresses the confrontation between the forces of evil (as an array of external maleficent beings under the control of Satan) and good (symbolised in the person of Jesus in the role of miracle worker). The latter conceptions – which accord largely with popular south Indian theodicies – are authenticated by reference to those sections of the New Testament which present the cosmic struggle as the central theme of the text and speak of the charismata conferred by the Holy Spirit. Fundamentalists see such powers working nowadays through divinely chosen and charismatically gifted individuals.

Such differing constructions of sacred history suggest that the exegetical propensities of fundamentalists are no less developed than those of modernists, although the former would insist on the integrity and inviolability of the text. This 'fiction' is often preserved by means of structures which invest religious leaders with the right to pronounce what is and what is not authoritative knowledge.

In asserting the divine inspiration of their texts, the fundamentalists assume the divinity of the knowledge they possess. Hence, they are inclined to proclaim certainties, to affirm universal, timeless moralities. They exemplify the 'one-hundred per cent mentality', as Hofstadter puts it, which 'tolerates no equivocations, no reservations...' (1964, pp. 118–19). In their opposition to the relativisation of knowledge, they offer the feeling of a secure reality. This contrasts with the doubts, hesitations and 'theorising' of the modernists (Webber, Chapter 5). This conviction in the incontestability of their claims allows fundamentalists to deny others the validity of their own beliefs. Within the Protestant fold the latter are frequently accused of not being 'true Christians', in the Islamic world they are 'infidels' or 'pagans', while for a Jewish fundamentalist, a 'modern Jew' is simply a contradiction in terms.

Fundamentalism must therefore be seen in its discursive aspect as an attempt to establish what Foucault (1980, p. 131) would call its 'regime of truth'. Where modernism prevails, the very idea of truth is seen to be the outcome of social and cultural conditions, and thus to be understood historically and contextually. Fundamentalism challenges this version, regarding truth as unchanging, substantive and so ultimately knowable as an object in the external world (see Marsden, 1980, pp. 114, 185). It is an essentialist view which claims to know 'what the world is truly like' (Hobart, 1985, p. 184). As such, fundamentalism both encompasses and transcends the religious domain, a theme to which both the Tappers and Taylor address themselves (Chapters 3 and 7).

If there is a common thread of argument running through the chapters which follow, it is that the character and contours of fundamentalism can best be drawn by reference to some notional and significant 'other'. This opposition may delineate and represent for the participants themselves a substantive arena of religious beliefs and practices, thus enabling them to establish definitive boundaries between themselves and other groups or sections in society. As observers, however, we might with greater profit utilise such a dualism primarily as a convenient, heuristic mechanism for thinking about the complex forms of religiosity which are conflated under the heading of fundamentalism. For only through such abstraction does the line dividing fundamentalism from modernism, paganism, fanaticism (or what have you) achieve a clear enough focus to allow the identification of alternative religious ideologies. In the everyday ethnographic contexts and historical conditions considered by each author, neither fundamentalism nor its classificatory alter emerges as monolithic; the actual boundaries separating them are vague and imprecise, allowing of continual overlap and trespass. This should suggest to us that an adequate understanding of fundamentalism requires us to acknowledge its potential in every movement or cause. Fundamentalism may therefore be regarded as a tendency which does not exclude and is not excluded by modernist or other contrary religious proclivities. We are all of us, to some degree and in some senses, fundamentalists.

Note

1. The influence of Professor James Barr's seminal monograph dealing with Protestant fundamentalism on several contributors to this symposium will become apparent in the course of the volume. Even those who do not agree with all aspects of his analysis acknowledge their considerable intellectual debt to his pioneering work.

References

Ahmad, I. (ed.) (1981), 'Introduction', *Ritual and Religion among Muslims in India* (Delhi: Manohar).

Amin, S. (1983), 'Is there a Political Economy of Islamic Fundamentalism?' *Jour. African Marxists*, 3, pp. 6–29.

Ardener, E. (1985), 'Social Anthropology and the Decline of Modernism', in J. Overing (ed.), *Reason and Morality* (London: Tavistock).

Aronoff, M. J. (1983), 'Gush Emunim: the institutionalization of a charismatic, messianic, religious-political revitalization movement in Israel', *Pol. Anthrop.*, 3, pp. 63–84.

Baharuddin, S. A. (1983), 'A Revival in the study of Islam in Malaysia', *Man*, 18, pp. 399–403.

Barr, J. (1977), *Fundamentalism* (London: SCM Press).

Carter, P. (1968), 'The fundamentalist defense of the faith', in J. Braeman, R. Bremner and D. Brody (eds), *Change and Continuity in twentieth-century America: the 1920's* (Columbus: Ohio State University Press).

Crawford, A. (1980), *Thunder on the Right: the 'New Right' and the politics of resentment* (New York: Pantheon).

Crick, M. (1976), *Explorations in Language and Meaning: towards a semantic anthropology* (London: Malaby).

Cudsi, A. S. and A. H. Dessouki, (eds) (1981) 'Introduction', *Islam and Power* (London: Croom Helm).

Dessouki, A. H. (1981), 'The resurgence of Islamic organisations in Egypt: an interpretation', in A. S. Cudsi and A. H. Dessouki (eds), *Islam and Power* (London: Croom Helm).

Dumont, L. (1971) 'Religion, politics, and society in the individualistic universe', *Proc. Royal Anthrop. Inst*, 1970, pp. 31–40.

Eisenstein, Z. (1982), 'The sexual politics of the new right: understanding the "crisis of liberalism" for the 1980s', *Signs*, 7, pp. 567–88.

Epstein, A. L. (1986), 'The millenium and the self: Jehovah's Witnesses on the Copperbelt in the '50s', *Anthropos*, 81.

Firth, R. (1981), 'Spiritual aroma: religion and politics', *Amer. Anthrop.*, 83, pp. 582–601.

Foucault, M. (1980), *Power/Knowledge: selected interviews and other writings 1972–1977*, ed. C. Gordon (Brighton: Harvester Press).

Frykenberg, R. E. (forthcoming), 'Revivalism and fundamentalism: some critical observations with special reference to politics in south Asia', in J. W. Bjorkman (ed.), *Fundamentalism, Revivalists and Violence in South Asia* (Riverdale, Md.: Riverdale Co.).

Hobart, M. (1985), 'Is God evil?', in D. J. Parkin (ed.), *The Anthropology of Evil* (Oxford: Basil Blackwell).

Hofstadter, R. (1964), *Anti-intellectualism in American Life* (London: Jonathan Cape).

Hollenweger, W. (1972), *The Pentecostals* (transl. R. Wilson) (London: SCM).

Humphreys, R. S. (1979), 'Islam and political values in Saudi Arabia, Egypt and Syria', *The Mid. East Rev.*, 33, pp. 1–19.

Lévi-Strauss, C. (1962), *Totemism* (transl. R. Needham) (London: Merlin).

Marsden, G. (1980), *Fundamentalism and American Culture: the shaping of twentieth-century evangelicalism, 1870–1925* (New York: Oxford University Press).

Mines, M. (1981), 'Islamization and Muslim ethnicity in South India', in I. Ahmad (ed.) *Ritual and Religion among Muslims in India* (Delhi: Manohar).

Nagata, J. (1979), 'Religious ideology and social change: the Islamic revival in Malaysia', *Pac. Affairs*, 52, pp. 405–39.

—— (1980), 'The new fundamentalism: Islam in contemporary Malaysia', *Asian Thought and Society*, 5, pp. 128–41.

Needham, R. (ed.) (1971), 'Introduction', *Rethinking Kinship and Marriage* (London: Tavistock).

—— (1975), 'Polythetic classification: convergence and consequences', *Man*, 10, pp. 349–69.

Overing, J. (ed.) (1985) 'Introduction', *Reason and Morality* (London: Tavistock).

Parkin, D. J. (ed.) (1985) 'Introduction', *The Anthropology of Evil* (Oxford: Basil Blackwell).

Parry, J. (1985), 'The Brahmanical tradition and the technology of the intellect', in *Reason and Morality*, ed. J. Overing (London: Tavistock).

Rivière, P. (1971), 'Marriage: a reassessment', in R. Needham (ed.), *Rethinking Kinship and Marriage* (London: Tavistock).

Robinson, J. (1963), *Honest to God* (London: SCM Press).

Ruth, S. (1983), 'A feminist analysis of the new right', *Women's Stud. Int'l. Forum*, 6, pp. 345–52.

Said, E. (1981), *Covering Islam: how the media and the experts determine how we see the rest of the world* (London: Routledge & Kegan Paul).

Sandeen, E. (1970), *The Roots of Fundamentalism: British and American millenarianism, 1800–1930* (Chicago: University of Chicago Press).

Shackle, C. (forthcoming), *Sikhism*, In S. Sutherland (ed.), *The world's Religions* (London: Croom Helm).

Van Buitenen, J. A. B. (1968), 'On the archaism of the Bhagavata Purana', in M. Singer (ed.), *Krishna: Myths, Rites and Attitudes* (Chicago: University of Chicago Press).

Vatikiotis, P. J. (1982), 'The rise of the clerisocracy', *Encounter*, 58, pp. 68–76.

Whitfield, S. J. (1982), '"One nation under God": the rise of the religious right', *Virginia Qtrly Rev.*, 58, pp. 557–74.

Williams, R. C. (1983), 'Scientific creationism: an exegesis for a religious doctrine', *Amer. Anthrop.*, 85, pp. 92–102.

2 The Quest for the Islamic State: Islamic Fundamentalism in Egypt and Iran
Sami Zubaida

INTRODUCTION

'Islamic fundamentalism' is a term which has gained wide currency in recent years, both in the scholarly literature and in the media. It is a term created in current discourses on the Middle East and elsewhere which has an identifiable but not strictly limited range of reference. It refers to modern political movements and ideas, mostly oppositional, which seek to establish, in one sense or another, an Islamic state. The model for an Islamic state is sought by these movements in a 'sacred history' of the original political community of the faithful established by the Prophet Muhammad in Medina in the seventh century and maintained under his four successors, the *rashidun* (rightly guided) caliphs (in Shi'i Islam, it is only the rule of one of them, Ali). Identifying the essential elements of this model, and the way in which they can be constructed into a contemporary state and society, varies widely according to different political and ideological positions. I would argue that all 'fundamentalism' is modern in that it attempts to reconstruct the fundamentals of an ideational system in modern society, in accordance with political and ideological positions taken in relation to current issues and discourses. Identification of the fundamentals and their combinations are effected in relation to these current political processes. In what follows I shall examine the development of themes and issues in Islamic political discourse and activity in two Middle East countries in which these developments have been prominent and influential, and which provide strikingly contrasting examples. I shall concentrate primarily on Egypt, concluding with a general sketch of religion and politics in Iran to draw out the main contrasts. I shall discuss these developments in the context of their relation to the ideas and realities of the modern nation-state, at first in anticipation of this political form and by

25

reference to European examples, and later in the project to Islamise the nation-state, or to deny it in favour of a universal conception of faith. In Egypt, modern political Islam started in the second half of the nineteenth century in anticipation of a modern state on the European model which it mostly welcomed, but constructed in terms of 'original' Islam, as against the degenerate religion of the dynastic polity it opposed. Subsequent movements in Egypt assumed the model of a modern nation-state and sought ways, intellectually and politically, to Islamise this model. Unlike Egypt, religious developments in Iran remained largely within the religious establishment, which feared and resisted the modern state (itself a very different pattern from the Egyptian), then acquiesced in its inevitability while retaining an important base of autonomy in relation to that state. This was to be a crucial factor in the leading role it came to play in recent political events.

The terms 'modern state' and 'nation-state' do not refer to an invarying common form, but more to combinations of elements and characteristics constituting perhaps an 'ideal type'. It was Max Weber who contributed most explicitly to the characterisation of the modern state.[1] The form of the state itself is 'legal-rational', in that government rests on codified law which regulates hierarchies of office with specified powers, obligations and limits, thus constituting a specific type of bureaucracy. Civil society which typically corresponds to this state and provides the conditions for it is one in which extensive social division of labour has led to individualisation of economic and political subjects from communal and collectivist organisation of tribe, village, kinship or other corporate forms. The constituents of the state are then individual citizens with legal personalities and specified rights and obligations. Whether such a state has a democratic representational form or not, its political processes and struggles involve the organisation and mobilisation of citizens in constituencies of support based on common interests or ideological commitments. A certain degree of general literacy is essential for the communications which form an important part of this form of politics. Literacy in a common language is also an important constituent of the ideological conceptions of common national belonging, which Dominic Anderson (1985) has called 'imagined communities'. In reality, as we all know, primordial loyalties of ethnicity, religion, regional origins and so forth play a very important part in the politics of modern states, but these loyalties are cast in the political idiom and mode of political parties employing methods of organisation and communication characteristic of this model of the modern state. I shall have occasion in what follows to elaborate on these different political modalities.

The currents of Islamic fundamentalism I shall discuss here have developed discourses and practices which refer, explicitly or implicitly, to the modern state. The creation or the transformation of the modern state along the lines of the 'sacred history' of Islam is a recurrent theme. There are fundamentalist currents which do not fit into this mould, most notably the Wahabi movement which culminated in the formation of modern Saudi Arabia (see Amselle in this volume, Chapter 4). I have argued elsewhere (Zubaida, 1985) that this is an example of a historical genre of tribal movements which start with religious zeal and culminate in a routinised dynastic state, which is precisely what happened in Saudi Arabia. It is quite distinct from Islamic politics in the context of the modern state (although it did have important intellectual effects in that context).

The event which above all others has focused world attention on 'fundamentalism' was the Iranian Revolution of 1979. For the European and American media and their audiences it was an object of fascination and fear: a demonstration to many that the deep rooted bases of 'traditional belief' cannot be overridden with 'modernisation' which is only a superficial veneer. To 'Third World' nationalists and some 'Third Worldists', it represented not merely an anti-imperialist revolution, but one with the special distinction of cultural authenticity, challenging the most insidious dimension of imperialism, the cultural. In other Islamic countries, especially in the Arab world, the impact was tremendous. Naturally enough, those already inclined to Islamic affiliations drew great inspiration and strength from the demonstration effect of the revolution; suddenly their ideas were firmly on the world stage and within the realms of political possibility. What is even more important, however, was the impact on other oppositional political groups and individuals, including those on the left, who have traditionally opposed Islamic currents, usually ranged to the far right of the political spectrum. Here was an Islamic revolution which was populist and anti-imperialist, which had sported some of the vocabularies and slogans of the left. For some it seemed that, unlike the 'imported' ideologies of Marxism or nationalism, Islam in its political and 'progressive' form is more accessible to the people, springing as it does from their historical cultural roots. Political Islam acquired many recruits, a political respectability and viability; it became firmly established in the political mainstream. This was to the embarrassment and discomfort of political regimes which had adopted or encouraged

Islam as a means of discipline and control (Saudi Arabia), or as a counter against the left (Sadat in Egypt).

The Iranian revolution underlined the salience of political Islam in current Middle East and world politics. But it is clearly neither the starting point of political Islam, which has a long history in the modern world, nor the political or sociological prototype of Islamic political movements elsewhere. It is important to emphasise this point, because it is often assumed, both by the Islamic propagandists themselves and by some Western commentators, that there is some unity underlying the Islamic phenomenon, provided by the receptivity of Middle Eastern peoples to religious appeals, which they understand and accept more readily than they would 'imported' politics and ideology. The argument I shall present here is that the significance and outcome of Islamic politics can only be determined in the contexts of particular institutions and struggles, which in the case of Egypt are vastly different. This difference, I shall show, cannot be explained in terms of the contrast between Sunni and Shi'i Islam. Let us turn to a consideration of these contexts and conjunctures.

THE HISTORICAL BACKGROUND

While the concern of this chapter is primarily with the modern world, a brief glance at the historical background is nevertheless essential. The very use of the term 'political Islam' may be at issue: what other form of Islam is there? Islam has been political since its inception, it may be argued, a unity of the state and the community of the faithful. That is at least the theory of Islamic jurisprudence, but the practice for most of the centuries of Islamic history is quite different, a fact also recognised in theology and jurisprudence. Islamic empires, at least since the time of the Umayyads, have maintained a *de facto* distinction between the state and society. Religion entered both but in different ways, and, except for brief periods, was neither dominant over nor coincident with either state or society. The state consisted of the ruling dynasty with their retainers, functionaries and soldiery. The early Islamic armies which conquered the vast territories which later constituted the Islamic empires, consisted of Arab tribesmen. Hence the Caliph could be seen as the chief of the community, the state as the political form of the community, and the soldiers as the faithful in arms. This state of affairs was not to survive dynastic rule, under which the Arab armies were disbanded and replaced by professional soldiers, mostly Turkish. This state, now structurally and socially separate from its subjects, remained theoretically the Islamic state. Its head still bore the title of Caliph (successor and deputy to the Prophet), who encouraged and facilitated Islamic worship, punished heresy and generally upheld the symbols and rituals of Islam. In the constitution of the state Islam was confined to particular institutions, almost exclusively the legal institutions. The law, however, was in practice only partially based on religious sources, and it only applied to limited spheres of mostly private and civil statuses and transactions. The ruler and his servants were bound by the law only in theory and in the most general ethical terms. Models and procedures of government were drawn from the pre-Islamic imperial traditions of Persia and Byzantium. The primary source of legislation was by decree of the ruler, although this in theory should not contradict the principles of *shari'a* (Islamic law). Some taxes are specified in *shari'a*, but most of the forms of taxation were in addition to those stipulated; some rulers even taxed the sale of alcoholic drinks, thus legally admitting what in religious terms was prohibited. In the sphere of the state, however, religion occupied a distinct but limited and subordinate position. Middle Eastern polities were in practice as Islamic as their European counterparts were Christian.

In the context of civil society, the first point to note is the diversity of religious manifestations. The most important divide is that between the city and the non-urban sphere of nomads and tribesmen of desert and mountain (in Middle Eastern geo-history, these are the two main spheres, the rural being an appendage of one or the other; see Zubaida, 1985). The nomadic was considered by the orthodox (often quite rightly) to be the sphere of heterodoxy and the refuge of heresy outside the reach of political and religious authority. Scriptural orthodoxy claimed pride of place in the city: it was the official state religion, and one of the main connecting links between state and civil society. The religious institutions of the state were manned by personnel drawn from the strata of urban notables, the same strata which included merchants and landowners. These were also the leaders of urban society and the intermediaries between the state and the other urban strata. Orthodoxy existed side by side with Sufism and, since about the eleventh century, in harmony with it. In terms of belief and ritual, Sufism is a mystical, spiritual and gnostic stream within Islam, but beyond this general characterisation exhibits, in turn, considerable diversity. To sum up, religion in civil society took diverse and overlapping forms, many of which bore only a tenuous relation to orthodox, scriptural Islam.

Modern Islamic political thought has to be seen in the context of a conjuncture between this historical background and the European impact. The reformist intellectuals of the Ottoman Empire and of Iran, concerned at the weakness and backwardness of their countries in the face of European might, believed that the superiority of the European powers (mainly Britain and France) did not depend solely on economic and military power. They were convinced that behind these factors lay a socio-political system which produced awareness and commitment among the people, and an effective organisation of state and society. Ottoman, including Egyptian Islamic, intellectuals argued that the perceived inferiority of their countries was not attributable to Islam as such, as Europeans may think, but to the degeneration and corruption of Islam. Islam was seen to have anticipated the European systems. This line of thought was shared by two major figures in the late nineteenth century, often cited as the founders of the reformist movement in Egypt, Jamal Eddin al-Afghani and Muhammad Abdu.

POLITICAL ISLAM IN EGYPT

Egypt was the Middle Eastern country which experienced the earliest direct European conquest and thereafter its continued presence and influence. It started with the Napoleonic invasion, soon followed by the modernising rule of Muhammad Ali, who attempted, with some success, economic and administrative reforms. These included institutions of modern education and scholarships for promising students to France. French and other European literature and social thought were eagerly taken up by a wide circle of intellectuals including, significantly, some with religious education and training. Muhammad Ali's successors (dynastic descendants) took Egypt into ever closer involvement with and dependence upon Britain and France, culminating in debt crises and more direct economic, military and political controls by these powers throughout the nineteenth century and for the first half of the twentieth. These developments included profound social and cultural effects: considerable measures of industrialisation and urbanisation, capitalist penetration of important sectors of agriculture, with consequent break-up or loosening of old communal bonds. Together with the limited development of education and literacy, these developments created more or less politicised publics, especially in the major cities, who were increasingly aware of the inequities of foreign domination, and of the gap between the promise of European ideas of liberty and the realities of continued restrictions under dynastic rule. Islamic political thought has to be considered in this context.

The picture of religion in relation to society and the state given in the foregoing historical sketch, still applied to nineteenth-century Egypt. Muhammad Abdu's reforms were aimed first at religious ideas and institutions, and then at the wider society.[2] Religious institutions, including the great university of al-Azhar in Cairo, were still partaking in the wisdom of the Middle Ages, and teaching medieval geography, mathematics and science as well as the religious studies of theology and jurisprudence. This archaic scholasticism existed side by side with popular religiosity imbued with magic and saint worship. Abdu, himself a prominent *alim* (a learned man of religion) succeeded in enlisting the support of the authorities in reforming and modernising these institutions. But the task which he and his mentor Afghani had set themselves was much wider: it was to liberate Islamic countries from their weakness and backwardness, and their subjugation to the European imperial powers. They attributed this weakness to the ignorance, corruption and fragmentation characteristic of Islamic polities and societies, including the religious institutions. But these failings, they argued, were certainly not intrinsic to Islam, quite the contrary; witness the glories of the Islamic past, both in knowledge and in might. In particular, the socio-political system which contributed so much to the might and civilisation of the West, was anticipated by Islam many centuries previously. The Islamic community founded by Muhammad in Medina in the seventh century exemplified all the principles of citizenship and democracy in a purer and clearer form. For while in Christianity religion is separated from the state, in Islam the state is one with the *umma*, the community of believers: religion, state and people form one body. In the Medinan community the state was but the plurality of its citizens unified by faith and obedience to the commands of God. No man could rule over another because rule belonged to God alone. The army was but the citizenry in arms. Institutions like *shura*, the imperative that the ruler consult his followers in all important matters, and *bay'a*, the collective oath of allegiance to a new leader before he could assume the *khilafa* (caliphate) – the succession to Muhammad as commander of the faithful – ensured representativeness and responsibility of rule in a form more original and direct than the equivalent institutions in modern Europe. What Muslims needed now was not so much to follow Europe, but to revive their original heritage, which had been subverted by the dynastic empires, and forgotten in the degeneration and corruption of religion in the later centuries.

It may be instructive to draw a parallel between Islamic thinkers seeking reform in the revival of original elements of their history with their European (especially German) equivalents in the eighteenth and nineteenth centuries. For Goethe, Schiller, Holderlin and Hegel,[3] the ancient Athenian republic fulfilled a similar function as the Medinan community for our Islamic thinkers. A model of the unity of the state and civil society, and the identity of private individual and citizen, in contrast to the social, political and psychological fragmentation which they perceived in their contemporary world. Some, like the young Hegel, saw in the French Revolution the possibilities of a regeneration at a higher level of the Athenian model. But it is the significance they attached to religion which is of particular interest here. They contrasted the subjective and individualistic elements of Christianity to the civic and folk religions of Greece and Rome, and attributed the fragmentation of life in contemporary society at least in part to the prevailing religious spirit. We do not know whether Abdu or any of his followers knew about this discussion, though we do know that Abdu was familiar with contemporary European thought, and was particularly impressed with Auguste Comte and Herbert Spencer.[4] What is interesting, however, is that he presented similar arguments when contrasting Christianity with Islam: Christianity separated religiosity from politics and public life, whereas Islam, as we have seen, he considered to be an eminently political and civic religion. But unlike the German thinkers who could not argue for a revival of ancient Greek religion, Abdu's Athenian republic was Islamic Medina; all he was doing was advocating a revival of true and original Islam.

Abdu is not normally identified as a fundamentalist but rather as a liberal reformer with a nineteenth-century faith in progress through enlightenment. The major contrast between Abdu and, say, the Muslim Brotherhood (see below) is his liberalism with regard to the application of Islamic law, particularly elements of the penal code and the restrictions on women.[5] At the present time the insistence on these elements of *shari'a* is the hallmark of fundamentalism, and by these criteria Abdu is not a fundamentalist. It may be argued that this insistence on the letter of the Quran is a defining characteristic of fundamentalism. But any call for the application of the *shari'a* must implicitly accept many interpretations and elaborations beyond the letter of the holy sources. Abdu was doing no more than the Islamic jurists have done throughout the ages in using very wide and vague principles of legal methodology of deduction and analogy in arriving at judgements. A fundamentalist position calling for the application of the *shari'a* must accept that any version will already contain many constructions which have a very tenuous connection to the holy sources. What underlies the contrast between Abdu and later fundamentalists are their different attitudes to European ideas and models: whereas for Abdu Europe, the oppressor, was at the same time the model for progress and strength, for the later fundamentalists the West was both oppressive and culturally threatening. The insistence on the Quranic penal code and on the restrictions on women are emotionally and symbolically potent proclamations of cultural identity and antagonism to the Westernised sectors of society who have betrayed this heritage. While Abdu is clearly not a fundamentalist in the current sense, his construction of the 'sacred history' as a model for the modern state was a very important episode in the quest for the Islamic state.

An event which symbolised the institution of the modern state in the former Ottoman lands was Ataturk's abolition of the Caliphate in 1924. The modern state which Abdu sought had arrived, but with hardly any Islamic trappings in its organisation or ideology. Ataturk's republic was explicitly anti-religious (see the Tappers in this volume, Chapter 3). Iraq, Palestine and Syria were under European mandates, and Egypt, while nominally independent, was in reality a European colony. Islamic presence within the state, in so far as it existed at all, was confined to the law of personal status. The loss of the Caliphate stimulated a pronounced reaction in India, where a movement for its restoration was started. In Egypt the most prominent response was that of Rashid Rida (d.1935),[6] a religious intellectual and disciple of Abdu. He sought a formula for re-establishing the Caliphate under modern conditions of separate nation states. His solution was a Caliph who would enjoy spiritual authority in all the Islamic lands by virtue of his learning and religious stature, and possibly of his descent from one of the respected Arab dynasties who claim the ancestry of the Prophet. This authority would be superimposed on independent sovereign governments, much like the Papacy in the Catholic world. Politically, Rida's advocacy came to nothing. Like Abdu, Rida exerted considerable intellectual influence, which had practical consequences in the religious and educational spheres. But neither of them succeeded in transferring his ideas into the field of political struggle or of incorporating them into the modern state. It was the Muslim Brotherhood which took the quest for the Islamic state into the political field of popular agitation and organisation.

The Muslim Brotherhood

This is the movement which, in one form or another, has been the most prominent fundamentalist current in Sunni Islam since its inception in Egypt in 1928.[7] While clearly influenced by the ideas of Abdu and Rida, it eschewed the European influences of Abdu's reformism and the intellectualism of Rida, aiming for a popular and populist appeal, with considerable success. The Brotherhood was founded by Hassan al-Banna, a school teacher in Isma'iliya in the Canal Zone. By all accounts al-Banna was a person endowed with great charisma and a prophetic zeal. He was struck by the corruption and degradation of Muslims, especially the young, of his time, and their subordination politically, economically and culturally to the dominant foreigners. He launched the Brotherhood as a movement for education and reform of hearts and minds. He taught the children in the daytime and their parents at night. The movement soon grew and spread to many parts of the country, and acquired premises and funds. It very soon acquired a political dimension, calling for the Islamic reform of society and government. It became bitterly opposed to the secular, liberal-constitutional parties, especially the Wafd (the main democractic party in Egypt before the Free Officers' revolution in 1952), and in the process was firmly identified with the right. At times the Brotherhood flirted with the Royal Palace and participated in its intrigues against the elected Wafd government. Its members participated in the nationalist agitations against the British in the Canal Zone and then as volunteers in the Palestine conflict. It clearly had a potent influence in the lower ranks of the armed forces. Eventually (early 1940s) it developed its own armed 'secret apparatus' and engaged in political assassinations, the most prominent victim being the prime minister of Egypt, al-Nuqrashi, killed in 1949. Al-Banna himself was soon to fall in what was evidently a reprisal killing by the secret police. The Brotherhood, it would seem, had close connections with the Free Officers movement which staged the *coup d'état* in 1952, and enjoyed official favour in the early days of the new regime. But they were soon to fall out with Nasser after he took over in 1954, and he was to become the target for an assassination attempt, after which the Brotherood was fiercely suppressed. In spite of the flourishes of Islamic rhetoric, Nasser's regime was essentially secular, and the dominant official ideas were those of nationalism and socialism. The bitter enmity between Nasser and the Brotherhood persisted and flared in another episode in 1965 when the police claimed to have discovered an armed plot against the government, arrested many of the cadres of the Brotherhood and executed some of the leaders, including Sayyid Qutb, theoretician of more recent trends to be discussed later in this chapter.

The original aim of the Brotherood was the reform of hearts and minds, to guide Muslims back to the true religion, and away from the corrupt aspirations and conduct created by European dominance. The early politicisation of the movement placed this objective in the context of a virtuous community and an Islamic political order. Hassan al-Banna, in an essay entitled 'The Reform of Self and Society', wrote:

> Our duty as Muslim Brothers is to work for the reform of selves [*nufus*], of hearts and souls by joining them to God the all-high; then to organise our society to be fit for the virtuous community which commands the good and forbids evil-doing, then from the community will arise the good state. (Hassan al-Banna, n.d.)

The main plank of their (rudimentary) political thought is a construction of the 'sacred history' similar to what we have already outlined, the recreation of the early Medinan community of the Prophet; their most persistent slogan is 'the Quran is our constitution'. But their model of the 'sacred history' is quite different from the liberal-constitutional image which emerges from Abdu's construction. In their version piety, order and authority play a central role. They advocate a presidential system with an elected *shura* (consultative) council, also part of the 'sacred history' model, postulated as an equivalent to a parliament. However, al-Banna strongly objected to political parties, arguing that they represent sectional and egoistic interests which divide and corrupt the body politic of the *umma*. This element in their thought reinforced their identification, by their opponents, with fascist organic-statist ideologies. The social and economic programme for such a regime is even more rudimentary and vague than the political thought. First is the axiomatic duty to facilitate and enforce the conditions and means for Islamic piety and ritual observance. This includes facilities for women, including working women, to maintain appropriate standards of dress and of insulation from contact with men. After that it is the maintenance of social justice as specified in the Quran. This of course gives wide scope for interpretation. Some thinkers from the ranks of the Muslim Brothers advocated Islamic socialism (see, for instance, Mohammad al-Ghazzali, 1951). These treatises always start with a denunciation of Marxism and materialism, then elaborate on the inequities of capitalism seen as a system of *riba*, usury, which is forbidden in Islamic law. Al-Ghazzali interprets the sacred sources as supporting a distrust of private property, all goods belonging to God and disposable by those who rule justly in His name, the Caliph or his equivalent in an Islamic order. Private property is only justified if it fulfils a social function. The programme of an Islamic government must, therefore, include nationalisation and land reform. Some commentators have remarked on the similarity of this picture to the Nasser regime's 'Arab socialism' which was to follow. But as we have seen, the Brothers were to denounce that regime as ungodly tyranny, and one that neglected all the tenets of Islam. These ideas of Islamic socialism have persisted in one form or another among progressive intellectuals with an Islamic orientation, but not so much among the Muslim Brothers as such. They have maintained vague notions of social justice, but have not used the vocabulary of socialism, or shown any hostility to private property. An obvious interpretation of this reticence regarding socialism is the maintenance of a clear ideological boundary against the rhetoric of the Nasser regime, and its apparent friendliness in foreign affairs to the socialist bloc. This hostility to socialism and to socialists has crystallised even more clearly in the ideas of the new Muslim Brotherhood which emerged into semi-legal public operation under Sadat in the 1970s and continues to the present day. Many of the leading personalities of the Brotherhood found refuge from Nasserite repression in Saudi Arabia, and the Saudi connection has been maintained as an important source of moral and financial support to the present time. This connection will no doubt have had significant political influence. It would seem that Sadat made an accurate political calculation in bringing the Brothers back to Egyptian public life, and allowing the publication of their magazine *Al-Da'wa*, as a counter to the Nasserites and the left.

In every respect the Muslim Brotherhood, from its inception, has operated as a political party, now legal, now clandestine. It is the first organised Islamic popular movement in a modern urban setting. Its organisation and ideology assume potential constituencies composed of individualised political subjects, a high proportion of whom are literate and approachable through the printed word. Its activities and strategies assume the space of a centralised modern state, and are directed at its institutions and powers. Part of its strategy is the infiltration of military and police establishments. The primary objective of the establishment of an Islamic state is construed within the context of a modern nation state. In fact, of all the political parties operating in recent Egyptian history the Muslim Brotherhood is one of the most modern in its assumptions and operations. Alongside the various small parties of the left, it relied primarily on organisation and mobilisation of support on ideological-political appeal and on an individual basis, as against the predominant politics of notables and of patronage networks characteristic of the general political scene, including many aspects of the organisation of support for the leading Wafd party. Nasserism in its heyday enjoyed widespread popular support and enthusiasm, but much of that was spontaneous and unorganised. And where it was organised, it was based on a government party closely interlinked with authority. Finally, in terms of the territorial scope of its operation, the Brotherhood shared the dilemma of Arab political ideologies in the oscillation between a particular national perspective (Egyptian) and a pan-Arab or, sometimes, pan-Islamic one. Its political organisation and activity was primarily in Egypt, but Brotherhood organisations were founded in other Arab countries, notably in Syria and Jordan, and more recently in the Gulf and in Tunisia. But while there is considerable contact and sometimes co-operation between these different national organisations, each constitutes a unit in the national politics of its location.[8] The political space of its operation is in effect the multitude of Arab political entities, each organised as a separate nation state, but with a formal commitment to 'unity' theoretically shared by all, in practice a dead letter. The most notable extra-Egyptian activity in the Brotherhood's history is its participation in the Palestinian conflict, in itself part of Egyptian national politics.

Recent fundamentalist currents

While the Muslim Brotherhood has maintained its position as a leading actor on the political stage in recent years, it was the other more militant Islamic groups, like the so-called *Takfir wal Hijra*, and *Jihad* which assumed the most spectacular roles, especially with the assassination of President Sadat in 1981. To understand properly the ideology and organisation of these groups and their difference from the Brotherhood, we have to consider the ideological strand which inspired them in the first place, the ideas of Sayyid Qutb.

Sayyid Qutb (1906–65) was one of the main intellectual figures in the Muslim Brotherhood. A school teacher who was also a known and respected man of letters, he spent two years in the United States (1949–51) on a training programme, and was familiar with the major strands in modern Western thought. He joined the Brotherhood in 1951 and was put in charge of *da'wa* ('missionary') activity. Under the Nasser repression he spent ten years in prison. He was released in 1964, only to be rearrested a few months later, implicated in an arms plot, condemned to death and executed in 1965. He wrote many books on Islamic religion and its modern social and political implications, including a highly original commentary on the Quran. *Ma'alim fil Tariq* ('Landmarks along the Path'; Qutb, 1980), was one of his last books. It contains the ideational basis for much subsequent radical thinking. Let us consider the main ideas of this work.

The project of re-enacting the episodes of the 'sacred history' features prominently in Qutb's thought, only the episodes follow early Islamic history more precisely. The 'first Islamic generation' of Muhammad and his followers constituted themselves as a nucleus of believers separate from the *jahili* (ignorant, barbaric) society around them. As such they strengthened themselves in faith and numbers in spite of the waves of persecution they suffered. When they were sufficiently strong and confident in their faith, they broke away from *jahili* society in a *hijra* (flight, migration) from Mecca to Medina, where support was already assured. From there they waged an armed assault, a *jihad* (holy war) against the unbelievers, and with the help of the Almighty, triumphed and prevailed. They instituted the rule of God (*hakimiyyet allah*) as against the theretofore prevalent rule of man. But this holy realm only lasted for a brief period, to be subverted after the death of the Prophet and his close companions into a dynastic corrupt rule of man by man. *Jahiliyya* was restored, and it prevails to the present day. The task of the believer now is to follow in the footsteps of this first Islamic generation. A vanguard of believers must be formed which would insulate itself from *jahili* society. Given that the believers will have to live within *jahili* society (as Muhammad and his early followers had to live within Meccan society), the insulation will have to be a psychic or emotional insulation (*in'izal shu'uri*). This vanguard, again following the example of the sacred history, would strengthen itself in faith and numbers, and then launch a *jihad* against *jahili* society, which will only end when the rule of God prevails throughout the world (and Qutb made it clear that he meant the whole world, and not just the Islamic world). This would not entail any coercion in converting people to the true faith, but only the removal of the coercion of the rule of man, and then individuals would be able freely to choose their faith. Qutb contended that Western civilisation, while successful in providing material wealth (which merited his approval, because Islam is not an ascetic religion, but enjoins the production and enjoyment of wealth), has reached a point of crisis because of spiritual bankruptcy. Communism is no solution, as it has proved itself to be a guise for tyranny and corruption. Only Islam can maintain the material achievements of the West, but in the good society, under the rule of God.

Qutb, however, was quite insistent that economic and social considerations were only secondary; Islam is not a social doctrine, its concern is not social justice or freedom or any other ideal, it is nothing but a faith. The sole object of the Islamic vanguard is to implant this faith in the hearts and minds of the believers. Part of this faith is to bring about the rulership of God, so it has a necessary political project: to overthrow the rule of man and end the state of *jahiliyya*. *Jihad* is, therefore, an integral part of the faith. The effect of this element of Qutb's thought is to rule out as irrelevant the comparisons of Islam to democracy, to socialism or any other 'ism': Islam is nothing but itself, a faith and a doctrine.

The political implications of Qutbic thought are quite startling. It departs radically from the central concerns of mainstream Islamic politics as represented in the different strands of the Muslim Brotherhood, or in reformist Islamic thinking. It implies that purportedly Islamic countries, like Egypt, are not really Islamic but part of the realm of *jahiliyya*. In terms of conventional religion it is a serious infraction to declare a Muslim (that is, one who declares himself Muslim) to be an infidel (*takfir al-muslim*). Politically, it requires an abandonment of the populist stance of the Brotherhood in favour of vanguardist secret politics of cells (the Brotherhood reserved this kind of politics for its 'secret apparatus', the armed conspiratorial branch). In our terms, it means an explicit rejection of the political idiom of the modern nation state and of modern political ideologies in favour of a universalist project based on faith. These implications were realised to various degrees by the radical groups of the 1970s and 1980s.

Modern radical groups

In the 1970s two main groups emerged on the political scene in Egypt: the 'Military Academy' (*al-faniyya al-askariyya*) group, deriving this name from the attack on the military academy in 1974 (as a prelude to a failed *coup d'état*), and the so-called *takfir wal hijra* (inadequately translated as 'repentance and holy flight'), but which referred to itself as *Jama'at al-Muslimin*, (the Society of Muslims).[9] This group came into prominence with the kidnap and then assassination of the Minister of Religious Foundations in 1977. The so-called *al-Jihad* (holy war) group, some of whose members were responsible for the assassination of President Sadat in 1981, is reckoned to be a continuation of the 'military academy' group. The founders and core members of these groups were among those incarcerated and tortured in Nasser's prisons. It is related that their jailers often ridiculed their convictions and taunted them that the Almighty was indifferent to their sufferings. These attitudes led many of the younger internees to the conviction that their jailers and the state which employed them could not be Muslims even when they professed Islam, they were *kuffar* (infidels). Sayyid Qutb's view of contemporary society as a *jahiliyya* from which the true believers must separate themselves until sufficiently strong to conquer it for Islam, gave a coherent theoretical expression to these sentiments. These ideas are at the basis of the doctrines of the modern radical groups.

Jama'at al-Muslimin was the group that took these ideas to their logical extreme. Under the leadership of Shukri Mustafa, they considered themselves to constitute the only true Muslims; anyone called to join who refuses is an infidel. The life and property of all infidels are licit to the believers. Their separation from *jahili* society was accomplished within urban spaces by housing their members in 'furnished apartments', a term which has specific significance in current Egyptian vocabulary. In modern Cairo, property values and rents are so high that to rent a house or a flat which is subject to rent control requires considerable capital outlay in 'key money'. The poorer entrants into the housing market, as well as various marginals like prostitutes and petty criminals are pushed into 'furnished apartments' (which do not in practice have much furniture), mostly located in the outer suburbs. It was in this space of marginality and transience that the true believers found their separation from *jahili* society. In common with the other radical groups they indicated their separation by refusing to recognise the religious and social institutions of *jahili* society. For instance, they refused to pray in the official mosques, and they arranged their own marriages without the customary monetary payments (*mahr*), or the parties and ceremonies. Some of the Society of Muslims went further and effected a total spatial separation, a *hijra* (following the example of the Prophet and the early followers in the sacred history) into the mountains and caves of upper Egypt, where they engaged in worship and physical training.

What is the political significance of this separation? First we must note an important difference between the two groups. While the Society of Muslims declared all the people outside their group to be infidels, the *jihad* group declared only the rulers to be infidels, while ordinary people were Muslims. Their task, therefore, consisted in attempting to remove these rulers and restore the rule of God (the assassination of Sadat was fully consistent with this view). The view of the Society of Muslims requires taking on the whole of society as *jahili* enemies, a much more difficult task. Both groups display characteristics of a messianic view of the world. This is not in the sense of postulating the coming of a messiah, but in aiming to achieve a perfect state of socio-political being without even a remotely realistic account of the current situation nor a strategy for achieving such a state, except perhaps a ritual one. An element of this ritual is their insistence on the imperative of *bay'ah*, the duty of every Muslim to swear allegiance to an *amir* and thereafter to obey his commands. In this step the group constitutes itself as a political society in the ritual sense of being subject to the rule of a Muslim prince, who will govern in accordance with God's commands. The question of how this microcosm of the Islamic body politic is to achieve its victory over *jahili* society and its rulers is answered primarily in terms of spectacular gestures.

All the Egyptian Islamic currents under consideration have been located outside the religious institutions and hierarchies, and often in opposition to them. But individual *alims* or *shaykhs* ('clerics', for lack of a better English equivalent) have participated in the leadership of movements: Abdu, as we have seen, was a *shaykh*, but one who found the religious establishment archaic, and embarked on a programme of reforms. More recently, some of the most vociforous demands for the application of the *shari'a* in Egypt have come from clerics. But these mavericks do not speak for the religious establishment, which is generally quiescent in relation to the government of the day. In this respect the religious institutions in Egypt still follow the Ottoman pattern of forming part of the state, for the most part supporting its policies, or at least not voicing strong opposition, unless some outrage is being committed against religion. To conclude the discussion, I want to identify a number of salient contrasts between the Egyptian context I have outlined and recent Islamic politics in Iran.

ISLAMIC POLITICS IN IRAN

The difference in religion between Iran and Egypt which immediately comes to mind is that between Shi'ism and Sunnism. There is a belief that Shi'i Islam is inherently revolutionary or dissident.[10] The recent revolution in Iran, followed by Shi'ite militant activism in various other parts of the world, notably the Lebanon, has lent credence to this opinion. I have argued elsewhere (Zubaida, 1982) against this view. The gist of the argument is that Shi'ism has not been a uniform phenomenon unified by a historical essence, but that many diverse groups, sects, movements and dynastic states have claimed the designation of Shi'ism, and that these diverse Shi'ites have for most of Islamic history been quietist, quiescent or active participants in government. This is not to deny the Shi'ite inspiration of many dissident and rebellious movements; they are part of the diversity.

The specific character of modern Iranian Shi'ism is not to be sought in some inherent essence of Shi'ism in general, but in the recent history of Iranian society and state. The key element, I would argue, is the mode of institutionalisation of religion in relation to the state. Whereas in the Ottoman world, including Egypt, religion was firmly attached to the state, in Qajar Iran religion, alongside other major social spheres, was autonomously instituted. The Qajar state (1796–1926) never managed to bring local and regional powers under its full control; it ruled primarily through the manipulation of alliances and loyalties, especially among the tribal factions, among whom the Qajar dynasty became *primus inter pares*. Religious magnates formed part of local power structures involving landlords, tribal chieftains, and sometimes wealthy merchants. These presided over intricate networks of tribal and urban factions, often including groups of armed retainers. *Mujtahids* (clerics of high rank) were often wealthy landlords in their own right, as well as controlling revenues from religious endowments (*waqfs*).[11] Every *mujtahid* had a network of followers who deferred to him in matters of belief and the regulation of daily life, in fact it was (and still remains) the duty of every believer to enter into a relationship of this kind (*taqlid*, imitation) with a *mujtahid*. This relationship entailed the payment of a religious tax, like the tithe in Europe, to the *mujtahid*, who would in turn dispense this revenue as he saw fit for charitable and religious purposes. Religious schools and their students were maintained partly from this source. In effect, through the control and dispensation of the various revenues, the *mujtahids* presided over considerable networks of patronage and following, including in some cases private armies composed of students and other dependents, who were sometimes employed in the collection of religious revenues from recalcitrant followers. It should be noted, however, that these *mujtahids* did not constitute a centralised church with overall control of religious matters; they were related to one another by informal bonds of kinship and marriage, mutual recognition of rank, and acceptance of each other's certification of students.

The notable aspect of Islamic politics in Iran is that, until the 1960s and 1970s, it was largely confined to the sphere of the clergy and the religious institutions. This is carried over to the Islamic Revolution of 1979, which was led by a prominent cleric and later dominated by the clergy. Until Khomeini first came to prominence in the early 1960s, the character of Islamic politics was largely reactive, that is the clergy reacted against social and political developments which limited their powers and privileges. Whatever reformist religious and political thought there may have been among the clergy remained subordinate and obscure; Iranian religion did not produce anyone remotely like Muhammad Abdu. Modernist intellectuals found no common grounds or sources of inspiration in religion, which they associated with reactive and reactionary clergy. The political alliance between liberal-nationalist intellectuals and sectors of the clergy in the Constitutional Revolution of 1906 was not based on any ideological affinity, but on common objectives against the absolutism of the Qajar monarchy and the increasing dominance of its European backers.

The course and the pace of development of the modern state in Iran is quite distinct from the Egyptian example.[12] European domination in nineteenth-century Iran was indirect, and while having important consequences for some sectors of trade and craft, did not extend far enough to create any major social dislocations or upheavals. The Qajar state remained rudimentary and decentralised, with little in the way of a state bureaucracy or standing army. The Constitutional Revolution of 1906 and the struggles which followed it represents perhaps, the preliminary steps in the formation of a modern state, but the establishment of centralised state powers and institutions only really took off after Reza Khan's (later Shah) takeover of government in 1924. He then proceeded to consolidate his power by eliminating, one by one, the alternative sources of power nourished under the Qajar state, starting with the tribes and the landed aristocracy. The religious sphere, too, lost many of its privileges and prerogatives, especially in the fields of law and education, as well as sectors of religious endowments. For the most part, the clergy acquiesced in the new status quo, and many of them lent voice and influence to positions of social and political conservatism which favoured the government. However, the bases for their institutional autonomy were not entirely eliminated: they still had the mosques, the religious schools, the religious charities, and the sources of revenue from the contributions of the pious. All these maintained bases for autonomy, organisation and networks of patronage and influence. These were to be crucial factors in facilitating their leading role in the Revolution.

The rule of the two Shahs of the Pahlavi dynasty maintained successfully repressive regimes which, for most of their rule, made organised political opposition difficult if not impossible. The exception was the period of the Second World War, when the British and the Russians deposed Reza Shah for fear of his sympathy with the Axis powers, and installed his young son on the throne in a regime more or less under their control. This was the period during which political organisation and activity flourished. The parties which came to prominence were the Tudeh (communist) party, and various nationalist and constitutionalist parties, allied after the war in the coalition called the National Front. It was the electoral success of this coalition which brought Mossadeq to power as the Prime Minister who nationalised Iranian oil in the early 1950s and provoked the CIA inspired *coup d'état* which restored the full powers of the Shah. After that, political repression proceeded apace, and during the 1960s and 1970s any oppositional political organisation was ruthlessly crushed, and even clandestine, underground organisation was successfully undermined.

Khomeini and his immediate followers among the clergy seem, in retrospect, to have effected a break with the defensive-then-acquiescent stance of their predecessors. They first came to public attention in 1963, in episodes of religious opposition to a number of proposed government acts: land reform, opposed by some on the grounds of incompatibility with Islamic protection of private property; extension of voting rights for women; and certain legal privileges and exemptions for US personnel in Iran. Khomeini's pronouncements were most emphatic and clear on the last two issues; his attitude to the first is not so clear. After his rise to prominence as a revolutionary leader with radical rhetoric in recent years, the balance of opinion seems to be that his position in 1963 was not opposed to land reform. Be that as it may, at that point religious opposition seemed to run along the traditional pattern of reactive resistance. But Khomeini showed none of the reserve of his predecessors in his vocabulary of denunciation of authority, including the person of the Shah. This earned him imprisonment and then exile, ultimately to the Shi'ite holy city of Najaf in Iraq, to a niche in the celebrated seminary there, a traditional refuge for Iranian clerics. It was at the Najaf seminary that he delivered the lectures on Islamic government which were to constitute his doctrine of *wilayat-i-faqih* (the guardianship of the jurist), which represented such a radical departure in religious political thought in Iran, in that it preached an alternative form of government based on Islamic law as promulgated and interpreted by a just and competent *faqih* (jurist): no longer merely a defence of the religious sphere, but a proposal for an alternative government within it. This doctrine was to be written into the Iranian revolutionary constitution for an Islamic *republic*: the Iranian clergy (or a section thereof) had finally entered the field in the ideological contest for the modern state. And their stance in this enterprise was 'fundamentalist', in that it evoked the supposedly original tenets and conditions of the Islam of the Prophet and of the Shi'i Imams.

I have argued elsewhere (Zubaida, 1982) that Khomeini's doctrine of government, although constructed in the vocabulary of Shi'ite discourses and authorities, and avoiding any reference to Western ideas or ideologies (except to denounce them in general), is nevertheless based on the assumptions of the modern state and nation, and in particular on the idea of modern forms of popular political action and mobilisation. His basic doctrine of *wilayat-i-faqih*, assigning the duty of government of Muslims to the just *faqih*, represents a radical departure from the mainstream of Islamic political ideas, Sunni or Shi'i, which had generally recognised and accepted the assumption of rule by princes who possess adequate power to maintain order and unity in the Islamic community, providing they are Muslims and enforce and facilitate Islamic worship. For the prince to be a *faqih* was never a required qualification. In this regard it is significant that Khomeini incorporated one European concept into his political vocabulary at the time of revolutionary agitation, that of the 'republic'. Perhaps Khomeini's modernist innovation, otherwise implicit, is manifested in the term 'Islamic Republic', a form of government never before conceived of in an Islamic history dominated by dynasties whose rule was for the most part accepted by Sunni and Shi'i jurists. Relying as he may have done on modern ideological assumptions, Khomeini never had the chance before the revolution of participating in modern forms of political organisation. The political organisation on which he relied during his exile and in the conduct of the revolution was that of the traditional networks already mentioned. During Khomeini's exile, a group of senior clerics associated with him maintained the networks of support and patronage, and collected the religious dues on his behalf (see Bakhash, 1985). Some were detected by the security services and suffered spells of persecution and imprisonment, but their organisation could not be eliminated, located as it was in the complex of mosques, bazaars and religious schools, which were never fully under the control of the regime. When the chance of open political action presented itself, the Islamic clergy was the only group that enjoyed organisation and resources which could be mobilised and directed in a concerted fashion. They also had leadership with great force and talent in the form of Khomeini. Alone of all the possible leaders he demanded the abdication of the Shah and the end of the monarchy in favour of an Islamic Republic, while all the secular leaders were making feeble demands for concessions on civil rights. He never hesitated or showed any inclination to compromise or prevaricate in spite of all the pressures. At the same time he gave vague indications of commitment to democracy and social justice, primarily through the radical vocabulary he adopted. His entourage in exile included many prominent Western-educated intellectuals like Bani Sadr and Yazdi, which strengthened the impression of a progressive openness to modern political objectives. These factors led many democractic and left forces to acquiesce in Khomeini's overall leadership with more or less enthusiasm. Thus a fundamentalist revolution was achieved with the full support of secular democratic forces who were later to become its victims.

The foregoing discussion raises the question of the extent to which the Islamic Revolution in Iran was based on popular support arising specifically from religious commitment. This is a very difficult issue to determine with any measure of confidence. The great majority of Iranians are Shi'i Muslims. Part of the legend and ritual of Shi'ism involves celebrations of the martyrdom of the Imam Hussein and his family and followers in the battle of Kerbala in the seventh century. Some writers have attributed great significance to this motif as symbolising the struggle of righteousness against oppression and tyranny, a view shared with the modern radical Shi'ites.[13] The fact of the matter is that Shi'ites throughout the world have been celebrating these rituals of mourning over the centuries without realising any necessary political implications, except on the occasions on which political interpretations are explicitly constructed in relation to contemporary struggles. This is precisely what happened in the agitations leading up to the revolution. At another level, many conservative religious figures, in and outside clerical circles, have maintained a distance from the revolution, and some have spoken up against Khomeini's political interpretations of Shi'ism. Radical Shi'i thought outside the clergy does not share Khomeini's specification of Islamic government (see Zubaida, 1982). As for the common people, the rural masses are not known for their piety or particular attachment to the clergy (often associated with landlords and authority). The old urban strata of merchants, craftsmen and the networks in which they are involved have had a long-standing association with the clergy, related by kinship and business association. These groups were clearly and significantly involved in the revolution, but not necessarily through religious commitment. It is difficult to ascertain the political commitments or religious faith of the recently urbanised inhabitants of the shanty towns around Teheran and the other major cities. We may guess that they were volatile and changeable, and certainly susceptible to agitation by any oppositional political group which could reach them, and the Islamic networks may have been the only avenue through which they could have been reached against the vigilance of SAVAK (acronym for the Shah's all powerful secret police). In any case, the degree of participation of these groups in revolutionary agitation is uncertain. The groups whose action was particularly important for the success of the revolution were the oil workers, the bank employees and the government workers, whose combined strike crippled the Shah's regime. These groups are not particularly known for their religious commitment. Many of the bureaucratic workers are modern educated, and though some may be personally religious, they would normally hold secular political objectives. Historically, the oil workers are known for their leftist inclinations, and constituted one of the most fruitful bases for communist organisation when it was possible. It would seem, therefore, that the significance of religious commitment for revolutionary support was a variable factor. It is certainly not a given disposition of a religious population to follow Islamic leaders and slogans. The leading role of religious ideas and personnel was politically and ideologically constructed in relation to a situation in which clerical forces were uniquely in possession of organisation and resources, while all other opposition groups were weak, unorganised and unprepared.

The revolution in Iran was made possible by the convergence of many economic and political contradictions. This is not the place to discuss them, and they have been widely covered in the literature. Like other revolutions it was not inevitable, but was produced by a favourable conjuncture of factors, one of the most important being Khomeini's powerful and uncompromising leadership supported by networks of organisations revolving around religious institutions and personnel. It was this conjuncture which made the revolution, and made it an Islamic revolution. I have tried to show that the importance of religion in the modern history of Iran was due to the fact that it remained the only major sphere not completely incorporated and controlled by the state, and as such retained the possibility of autonomous action and organisation. This is quite different from the popular explanation of the Islamic revolution in terms of the effect of some religious essence inherent in Iranian culture and most readily appealing to the hearts and minds of Iranians.

CONCLUSION

I have surveyed the currents of Islamic fundamentalism in Egypt and, to provide a contrast, in Iran in the contexts of their ideological and political relations to the modern state. I have argued that the differences between the movements and ideologies in the two countries are not reducible to the differences between Sunni and Shi'i Islam, although some aspects of this difference are significant, such as the Shi'i doctrine of the imamate, and the Shi'i cult of martyrs. But these distinctions cannot explain the varying characters of Islamic movements in the two countries and the political significance of these movements. I have tried to explain them in terms of the different histories of the development of the modern state in the two countries, and the modes of institutionalisation of religion in relation to the state. I have also argued that these Islamic discourses and politics are modern in so far as they involve the construction of the sacred history of Islam in forms which relate to models of the modern state.

The argument in the paper was aimed against the view of Islamic movements as expressions of a deeply-rooted religiosity among the peoples of the Middle East, who are impervious or unreceptive to secular ideological currents of Western origin, but eager to assert their identity in terms of faith. The main activists in the Islamic movements in both Egypt and Iran are the young intelligentsia, what may be termed the intellectual proletariat of students, teachers and minor functionaries, together with some elements drawn from the urban working class and 'petty bourgeois' shopkeepers and artisans (these latter elements constituting a numerical minority). These are the same social groups from whom support is drawn for all oppositional politics, left and right, religious and secular. As for the urban poor, the indications are that their participation is sporadic, little organised and probably dependent on bandwagon effects, which, again, is consistent with the general character of these groups, at least in the Middle East, with regard to *any* political agitations. In this respect the Islamic movements cannot be distinguished or explained in terms of the sociology of their constituencies of support, nor in terms of a given religious essence predisposing the common people to support political Islamic movements. Islamic politics, like all other forms of politics, are constructed in relation to particular institutional contexts and historical conjunctures. The aim of this paper has been to clarify some aspects of these institutions and conjunctures.

Notes

1. For a discussion of Max Weber's characterisation of the modern state see Beetham (1985).
2. For an account of Abdu's thought see Hourani (1962, pp. 130–60).
3. See Plant (1983, pp. 16–40).
4. Hourani (1962, pp. 135–40).
5. While committed to the ultimate implementation of the Quranic penal code, some Muslim Brothers (see al-Ghazzali, 1948) have held that these prescriptions would only be just under conditions of general social justice in a truly Islamic society.
6. See Enayat (1982, pp. 69–83).
7. For a history of the Syrian Muslim Brotherhood, see Mitchell (1969).
8. The politics of the Syrian Muslim Brotherhood, for instance, is significantly influenced by the sectarian (Alawite) composition of the ruling Ba'th faction in a predominantly Sunni country.
9. More detailed accounts of these groups and their activities can be found in Ibrahim (1980), al-Ansari (1984), and Kepel (1985).
10. A recent statement of this view is contained in Lewis (1985).
11. For an account of the relation of the *ulama* to the Qajar state see Algar (1980).

12. For an analytical history of modern Iran see Abrahamian (1982).
13. For a discussion of the political significance of mourning rituals see Fischer (1980, pp. 12–27, 170–80, 213–16).

References

Abrahamian E. (1982), _Iran Between Two Revolutions_ (Princeton University Press).

al-Ansari, H. (1984), 'The Islamic militants in the politics of Egypt', _International Journal of Middle East Studies_, 16, pp. 123–44.

al-Banna, H. (n.d.), _Islah al-Nafs Wal Mujtama'_ (The Reform of Self and Society; Cairo).

al-Ghazzali, M. (1948), _Min Huna Na'lam_ (From Here We Learn; Cairo: Dar al-Kutub al-Haditha).

—— (1951), _al-Islam Wal Manahij al-Ishtirakiyya_ (Islam and Socialism; Cairo: Dar al-Kutub al-Haditha).

Algar, H. (1980), _Religion and the State in Iran 1785–1906_ (Berkeley: University of California Press).

Anderson, D. (1985), _Imagined Communities_ (London: Verso).

Bakhash, S. (1984), _The Reign of the Ayatollahs_ (New York: Basic Books).

Beetham, D. (1985), _Max Weber and the Theory of Modern Politics_ (Cambridge: Polity Press).

Enayat, H. (1982), _Modern Islamic Political Thought_ (London: Macmillan).

Fischer, M. M. J. (1980), _Iran: From Religious Dispute to Revolution_ (London: Harvard University Press).

Hourani, A. (1962), _Arabic Thought in the Liberal Age 1798–1939_ (Oxford University Press).

Ibrahim, S. E. (1980), 'Anatomy of Egypt's militant Islamic groups: methodological notes and preliminary findings', _International Journal of Middle East Studies_ 12, pp. 423–53.

Kepel, G. (1985), _The Prophet and Pharoah: Muslim Extremism in Egypt_ (London: al-Saqi).

Lewis, B. (1985), 'The Shi'a, _New York Review of Books_, 32, pp. 7–10.

Mitchell, R. P. (1969), _The Society of Muslim Brothers_ (Oxford University Press).

Plant, R. (1983), _Hegel: An Introduction_ (Oxford: Basil Blackwell).

Qutb, S. (1980), _Ma'alim Fil Tariq_ (Landmarks along the Path; Cairo: Dar al-Shuruq).

Zubaida, S. (1982) 'The ideological conditions for Khomeini's doctrine of government'. _Economy and Society_, 11, pp. 138–72.

—— (1985). 'The city and its "other" in Islamic political ideas and movements', _Economy and Society_, 14, pp. 313–30.

3 'Thank God We're Secular!' Aspects of Fundamentalism in a Turkish Town

Richard Tapper and Nancy Tapper

INTRODUCTION

Our title comes from a cartoon in *Cumhuriyet*, the Turkish national newspaper of the centre-left. It shows the President of the Republic bowing Muslim-fashion and saying 'Thank God we're secular'; here, the old joke is poking mild fun at the secular state's relation to Islam, a relation which has been a touchy subject since the foundation of the Turkish Republic in 1923.

This chapter approaches fundamentalism from what is perhaps an unusual angle. First, we tackle the notion of fundamentalism itself, by examining its characteristics in its original context of Protestant Christianity, and asking how far these can apply also in the case of Islam. Secondly, we look at fundamentalist tendencies in nationalism. Thirdly, we examine fundamentalist aspects of Islamic and nationalist ideologies in Turkey, a country not usually associated with the notion of Islamic fundamentalism. We hope to offer some insights into the current political and social situation not only in Turkey but elsewhere in the Muslim world. To help us in the search for insights, we follow Barr's discussion of Protestant fundamentalism,[1] which has been useful and thought-provoking when applied to the Turkish case.

It will soon become clear that we want to treat 'fundamentalism' not as a single, discrete idea, but rather as a continuum of *closed ideologies*, which may vary in degree from one extreme where they are associated with exclusive, ruthless, dogmatic behaviour, to the other where the ideology is more or less open in its structure, where it is 'wet', liberal, relativistic, and ecumenical or international in emphasis. Clearly associated with this continuum are different emphases on boundedness and on the control of individuals. In other words, the degrees of cognitive coherence and social coherence are related.

51

Clearly of relevance here is Mary Douglas's (1970) 'grid-group' approach: the more closed the ideology, the more the body is controlled: hence veiling women, cutting off the hands of thieves, and so on, which are often associated with Islamic fundamentalism.

So how are we to define this notion of 'fundamentalism'? First, we think that no useful analytical category can be derived from the term 'fundamentalism' as it tends to be used in everyday speech and in the Western media: for example, in an article in the *Guardian* ('Third World Review', 18 January, 1985) entitled 'The New Islam signals danger in Paradise' (that is, Malaysia), Islamic fundamentalism is characterised as radical, extremist, anti-Western, anti-secular, anti-consumerist; it is associated with veiled women, and its appeal is said to be very powerful; but what this 'new' Islam is we are never told. This use of the word fundamentalism is itself a datum which can be understood only in terms of its, often only implied, opposites: in this typical example, Western secularism, unveiled women, and so on. In such usage, 'fundamentalism' is a label used by outsiders, usually disparagingly, for phenomena which have little or nothing in common except the outsider's wish to discredit them. In this sense, 'fundamentalism' is a problem for the twentieth-century West, but not for the people who may be so labelled. For these, a return to basics is seen as a wise, rational strategy; they deny extremism, but easily find others around to label in this way.

So our aims in this discussion are not helped by the use of the word 'fundamentalism' as an outsiders' label, though studying just this usage would itself be interesting. We need to start again: we look at the structure of the ideology Barr describes – he sets out to reveal the structure and logic of Protestant fundamentalism, much as Evans-Pritchard did for Azande witchcraft (1937) – and then consider how that ideology fits with the discourse of power and authority in Islam. We suggest that a key to Islamic fundamentalisms lies in their relation with nationalism. Then we turn to the Turkish case, which in some ways is the exception that proves the rule.

Our fieldwork in Turkey was done in the town of Eğirdir in the province of Isparta. Eğirdir is comparatively prosperous, experienced no civil strife in the troubles during the period to 1980, and contains very few 'extremists' on either left or right. The townspeople see themselves, indeed, as admirably fulfilling the expectations of the Turkish Revolution of the 1920s, when Ataturk created a strong, secular republic from what remained of the Ottoman Empire at the end of the First World War. Townspeople treat republicanism and

Islam as two discrete sets of values and associated activities, but our data suggest that there are close underlying links between them, and that it is useful to think of them as aspects of a single ideology, which shares many characteristics with the Protestant fundamentalism analysed by Barr.

By way of the Turkish example, where there is a controlled separation between religious institutions and the state, we re-examine the proposition about the general relation between fundamentalism and nationalism, and ask what factors are associated with the variations between ideological and practical forms of Islamic fundamentalism. Our provisional answer is in terms of the homogeneity and prosperity of a community, and the extent to which it sees its way of life threatened by outside forces.

BARR'S APPROACH TO FUNDAMENTALISM

Though he nowhere makes the distinction specific, Barr uses the word 'fundamentalism' in two distinct senses. His study focuses on Protestant fundamentalism *per se*, but treats it as a particular religious example of a more general class of 'self-enclosing' (p. 341) fundamentalist ideologies which include political and other ideologies as well as religious ones. Throughout the book, fundamentalism in both these senses, the particular and the general, is treated as a polythetic class (pp. 185, 315). The main force of the book is his detailed investigation of the bundles of attributes associated with Protestant fundamentalism; those he isolates are treated as more or less pronounced in different fundamentalisms; that is, as if each attribute could be used as the basis of a continuum (pp. 187, 207).

In the general sense of fundamentalism, two key features seem relevant: the first is the *exclusivity* these ideologies engender. That is, doctrinal and social exclusivity go hand in hand. Agreement with the main dogmas of the ideology is used as a test, to measure the commitment of an individual who, if acceptable, may gain membership in a tight-knit group (p. 318) which sees itself as part of a larger category of 'true believers'. Clearly exclusivity is a characteristic of all groups: the dimension that is important here is the degree to which social exclusiveness is determined by *belief* in a closed ideology.

A second feature of the general class of fundamentalist ideologies is their *oppositional* character (p. 208); that is, the degree to which they define believers in terms of what they are not. In this respect, the committed always take on the character of a *minority* (pp. 104, 164), and there is an emphasis on the existence of a threat to both beliefs and believers (p. 315). Barr notes a major, characteristic paradox: in spite of this emphasis on the threat and hostility of non-believers, fundamentalist beliefs are often used as a 'weapon of ideological conquest' (p. 341) and many of the activities associated with such ideologies are directed towards the domination of others. Further, when such ideologies *do* dominate in a community, the element of perceived threat continues to operate to repress criticism (pp. xiii, 316). Barr also notes that when such ideologies are socially dominant, they tend to become 'tired, moralistic and puritanical' (p. 321).

If we are right in suggesting that exclusivity and opposition are the key characteristics of the general class of fundamentalist ideologies, it is clear that such a class can subsume not only certain religious ideologies but also ideologies of ethnicity and nationalism as well.

Before discussing nationalist ideologies, let us first consider some of the specific attributes of the ideology of Protestant fundamentalism. It is worth going into some detail here because, as Barr suggests, it is clear that many elements of contemporary Christian fundamentalism are deeply embedded in the structure of Semitic religions generally (pp. 180, 182). It is largely because of this common historical tradition that discussions of 'fundamentalist' Islam make sense.

There seem to be four important features of Barr's category of Protestant fundamentalism. First is the central dogma of the *inerrancy* (p. 47) of the Bible, where the Bible itself becomes a key symbol of the religion (pp. 36–7). This belief in inerrancy is the key to the whole ideological system and is protected against criticism by a web of secondary elaboration. In practice, one important way that the system is closed is by focusing on the belief in inerrancy as a test of faith. That is, believers must accept that the Bible is inspired and without error (because it says so; p. 260), but after the 'test of faith' is passed, the Bible is used devotionally (p. 306), and access to the divine is through Jesus Christ, as mediated by various human authorities. Barr argues that Protestant fundamentalism has no theology; and though it is authority-centred, it is also fragmented, didactic and apologetic in character (p. 161).

A second feature of Protestant fundamentalism is the prominent place accorded to *soteriological* and *eschatological* beliefs. That is, it is salvationist and millenial in character. It is important to Barr's argument and, as we shall see, to our understanding of fundamentalism in Turkey, and probably elsewhere, that salvation is seen as personal and individual – it is not associated with membership in a social group. A corollary of this individualist focus on the world to come is that interest in contemporary life tends to focus on the sin and wickedness of the world, and there is an absence of any elaborate programme of temporal reform.

The intellectual and social consequence of this construction is that religion is compartmentalised (pp. 108, 111) and kept separate from a wide variety of everyday activities. In so far as any connection is made between the two, it is held that the individual acts alone, as a 'witness' (p. 113) for belief and not as a member of a religious pressure group. In other words, the fundamentalist believer can also be comfortable as, for example, an 'honest' businessman, and experiences no contradiction between belief and everyday activity (p. 100). A focus on individual salvation, and the compartmentalisation of religion, lead to a tendency for Protestant fundamentalism to be conservative and to support the economic and political establishment in the community (pp. 110, 111), in spite of elements like a lack of ritualism which make it similar to religions of the dispossessed.

Third, Protestant fundamentalism is *ahistorical*. That is, in spite of the importance of narrative history in Western European culture (pp. 102, 334), the authority and legitimacy of Protestant fundamentalist dogmas lie in their apparent creation *ex nihilo*. There is a concealment of traditional sources, and of changes and development in the meaning of key religious concepts. So, for instance, the Bible is treated as timeless, out-of-time; and a central concern is to return to the golden age of early Christian beliefs and practices.

Fourth, Protestant fundamentalism gives prominence to '*reason and rationality*' (pp. 12, 13, 122, 220, 271). This, according to Barr, is one of the differences between contemporary and earlier closed systems of Christian belief: Protestant fundamentalism is a *modern* ideology (pp. 173, 182). The emphasis on reason is clearly congruent with much of contemporary philosophy, and in particular, it allows for an easy accommodation with modern science. It is an emphasis which plays down all forms of emotionalism, and denies the miraculous or supernatural an important place in the belief system. In Barr's words, the Protestant fundamentalist is often profoundly *secular* (that is, non-mystical) in his/her beliefs (pp. 238–9, 242).

We return to Barr's detailed characterisation of Protestant fundamentalism below, but first let us consider several broader issues. His general sense of fundamentalism fits well with certain versions of practised Islam and various forms of nationalism. Undoubtedly this derives from the similarities of certain core concepts and from the historical connections between them.

ISLAM AND NATIONALISM AS FUNDAMENTALISMS

Islam has been tied to Christianity and Judaism from the outset, and the continuing relations between the three traditions have been an important factor in their history and development. Equally, the similarities between nationalism and Protestantism as ideologies stem, in large part, from their development in the same social and political environment of the sixteenth century, and from the continuing interaction between them. Thus modern nationalist forms were confirmed with the Treaties of Westphalia (1648) and the rise of popular sovereignty movements after 1789 (Hager, 1983, p. 84), and it is no mere coincidence that Barr sees the Protestant fundamentalism he describes as emerging in the eighteenth century (p. 183).

What all these ideologies, whether religious or political, have in common, is their general fundamentalist potential: a strong tendency to exclusivity and oppositionalism is inherent in them all. Islam, Christianity and Judaism share an aggressive monotheism, in which doctrinal and social exclusivity are central, and alternative beliefs, allegiances or paths to salvation can be seen as heretical. And the narrative histories of the three religious traditions emphasise opposi- tional themes that have frequently been used to create or validate a sense of threat.

By the same token, exclusivity and oppositionalism are strong tendencies in what we normally understand as *nationalism*. Here we use 'nationalism' to mean the ideology of a modern, complex, heterogeneous, territorial state which promotes social integration and loyalty to the state above any particular loyalties to class, ethnic group and so on. To do this effectively, the state fosters, and indeed frequently invents, notions of a common culture and language, if not also a common religion and history.

At first sight, nationalism thus described seems inward-looking, but in fact it can be understood only in terms of a state whose existence depends on the control of a discrete territory and recognition by other states. That is, its existence depends in part on what we can call its general fundamentalist potential – its exclusivity and opposition to other states.

All this is not to deny that other (non-fundamentalist) potential emphases are also embedded in the Semitic religions and nationalism. Of course they are: in religious discourse it is as possible to emphasise ideas of common humanity or to focus on ecumenical goals as it is to use religious dogmas to exclude; so too, nation states can define their self-interest in extra-national ways: military alliances, the EEC, the UN, provide examples of how this may be done. However, our interest here is in their fundamentalist aspects, rather than their potential for generating more open, universalistic kinds of ideologies.

There are today many varieties of Islamic ideology to which the four features in Barr's specific characterisation of Protestant fundamentalism apply, including the cases of Iran and Egypt described by Zubaida in this volume (Chapter 2). However, the standard sociological analyses of Islamic ideologies do not help us to understand why this should be so.[2] This suggests that we need some other dimension to our argument if we are to understand when, where and why these 'Barr-type' fundamentalist ideologies turn up. Barr sees them as modern; and it is worth seeking the missing factor in recent history.[3]

We argue that the incidence and character of Islamic fundamentalist ideologies depend on the character of the polities in which and in relation to which they emerge. In other words, we feel that fundamentalist ideologies must be explained in terms of a discourse of authority, and we suggest that fundamentalisms of the kind we have been discussing are linked to this discourse of authority as it relates to differences between nation-states and empires.

Modern states, concerned to defend their territorial and cultural integrity, adopt nationalist ideologies, with their potential for fundamentalism. By contrast, modern empires, which are inherently expansionist (whether seeking territorial/political control, economic markets, or cultural influence) must operate with universalistic, non-fundamentalist ideologies that allow subordinate states or ethnic groups diversity and partial autonomy, for example through indirect rule.

Most modern territorial states include minority cultural/ethnic groups, with more or less active 'nationalist' political aims of their own. Towards these, a state has several possible policies, and may use more than one: (a) it can deny the existence or importance of the minorities and insist on their integration as citizens within the dominant culture; (b) it can deal 'imperially' with minorities and allow a degree of cultural autonomy; (c) to the extent that the state perceives minority political activity as a threat, it can blame this on outside instigation, and adopt a more fundamentalist attitude in its own national ideology; (d) further, the more the state feels itself subject to imperialist pressures from outside, the more effectively it can organise resistance by appeal to a fundamentalist nationalist ideology.

In states where the dominant religion is of Semitic origin, we find one reaction to perceived external threat is the adoption of a religious fundamentalism, paralleling a move to an extreme nationalist stance. Such an argument fits a number of cases. The rhetoric of the Iranian revolution at the beginning was directed almost entirely against American imperialists and their agents, and it continues today against Iraqi and Israeli imperialisms. In Afghanistan in the present century, the importance of fundamentalist Islam in the political and social life of the country has fluctuated directly with the degree of foreign threats to the integrity of the state – since the Soviet invasion, nationalists wanting to regain control of their country have predominantly adopted an Islamic fundamentalist stance.

The argument applies elsewhere too, including cases of reaction to more economic forms of imperialism (as in the Malaysian case mentioned earlier). As Gellner points out, Islamic fundamentalism 'has certain conspicuous traits – strict unitarianism, sobriety, orderliness, scripturalism, egalitarianism – which are consonant with the organization and ideological requirements of an industrialising age' (1984, p. 30). Muslims are fortunate in that they can 'define and reform themselves in the name of a genuinely indigenous and quasi-modern set of beliefs and values, not visibly indebted to the West...' (ibid.). Islamic fundamentalism is a powerful ideology for a Third World country to adopt, not least because it can be seen as separate and independent of the ideologies of both Western and Eastern bloc imperialisms. Moreover, using insights from Barr's analysis, we can see clearly what it is that makes these Islamic ideologies in Gellner's words 'quasi-modern', and by looking at the locus of power associated with nationalism we can understand what generates the need for a modernist response. Today, the upshot of imperial designs and nationalistic responses depends on a command of technologies of great sophistication, and it is clear that any ideology akin to Protestant fundamentalism that treats men as individual competitors but encourages the domestication of women, that allows for the compartmentalisation of religion, and that uses an enlightenment notion of rationalism to accommodate modern science, can lead to technological competence and effective competition and/or confrontation with the West and/or the Soviets (cf. Sayarı, 1984).

Let us apply this general perspective to a particular case that is not usually associated with Islamic fundamentalism at all: Turkey.

A TURKISH CASE STUDY

Secularism ('laicism') emerged as one of the key principles of Ataturk's new state. Laicism meant a separation of religion from the state and state control over all organised religion in the country. There are all kinds of historical reasons why this particular configuration came about in Turkey. Suffice it to say that to form a nation-state from the remains of the Ottoman empire necessarily required a drastic change in the role and character of Islam, since both pan-Islamic institutions like the Caliphate, and the open, tolerant religious ideology associated with it, were inconsistent with a movement for national independence based on a distinctive Turkish culture.[4] In the war of independence the Turks learned to see themselves as a discrete nation threatened on all sides by many different enemies. However, Kemalism, as Berkes writes, actually lacked a political creed and a positive doctrine and was at its most articulate when negative and in opposition (1964, p. 502).

Since the republican revolution, Islam in Turkey has been redefined. The Caliphate was abolished, the powerful Sufi brotherhoods were outlawed, and mystical forms of Islam were discouraged. In effect, Islam has become more standardised, narrowed and compartmentalised, while the republican ideology and its associated institutions have come to dominate much of everyday life. This construction of Islam seems to coincide with the secular ambitions of the state, which, because they focus on the institutional manifestations of religion, may best be considered as part of a national 'myth of secularisation' (cf. Glasner, 1977, p. 5ff.).

Changes in provincial towns like Eğirdir have reflected the wider changes of the last sixty years and indeed such towns may have played a crucial mediating role in reinterpreting the relation between the secular state and Islamic beliefs and practices. Eğirdir is a market and administrative centre for a region of some forty villages.[5] The town itself has a population of about 9000, brought to a total of over 12 000 by two substantial national institutions, the Army Commando School and an Orthopaedic Hospital. The town lies on the shores of a large lake, and fishing still brings a proportion of the income, but nowadays the economy of the town is based on the international export of locally grown apples. Until the 1920s Eğirdir was a poor local centre, dominated by a few families of powerful landlords, wealthy merchants and religious leaders associated with the many religious schools in the town. Eğirdir was also a centre for active branches of the Bektashi, Naqshbandi and Mevlevi Sufi orders. During the late Ottoman period, most of the population of the town, including a Greek minority, were involved in small-scale crafts and trade; the labouring sector was small, though in the villages many people worked for the landlord families.

The town's development is largely due to the spread of education, improved communications in the country as a whole, and the entrepreneurial efforts of local residents themselves. The apple economy started in the 1950s and took off in the 1970s. All Eğirdir families traditionally owned orchard land outside the town, and all have benefited to some degree from the apple boom, though large differences in wealth are now emerging. There are, in terms of socio-economic status and life-style, distinct strata in the town which one is inclined to call 'classes'; but the townspeople themselves maintain a self-image of classlessness. All but the poorest consider themselves to be 'middle class', and they deny there is anything in the way of 'class conflict' in the town. The really quite remarkable peacefulness of the town seems due to the fact that there are few very rich or very poor among local people. The relative prosperity of the town is due to people's respect for hard work and education (local children have, for example, had unusual success in gaining university entrance). The town's apparent homogeneity is also due, first, to the fact that the small 'proletariat' is socially invisible (most manual labour is done by supposedly transient Kurdish immigrants from the east), and secondly to the dense and continuous network of kinship and marriage linking the 7000–8000 locals (*yerli*, an indigenous category opposed to *yabancı*, strangers, including Kurds, bureaucrats and other outsiders). This means that individuals count as relatives people from all 'classes'. The kinship network is undoubtedly a powerful mechanism for social control; it has also served to exclude strangers of all kinds, who find the locals unfriendly and grasping.

Eğirdir people vote predominantly for the main right-of-centre national political party (formerly the Justice Party, now the True Path Party), but have frequently chosen local officials (including their most successful mayor) from the main left-of-centre party (Republican People's Party).

By and large, Eğirdir people are religious. One dentist who closes his office during Ramazan because dental treatment is held to break the fast, estimated that 50 per cent of all men in town, and probably many more women, scrupulously keep the fast, but that another 30–35 per cent of all men make a show of doing so. The least religious people in town are the high-status bureaucrat outsiders, while the most pious are reckoned to be found among the small traders and craftsmen of the bazaar (the *esnaf*).

The townspeople are committed republicans and they see republican values as underwriting most of their activities in this world, whereas they see Islam (and they are all also committed Muslims) as mostly about the life hereafter. They often talk about a division between material (*maddi*) and spiritual (*manevi*) domains, and they treat republicanism and Islam as two separate ideologies, of which the former is of wider temporal scope.

This perspective leaves the townspeople unaware of, or actually inhibited by various taboos from seeing, the many areas which suggest that republicanism and Islam in Eğirdir today are aspects of a single ideology. One of the most salient features of the relation between republicanism and Islam is its location at the centre of town values and activities. The ideology is utterly and thoroughly establishment in character. It creates and reproduces an orthodoxy and homogeneity in which ideas about Turkey as nation state and ideas about Islam are mutually reinforcing.[6]

Dissent from such a strong, unitary, centralising value system is muted, or is likely to resemble treason, or heresy, or both. About two dozen people, many of them of recent village origins, are considered by townspeople as 'extremists' (*aşırı*); they include adherents or sympathisers of the former main political parties of the extreme right and left as well as religious fanatics (*yobaz*). What is interesting is how, locally at least, these extremists adopt various strategies to avoid accusations of treason or heresy. Those of the right carry political orthodoxy to an extreme; those of the left adopt a diffuse, boundariless, heterodox ideology, a quasi-mysticism. The religious fanatics, such as members of the two clandestine Islamic sects, the Nurcus and the Suleymancıs, do both: in their behaviour (for example, their clothing and insistence on sexual segregation) they resemble Western stereotypes of Islamic fundamentalists, but their beliefs are theistic and ecumenical in character.[7] In other words, in Eğirdir and probably widely in Turkey, the structure of the value system held by those considered by most people as 'fanatics' ('fundamentalists') can only be understood in terms of the value system of the local establishment, which itself has certain fundamentalist characteristics, of both a general and a more particular, Protestant kind.

We argue then that in Eğirdir, and probably elsewhere in Turkey, nationalism is associated with Islam in the form of a fundamentalist ideology. In Eğirdir this ideology takes a relatively mild, open-ended form, but it is potentially hard-line, like that which surfaced in many Turkish communities before the 1980 military intervention. At present, its most obvious manifestation is the way in which conversations between townspeople on a wide variety of topics veer either into diatribes against Kurds, Armenians or Greeks as threats to the integrity of the Turkish state, or into a paean for the unassailable virtues of Islam.[8]

HIDDEN AND EXPLICIT IDEOLOGICAL ACCOMMODATIONS

The townspeople tend to treat both republicanism and Islam as separate monolithic wholes; there are, however, a number of important types of accommodation between them. First, there are key social values to which everyone in the town subscribes, and which, because they are so general and all-embracing, seem to contain or deflect any specific republican *or* Islamic interpretation that might be placed on them. Such concepts include humanity, friendship, generosity, civilisation, sophistication, hospitality and community service. It is perhaps significant that all these concepts are expressed in words of Arabic or Persian, not Turkish origin, in spite of the efforts of fifty years to purge modern Turkish of such 'loan' words. This linguistic continuity suggests important social continuity with Ottoman values and forms of social control.[9] All these values, and indeed a further extensive range of ideas, including notions of duty, respect, purity and discipline, allow for a wide area of agreement that can hide the complicated relation between specific customs and activities which people do label as either national (*milli*) or religious (*dinî*).

However, if one asks a question of republicanism and Islam which implies a comparison between them, one is liable to get an answer cast wholly in republican terms, in which Islam is associated with all that was formally outlawed by Ataturk: superstition, local custom, Sufi mysticism and so on. There is also a tendency for people to apologise for Islam and religious allegiance by emphasising that it is possible to be both a good Turk and a good Muslim. At first sight, loyalty to the state comes first and is the standard and foil against which religious allegiance is judged; as one notable republican leader was able to say, 'our way of [religious] worship (*ibadet*) is to respect Ataturk'.

In explicit statements, republican values appear to dominate social life, while the values that people would label explicitly religious are stated less often, less publicly, and in a more qualified manner. So, for instance, on national holidays and in public places throughout the town, banners, posters and inscriptions are displayed that express republican sentiments, often using Ataturk's own words. Perhaps the most well-known of these is inscribed on the back of the main Ataturk statue in town, and reads: 'How happy he who can say "I'm a Turk"'; and this sentiment is shouted out by school-children twice a day in their pledge of allegiance. By contrast, wherever religious ornaments are displayed, in shops or restaurants, a picture of Ataturk is even more prominently shown. Indeed, an exception that in effect proves this rule of the qualification of things religious by things republican, is found in a few religious activities associated exclusively with women and which take place in the privacy of their homes.

The townspeople are well aware that there have been considerable changes in the character of Islam since the coming of the Republic; and of course an important republican concern has been secular 'consciousness-raising'. For most people, however, these efforts seem to relate to only a few specific areas of life, such as education, where they consider that traditional (religious) learning occurred only because children feared the physical punishment meted out by teachers; or the family, where men and women agree that in the past, with the sanction of Islam, relations between them and between adults and children were oppressive and tyrannical. No one regrets such changes.

In effect, the notion of republicanism has expanded, and is often treated as more or less synonymous with anything and everything that is thought new and different. It is as if the changes people have experienced have no antecedents in Ottoman history, and the Republic arrived all of a piece. So, for instance, there is an absence of detail or social realism in school textbook accounts or televised depictions of nineteenth-century Ottoman history, or even of the early Republic, which many people have experienced themselves.

Moreover, because republican efforts at re-education focus on day-to-day social relations where those key values like humanism and friendship can apply, the townspeople fail to see other areas in which religious experience has also changed. For instance, few people seem aware that many of the town's shrines have gone, and that the complex sacred geography of the town has now altered and become very mosque-centred; or that some of the religious activities of individuals have become, paradoxically, more ostentatious during the same period. For example, inscribed tombstones are becoming fashionable among ordinary people, and nowadays charitable gifts which would previously have remained anonymous are often treated as news in local papers.

Since the Republic, the townspeople's religious experience has become much less shrine-centred, less ritualistic and more individualistic. Moreover, people's ideas about what constitutes 'religion' have narrowed. Now, normal accepted religious values and activities are seen as those which neither support nor impinge on republicanism.

Mevlûd recitals provide a good example of a compartmentalised religious activity that none the less allows for complex, varied statements of social identity. The *mevlûd* poem is a narrative account of the birth and life of the Prophet Muhammad, and *mevlûd* recitals are arguably the most prominent religious services held in Turkey today. When they are performed in private homes as part of marriage and circumcision ceremonies, they have a confirmatory character and are particularly associated with men, as are those recitals sponsored on Islamic festivals by the local religious establishment and performed in local mosques to coincide with a nationally broadcast *mevlûd* on Turkish television. Most *mevlûd* recitals, however, are part of funeral and mourning rituals, and have a piacular character. Women are particularly associated with these mourning *mevlûds*, but this very fact emphasises the compartmentalisation of religion in town life. Men tend to adopt the 'official' line in which the *mevlûd* poem and the associated hymns are said to be 'beautiful but unimportant' because not in the Quran. Indeed, for most men the only value of the *mevlûd* services lies in the extent to which they serve as occasions for Quranic readings. Women insist that their services, and the rituals and hymn-singing associated with them, demonstrate that they are more caring and consciously religious than men. But the women's piety, and even the threat it might pose to state secularism, are dismissed by men as spurious, and the traditional stereotypes of women's social and religious inferiority are confirmed.[10]

Townspeople are aware of accommodation between republicanism and Islam in only certain limited areas. Three types of accommodation seem particularly common. The first involves the suggestion that some specific Islamic injunction was associated with a particular historical period or social problem, and that other Islamic values are more appropriate today: for instance, we were told that the Prophet forbade alcohol because he found all Arabs to be drunkards and could discover no other remedy for their excesses, but in fact Islam favours moderation in all things, and if one can imbibe sparingly then one has no need to fear for one's soul.

A second type of accommodation is managed by arguing that republican institutions function in exactly the same ways as Islamic ones did and therefore are acceptable substitutes for them: for instance, people note that income and other taxes paid to the state go to support hospitals, education, the salaries of religious teachers and so on, and thus replace the Islamic alms and tithes.

A third type of accommodation is where religious values or customs are rationalised, or explained by an appeal to 'modern' secular values. Thus prayer, or fasting during Ramazan, are said to be excellent for the health, to lead to regular exercise, to purge the body, and so on. Such explanations imply that Islamic wisdom long anticipated current scientific ideas which serve to verify it.

This third type of accommodation can be reversed and people may declare that, in all important essentials, republicanism is close to Islam. Such an argument is tricky because of problems of historical fact, such as Ataturk's known personal antipathy to Islam. None the less these problems are ignored, almost as if Ataturk, to have achieved so much, must have been on God's side. So, for instance, stories from early republican local history label as 'atheists' those who fought against Ataturk and for the Sultan-Caliph and traditional Ottoman-Islamic rule. Or the townspeople explain that Ataturk was not originally against religion but when religious fanatics threatened the new Republic he was forced to turn to secularism (cf. Jacob, 1982, p. 84 n. 155).

This latter gloss on republican history is not so much wrong as oversimplified. What is interesting about it is the way fanaticism is condemned. All townspeople (including the two dozen or so 'extremists') reject fanaticism, past or present. Traditional religious leaders are described as having been ignorant, while contemporary 'extremists', whether in Iran or from Turkish sects, are seen both as ridiculous, unthinking puppets manipulated by outsiders for political purposes, and as Machiavellian opportunists who would cheerfully sell heaven for their personal gain. It is important to realise that the same scorn and repugnance is also directed against political fanaticism of both right and left. Looked at the other way, the general notion of 'fanaticism' is a foil which makes both republicanism and Islam seem monolithic, moderate orthodoxies.

So far, we have described ways in which townspeople treat Republican and Islamic ideologies as distinct and separate, if complementary, in those areas where they can make the type of accommodating arguments we have outlined. Such accommodating explanations are popular, unquestioned, and used as evidence that neither Islam nor republicanism poses a serious threat to the other.

The notion that there is a balance between the two distinct ideologies and associated institutions comes out clearly where either balance, or discreteness, are felt to be at risk. For instance, people are well aware that since the 1980 military intervention there has been a considerable increase in republican propaganda, much of which focuses on Ataturk himself, resurrecting and perpetuating his example and image. Many see this propaganda as unnecessary and boring: as one man said: 'Even our Prophet Muhammad is dead and his bones in a box!' But equally, President Evren's recent attempts to buttress the regime by using religious slogans and arguments is also seen as ridiculous and hypocritical; hence the cartoon whose caption is used in our title.

Finally there are the cases where people are aware they are mixing religious and secular issues which ought, they feel, to be kept separate, but they do it anyway. So, for example, all important new enterprises (buying a new car, opening a shop, laying foundations of a new house and so on) should be initiated with a sacrifice; but if one asks more about such sacrifices, people usually talk sheepishly about custom and superstition (*bâtıl inanç*), and how such sacrifices have little or nothing to do with Islam.[11]

Such types of accommodation townspeople recognise explicitly. In other areas, of which they seem unaware, republican and Islamic values and forms are juxtaposed in complex ways such that they can best be understood as parts of a single ideological structure. These areas range from what Firth would call 'religious contact' (1959, p. 139), such as the constant conversational references to God ('praise-God', 'God-willing', and so on) to the structural similarities between civic and Islamic rituals. We have mentioned notions like 'humanism' and 'friendship', which townspeople readily volunteered as key values by which they live and to which they gave neither republican nor Islamic labels. However, people are more or less oblivious of the further extensive vocabulary of values which they use constantly in both religious and republican contexts, and which includes key concepts like respect, duty, purity and discipline. Similarly, the popular use of nearly identical aphorisms in different contexts confirms local belief in the separation of religion and the state while enhancing and multiplying the meanings of particular values. For example, the saying 'Find learning wherever you can' is attributed to Muhammad, while posters quote Ataturk as saying 'In life the truest [religious] teacher [*mürşid*] is knowledge'; and the Commando School has fashioned in huge letters on the mountainside above the town the slogan 'Knowledge is power'.[12]

Three broad areas where this juxtaposition takes place indicate the centrality of the single ideology. The first concerns the pervasive, almost puritanical, work ethic to which townspeople subscribe and which has, without doubt, been an important element in their material prosperity. Hard work is a key republican virtue.[13] School children promise twice daily in their oath of allegiance to work hard; and perhaps the most widely reproduced Ataturk saying of all (it appears under his bust on the main square and in innumerable other places), runs 'Be proud, hard-working, confident'. The value of hard work turns up in quite other secular contexts as well: townspeople tend to see Kurds as potential arch-traitors to the state, and they also assert that, unlike the hardworking Turks, Kurds are lazy and shiftless and make their women do the work. But hard work is also part of the religious ethic. An individual's prosperity can be explained by phrases like 'God gives to the hard worker'. A well-known moral injunction runs: 'Prepare for death as if you will die tomorrow, but work as if you will live for ever'. In fact, people are keen to assert that Islam does not encourage fatalism, but demands of Muslims hard work and self-improvement. There is even a category of the 'deserving poor' (*gizli fakir*) to whom alms should be given. The work ethic is further fuelled by egalitarian ideals drawn from both republicanism and Islam. Ideally, the secular system is a meritocracy where a competitive, Western-type educational system reinforces individualistic capitalism. Parallel to this system is a path to personal salvation based on gaining merit (*sevab*) and cancelling out sin (*günah*), which is a central goal of religious activity. It is essential to aspirations and choices in both systems that merits and faults can be and are given measureable values. (In practice, of course, the intangible factors of influence and connection (*torpil*) are sources of inequality in the secular system, and the pursuit of religious merit is qualified by the notion of pious intention and the belief that salvation depends ultimately on God's unknowable will.)

Secondly, there is a similar parallelism throughout the whole range of religious and civic rituals. Maurice Bloch has proposed (in discussion) two basic models of ways Muslims can contact the divine: in the *sacrifice* model the divine is brought into temporal life and associated with fertility and prosperity on earth; in the *funeral* model the divine is separated into the afterlife. This second model is salvationist, sometimes millenial in character. In this light, it is fascinating that in Eğirdir both religious and civic rituals use both models. Many civic rituals focus on the sacrifice of republican martyrs, and we were told that when the head of state travels around Turkey so many animals are sacrificed in front of his car that he leaves a bloody shambles in his wake; but townspeople agree that the most important civic ritual is that which commemorates Ataturk's death. Among religious rituals, the *mevlûd* is most frequently and movingly heard in the context of death; funerals are prominent among life-cycle rituals; yet townspeople agree that the most important event of the Islamic year is the feast of Sacrifice (*Kurban*).

The question of ritual parallels is a vast one: here we can mention only one other thread. Throughout civic and religious rituals there is a juxtaposition of egalitarian and authoritarian values. There are, for instance, many occasions (for example, in communal prayers and in the processions on national holidays) when people act as equals and move and articulate in unison, and which emphasise some notion of the mechanical solidarity between individuals in the community, as well as other more explicit values such as self-discipline and will-power. But these rituals also express acceptance of a kind of authority (political or religious) which is hierarchical, and generated and imposed from the top down. It is surely not coincidence that the voice of authority in Turkish often sounds the same: the teacher addressing a class, the Imam giving a sermon, the local dignitary making a speech, the officer giving commands to a subordinate – all use the same style and intonation.

The third and most striking juxtaposition, and the one which townspeople find quite unthinkable, involves the similarities that struck us in attitudes and behaviour towards Ataturk as founder of the Republic, on the one hand, and the Prophet Muhammad, as founder of Islam, on the other.[14] Both are 'great men'. Ataturk is spoken of as deathless and as a judge of all that goes on in Turkey today; his role in these respects is like that of Muhammad in heaven. Both men deserve the utmost honour for the legacy they have bequeathed ordinary people. In each case, moreover, this heritage was gained in battle. The military campaigns of Ataturk and Muhammad are the most widely known and understood parts of their respective biographies. In many ways the history of Ataturk's journey from Samsun to Ankara and around the country until the expulsion of the Greek army from the mainland, replicates the *hijra* (*hicret* in Turkish) when Muhammad left Mecca for Medina, whence he was later able to conquer Mecca by force. The similarities come out not only in biographic details, but in ritual as well: Islam forbids the depiction of the figure of Muhammad, and it is not illustrated in current Turkish iconography, while in the Hollywood-style biopic 'The Messenger', based on the life of the Prophet, which was shown to general approval on Turkish TV during Ramazan 1984, Muhammad was always present just off camera. By contrast, pictures and statues of Ataturk are ubiquitous in private and public places; yet, in the tableau of the Independence War presented to the town on the national holiday of 19 May, Ataturk's presence was represented by a bust carried by soldiers. When we asked, in both cases, why no actor played the part of Muhammad or Ataturk, we were told, not surprisingly, that respect made such an idea unthinkable: 'What men could possibly play such parts?'

BARR'S MODEL AND THE TURKISH CASE

How do the four elements of Barr's model of Protestant fundamentalism fit our Turkish material?

The sayings of Ataturk, and certain details of his personal biography, are used in schools and elsewhere as *inerrant texts*. They are uncriticised, and presented as without precedent or wider social context. They are a central part of the mythology of the Turkish republic (and have their ritual counterpart in the use of photographs, film and pageantry on television and in civic rituals). Similar treatment is given to the sayings of Muhammad and stories of the Prophet's life, especially in the *mevlûd*. The mediatory and personalising roles of both Ataturk and Muhammad have many implications; here it is enough to say that in the use of their sayings and biographies as texts, there is an extreme formalisation of language, which, as Bloch (1974) describes, can be directly associated with traditional authority and social control. Further, in Barr's terms, acceptance of the text can be used as a test of faith; but among believers, the text is used devotionally, and often becomes an invocation or icon itself.

Secondly, access to the central values of both the state and Islam are mediated by visionary generals. Of the utmost importance is the *salvationist* role which is ascribed to them both. Ataturk saved the Turkish nation from being devoured by the Western powers at the end of the First World War; he gave the Turks an identity and the chance and duty to defend it against all comers. So too, Muhammad showed men a way of finding eternal salvation and gave Muslims all the privileges and responsibilities associated with their faith. A pervasive theme to which townspeople return again and again is that only through constant effort and vigilance can they hope to maintain and protect their way of life and the promise of an afterlife against the forces of evil and the sources of sin.

We have already touched on the third issue, *ahistoricity*, as related to the present treatment of Ottoman and early republican history. In this respect, Ataturk is the source of values which should guide Turkey through all time: he is the 'eternal leader'. Political rhetoric in the town is almost invariably based on themes of returning to origins, that is, Ataturk's example, and is often about which party most truly follows the republican tradition. The same ahistoricity is seen in townspeople's approach to Islam: they constantly repeated to us how the messages of the Jewish and Christian prophets had been corrupted and that Muhammad's message had to introduce people to the work of God completely afresh. Moreover, in the practice of Islam in the town, one finds that, rather than some idea of returning to an Islamic golden age (which would bring with it embarrassing issues to do with the Caliphate and Ottoman relations with the Arabs), what seems to happen is that Muhammad's life is the focus of devotion and, in the *mevlûd* recitations, it is made to seem as if he lived only yesterday.

Finally, there is the issue of *rationality* raised by Barr. Ataturk himself seems to have regarded Islam as a 'natural', rational religion (Berkes, 1964, p. 483); and it seems clear that his early intention was to rid Islam of 'superstitions' and local customs, and to initiate a period of religious enlightenment, in Berkes' words to 'rationalize or Turkicize Islam' by such measures as translating the Quran into Turkish and insisting that sermons also be delivered in Turkish. Such aims are now central to the bureaucracy that controls religious teachers, Imams and other officials; they are also accepted without question by virtually all Eğirdir townspeople. It is interesting that those few Nurcus and Suleymancıs whom the other townspeople regard as 'fanatics' are also those who go to extremes to show how modern science proves Islam right: yet their main texts, apart from the Quran, are the obscure writings of a twentieth-century Kurdish mystic.

CONCLUSIONS

In conclusion, we may consider what has been learned from this application of Barr's analysis of features of Protestant fundamentalism to the case of provincial Turkish nationalism and Islam.

We have argued that both nationalist ideologies and the traditions of the Semitic religions have a general fundamentalist potential for exclusivity and opposition. We continued by suggesting that in the Muslim world nationalism, and particularly the degree of outside threat perceived by a community, is an important factor in the appearance of religious ideologies which are very similar to that described by Barr as Protestant fundamentalism. In large part, this response is a reaction to threats believed to be posed by Western and Soviet imperialisms; it is not inappropriate that Islamic fundamental-isms offer tight, authoritarian control over populations and at the same time encourage values and behaviours that are likely to lead to competence in economic, military and other technologies.

Turkey, which is proudly nationalistic, seems, because of the explicit secularism of the state, to be an exception to our argument. The data from Eğirdir suggest, however, that an 'Islamic' fundamen-talism does underwrite many contemporary values and activities and is an important covert prop of the state. But the townspeople are very reluctant to acknowledge any such connection. This taboo is due to republican teaching, and is certainly related to the fact that national-ism on a Western model could not have been created without shedding many imperial traditions, and with them the hierarchical, tolerant Islam of the Caliphate. Nowadays Turkish Islam has a definite 'Protestant' character, which parallels other establishment orthodox-ies, yet appears discrete and separate from the secular state.

We suggested how fundamentalisms might be linked to the experience of power in a nation-state. What of the degree to which outside threats are perceived in the community? Here too the Turkish ethnography provides some clues.

By and large the people of Eğirdir are mild, tolerant and aware of and sensitive to international opinion and issues. Equally, it is a peaceful town. It differs in degree from other such towns in Turkey in two respects: it is relatively both prosperous and homogeneous. We agree with local opinion, that peace in the town stems directly from both these factors, and we suggest that the open, tolerant fundamentalism we found there also derives from them. Homogeneity means that threats to the community tend to be located outside; it also means that virtually the whole community participates in a prosperity that might be jeopardised by an extreme fundamentalism. As they say themselves, 'we keep the hungry dog from our kitchen'. In Eğirdir the fundamentalist ideology has not so far been associated with extremes of political action. However, other towns in the province were not so quiet in the years before the 1980 military intervention. Civil disturbances in towns such as Yalvaç or Senirkent, for example, took a variety of political and religious forms, but opponents of all shades were generically labelled 'fanatics', thus suggesting something of both the richness and centrality of the ideology itself and the need to explain extremist reactions in terms of their specific local context.[15]

Can we generalise to the national level? Turkey was the first republican state with a predominantly Muslim population. For reasons of geography and because of its sophisticated imperial background, the Turkish state had an early start both in creating a cultural uniformity among its population and in offering them the possibility of Western-type prosperity.

To date the development of the public rhetoric and civic rituals of the Turkish Republic remains obscure. It is not clear how, when and at what levels detailed policies relating to civic, educational and military idioms, etiquette and ceremonial were formulated and established.[16] It is certainly the case, however, that by the mid-1930s celebrations of national holidays in the provincial capital of Isparta were at base similar to today. This suggests that such celebrations have drawn on sources closely related to the stability of the Turkish state and the people's commitment to it.

Many accounts have described how the state formally redefined Islam and determined its character, but the very fact of the state's determination to dominate religion makes it difficult to discern the subtle ways in which Islamic beliefs and practices have simultaneously determined the character of the state. Our hypothesis is that Turkish Islam and Turkish republicanism/nationalism today are both expressions of a single underlying ideology of social control. This ideology, which shows through in the ritual and symbolic parallels between the officially separate Islamic and republican ideologies as they are popularly perceived and articulated, is fundamentalist in character though at present remote from the extreme 'fundamentalism' of the media. The fundamentalism of the ideology is best revealed by the shifts in emphasis which have followed a variety of internal and external threats over the sixty years of the Republic. Indeed, recent changes have led other observers to remark on the fundamentalist character of this establishment ideology.

Today Turks would risk a great deal if they adopted an extreme fundamentalism which transformed their relations with the West and with the Soviet empire. However, it is just those relations, and the threat seen to be posed by Kurds, Greeks and Armenians, which lie behind the degree of fundamentalism associated with the dominant ideology of the state. Dissidents of left and right who created the terror of the late 1970s were seen as agents of outside powers. And to vanquish them after the intervention of 1980, the state, with its Islamic props, moved to a rather more hard-line national-fundamentalism.

Notes

Our fieldwork in Turkey was done jointly. Preparations for fieldwork were begun in 1979, after which we spent some 15 months in Turkey, completing the field research in November 1984. Richard Tapper was supported by grants from the School of Oriental and African Studies, the Nuffield Foundation, and the Economic and Social Science Research Council (HR 8851); Nancy Tapper's research was an SSRC/ESRC Project (HR 7410). Our gratitude and obligation to the authorities and to countless private individuals in Turkey are considerable and will be acknowledged more fully in a later publication.

This paper was prepared for the Inter-Collegiate Seminar on 'Fundamentalism' held at SOAS in spring 1985. It was also read at a seminar in the University of Cambridge and at the 1985 conference of the British Society for Middle East Studies at Edinburgh. We are grateful for the many helpful comments received on all these occasions. We would like particularly to thank Professor Şerif Mardin for both his general encouragement over many years and his incisive remarks on this paper. Some of the connections we explore in this paper are anticipated in his works, for example his 'Youth and Violence in Turkey' (1978).

1. We rely heavily on James Barr's now classic study (1977) as a foil for the treatment of our Turkish material. To simplify the text we hereafter refer, by page number only, to the second edition (1981).
2. Neither Gellner's 'pendulum-swing' theory of a hierarchical, ritualistic Islam of the hinterlands confronting an egalitarian, rule-bound Islam of the urban centres (1969), nor his more recent dichotomy between

'sober', legalistic Sunnism and the personality cult and religious mysteries of Shi'ism (1984), explain the presence or absence of our four features. See also, for example, Geertz's now classic study (1968) and more recent contributions by Gilsenan (1982) and MacEoin (1983).

3. Thus, like Webber and Taylor in this volume (Chapters 5 and 7), we consider fundamentalism to be a historiographical category and a corollary of the notion of modernism, if not imperialism. We are less concerned here, however, with the structures that generate references to 'fundamentalism' (Webber) or with the historical unfolding of a religious-cum-political movement (Taylor), than with the specific structure of the state-supported ideology in contemporary Turkey.

4. See, for example, Rosenthal (1965, Chapters 3 and 10), and particularly Mardin, who insists that modern Turkish secularisation cannot be understood apart from the character of Ottoman Islam, including its extensive politicisation and bureaucratisation (1982, p. 171).

5. See Yiğitbaşı's detailed local history of Eğirdir (1972) as well as Sami's history of Isparta (1983).

6. See Ajami's study of religion and authority in Egypt (1983); and cf. Bocock's comment on other modern ideologies which mix political and religious values and symbols (1985). Martin's account (1978) of the 'secular monopolies' in Poland and the USSR and the character of religious expression these have fostered is of considerable comparative interest and has now been supplemented by Ramet (1984), while the works of Binns (1979, 1980) and Lane (1981) treat aspects of state ceremony in the Soviet Union in ways that are directly relevant to our Turkish material.

7. Cf. Yalman (1969, 1979), *Arabia* (1985) and Alkan (1984). See Mardin (1982, p. 187ff.) for a summary of some of the complexities of these associations for Turkey as a whole.

8. A wide variety of circumstances may cause embarrassment and intellectual confusion and provoke such defensive reactions. It seems likely that these reactions are directly related to those elements of the fundamentalist ideology that concern the social construction of the self and personal identity. Certainly, patterns of socialisation (in the home, in schools and in both religious and military training) are often arbitrary and authoritarian and emphasise an individual's personal duties to the state or to God rather than a commitment to a broader social ethic. Failure and threats of all kinds are often explained in terms of outsiders or external forces; where specific insiders are held responsible for anti-social actions, their behaviour is often concealed and ignored or the individual concerned may literally be ostracised from the town.

9. Republican changes should have made irrelevant some of the traditional stumbling-blocks for non-Arab Muslims such as the 'Arabic Quran', but ironically the translation of the Quran into Turkish and the use of Turkish in the call to prayer were received with widespread hostility. However, the fact that sermons and religious instruction in the mosques are now always given in Turkish is an important element in the juxtaposition of 'religious' and 'secular' values and practices. The same point can be made with regard to the use of the Romanised Turkish

script. In effect the religious aesthetic has changed and become accessible to a wider public. Today, many well-educated Turks cannot even distinguish between the words 'Allah' and 'Muhammad' in Arabic script, but of course they read these names in Romanised script constantly, on religious posters and in both religious and secular publications of all kinds. Ataturk, by introducing the new script and establishing the Türk Dil Kurumu with responsibility for purifying Turkish and ridding it of all foreign (including Arabic) loanwords, sought to control and manage language in ways not unlike the founder-heroes of many other cultures.

10. For detailed analysis of *mevlûd* performances, see Tapper and Tapper (1987). Preliminary discussions of gender and religion in Eğirdir may be found in N. Tapper (1983). There is, however, much more to be said about the specific place of gender issues in the fundamentalist ideology we identify, not least because all too often in women's studies, whether of the Middle East generally or Turkey in particular, it is the differences between 'secular' and 'religious' ideologies that are stressed, and not their similarities (cf. Kandiyoti, 1982).

11. For example, the night after a new bulldozer was bought and inaugurated by the municipality, we chanced to see council workmen repairing two burst tyres by flashlight; shamefacedly, they explained that there had been no sacrifice and it might look as though the machine had been struck by evil eye, so they very much wanted to avoid public comment.

12. We could quote a range of other examples of the juxtaposition of republican and Islamic concepts; for example, see Mardin's comment that republican laicism was a 'Janus-like affair' and though the Caliphate had been eliminated in 1924, army training in the 1950s 'still culminated with the storming of a hill with cries of "Allah, Allah!"' (1971, p. 208). Norton describes contemporary Bektashi ceremonies which have departed from the universalising Sufism of the early twentieth-century and have become nationalistic – Hajji Bektash is treated as a sort of patron saint of Turkey who claimed that 'the Turkish nation was created to rule the world' and that even Muhammad and Ali were Turks (1983, p. 80f.). Or compare Olson's recent article discussing ideological conflict conventionally in terms of 'Turkish nationalism versus Muslim identity' and 'secularism versus Islamic society' (1985, p. 165), but with data on women's head coverings illustrating intrinsic relations between these different perspectives.

13. See Webster's comment on the new motto, 'we work [*çalışırız*]', which replaced traditional phrases referring to fate (1939, p. 289).

14. Compare the complementary and supportive relationship we are suggesting, with Mardin's comments on the cult of Ataturk (1982, p. 181), Fallers' remarks on the cult of the beloved Prophet (1971, p. 12), and Webster's early account of the quasi-deification of Ataturk (1939, pp. 146f., 196, 281). Though the association between Ataturk and Muhammad is vehemently denied by the townspeople, it is reproduced in data from other sources. Compare the text of the *mevlûd* (MacCallum, 1943; and see N. and R. Tapper, 1987) with, for instance, Koopman's account of poems about Ataturk which have appeared in the

Western European Turkish press. In these poems a variety of honorifics with religious connotations are used for Ataturk, including 'the saviour' and 'the mighty Mustafa'; he is treated as if he were asleep and could rise up and cleanse the nation and restore order; in others there is the suggestion of his messianic second coming (Koopman, 1981). The taboo on the explicit identification of Ataturk and Muhammad contrasts dramatically with Muhammad Reza Shah Pahlavi's deliberate strategy for managing the religious commitment of the Iranian people, by associating himself and his family with the supernatural and charismatic figures of Shi'ite Islam (see Braswell, 1975, pp. 206f., 237).

15. Cf.Magnarella (1982) who suggests crimes of honour and blood feud as sources of the violence in Turkish society today. We would point out that these are now anachronistic for much of Western Turkey at least and probably always had a semi-mythical status; we argue that more important sources of violence today are the dual emphases on the military history of the Republic and on Muhammad's military prowess and notions of an embattled Islam, which are collapsed into the single fundamentalism we discuss here. For an authoritative and much broader discussion of violence in Turkish society, see Mardin, who emphasises the 'identification with and internalization of the role of the epic hero' (1978, p. 252).

16. In this respect, Webster's chapters on propaganda and education are of considerable importance (1939, p. 181f.).

References

Ajami, F. (1983), 'In the Pharaoh's Shadow: Religion and Authority in Egypt', in J. Piscatori (ed.), *Islam in the Political Process* (London: Cambridge University Press).

Alkan, T. (1984), 'The National Salvation Party in Turkey', in M. Heper and R. Israeli, (eds), *Islam and Politics in the Modern Middle East* (London: Croom Helm).

Arabia (1985), 'Politics, Turkey – water under the bridge?', *Arabia*, August, pp. 42–3.

Barr, J. (1981), *Fundamentalism* (2nd edn; first published 1977) (London: SCM Press).

Berkes, N. (1964), *The Development of Secularism in Turkey* (Montreal: McGill University Press).

Binns, C. A. P. (1979, 1980), 'The changing face of power: revolution and accommodation in the development of the Soviet ceremonial system', Pt. I, *Man (N.S.)*, 14, pp. 585–606; Pt. II, *Man (N.S.)*, 15, pp. 170–87.

Bloch, M. (1974), 'Symbols, song, dance and features of articulation. Is religion an extreme form of traditional authority?', *Eur. J. Sociology*, 15, pp. 55–81.

Bocock, R. (1985), 'Religion in modern Britain', in R. Bocock and K. Thompson (eds), *Religion and Ideology* (London: The Open University).

Braswell, G. W. (1975), *A Mosaic of Mullahs and Mosques: Religion ana Politics in Iranian Shiah Islam* (Chapel Hill, N.C.: unpubl. Ph. D. thesis).

Richard Tapper and Nancy Tapper

77

Douglas, M. (1970), Natural Symbols (London: Barrie & Rockliff).
Evans-Pritchard, E. E. (1937), Witchcraft, Oracles and Magic among the Azande (London: Oxford University Press).
Fallers, L. (1971), Turkish Islam, unpublished paper given at University of Chicago.
Firth, R. (1959), 'Problem and assumption in an anthropological study of religion', J. Roy. Anthrop. Inst., 89, pp. 129–47.
Geertz, C. (1968), Islam Observed (Chicago University Press).
Gellner, E. (1969), 'A pendulum swing theory of Islam', in R. Robertson (ed.), Sociology of Religion (Harmondsworth: Penguin).
—— (1984), 'Inside Khomeini's mind', The New Republic, no. 3622, 18 June, pp. 27–33.
Gilsenan, M. (1982), Recognizing Islam (London: Croom Helm).
Glasner, P. (1977), The Sociology of Secularisation (London: Routledge & Kegan Paul).
Hager, R. (1983), 'State, tribe and empire in Afghan inter-polity relations', in R. Tapper (ed.) The Conflict of Tribe and State in Iran and Afghanistan (London: Croom Helm).
Jacob, P. X. (1982), L'enseignement religieux dans la Turquie moderne (Berlin: Klaus Schwarz).
Kandiyoti, D. (1982), 'Islam e politiche nazionali: riflessioni sulla Turchia', Donna, Woman, Femme (DWF), 22, pp. 7–22.
Koopman, D. (1981), 'Ataturk as seen by Turkish workers in Europe', Anatolica, 8, pp. 159–77.
Lane, C. (1981), The Rites of Rulers (Cambridge University Press).
MacCallum, F. L. (1943), The Mevlidi Sherif by Suleyman Chelebi (London: John Murray).
MacEoin, D. (1983), 'Introduction' to D. MacEoin and A. Al-Shahi (eds), Islam in the Modern World (London: Croom Helm).
Magnarella, P. J. (1982), 'Civil violence in Turkey: its infrastructural, social and cultural foundations', in C. Kağitçibaşi (ed.), Sex Roles, Family and Community in Turkey (Bloomington: Indiana University Turkish Studies, 3).
Mardin, Ş. (1971), 'Ideology and religion in the Turkish revolution', Int. J. Middle East Studs., 2, pp. 197–211.
—— (1978), 'Youth and violence in Turkey', Eur. J. Sociology, 19, pp. 229–54.
—— (1982), 'Turkey, Islam and Westernization', in C. Caldarola (ed.), Religion and Societies: Asia and the Middle East (Berlin: Mouton).
Martin, D. (1978), A General Theory of Secularization (Oxford: Basil Blackwell).
Norton, J. (1983), 'Bektashis in Turkey', in D. MacEoin and A. Al-Shahi (eds), Islam in the Modern World (London: Croom Helm).
Olson, E. (1985), 'Muslim identity and secularism in contemporary Turkey: the headscarf dispute', Anthr. Quarterly, 58, pp. 161–70.
Ramet, P. (ed.) (1984), Religion and Nationalism in Soviet and Eastern European Politics (Durham, N.C.: Duke University Press Policy Studies).
Rosenthal, E. I. J. (1965), Islam and the Modern National State (London: Cambridge University Press).
Sami, S. (1983), Isparta Tarihi (Istanbul: Serenler).

Sayarı, S. (1984), 'Politicization of Islamic re-traditionalism: some preliminary notes', in M. Heper and R. Israeli (eds), *Islam and Politics in the Modern Middle East* (London: Croom Helm).

Tapper, N. (1983), 'Gender and religion in a Turkish town: a comparison of two types of formal women's gatherings', in P. Holden (ed.), *Women's Religious Experience* (London: Croom Helm).

Tapper, N. and R. Tapper (1987), 'The birth of the Prophet: ritual and gender in Turkish Islam', *Man*, n.s., 22.

Webster, D. (1939), *The Turkey of Ataturk* (Philadelphia: American Academy of Political and Social Science).

Yalman, N. (1969) 'Islamic reform and the mystic tradition in eastern Turkey', *Eur. J. Sociol.*, 10, pp. 41–60.

—— (1979), 'The center and the periphery: the reform of religious institutions in Turkey', *Current Turkish Thought*, 38, pp. 1–23.

Yiğitbaşı, S. S. (1972), *Eğirdir-Felekâbad Tarihi* (Istanbul: Çeltüt).

4 A Case of Fundamentalism in West Africa: Wahabism in Bamako

Jean-Loup Amselle
(translated by Donald Taylor)

Even though it is not possible to trace a direct historical link between Wahabism and the phases of reform that preceded it in West Africa, it is nevertheless possible to assert that Wahabism is part of a recurrent movement in which Islam seeks to return to its origins, part of the struggle against the mingling (*shirk*) of pagan practices with Islam, and part of the rejection of any compromise between the *ulama* (learned men of religion) and holders of political power (Levtzion, 1978).

This movement which periodically reappears in Islam was started in West Africa by al-Maghili, adviser to Askia Muhammad, King of Sonrai (Cuoq, 1975). It was then taken up again by Usman dan Fodio in the north of Nigeria and by Al Hajj Umar in his struggle against Masina (Mahibou and Triaud, 1983).

If we accept that these different phases of Islamic reform constitute a unity then we can say that the unity itself is a type of fundamentalism because it is patterned in the same way.

BACKGROUND

Wahabism originated in the Arabian peninsula in the eighteenth century. The founder was Muhammad b.Abd al-Wahhab (1703–93), who was born into a family of legal experts, and who had been greatly influenced by the ideas of Ibn Hanbal and Ibn Taimiya. He developed a unified doctrine centred upon the oneness of God which at the same time criticised the cult of saints, Sufism and the non-Sunni sects within Islam.

Wahabism was both a religious and political movement, Arab and Islamic, that responded to the decline of the Ottoman Empire, on the one hand, and the increasing acceptance of Shi'ism in Iran, on the other. It sought to set up a Sunni state among Arab countries and to restore Islam to its original purity by driving out all innovations and superstitions and adopting a policy of expansion. Thanks to the pact of Dariya made in 1744 between Muhammad b. Abd al-Wahhab and Muhammad b. Saud, Wahabism became the official ideology of the Saud dynasty, thus turning this bedouin principality into a theocracy. Since then the destinies of Wahabism and of the Saudis have been inseparably bound together (Laoust, 1983, pp. 321–32).

Even though its influence was no doubt felt in West Africa before the colonial period (Kaba, 1974, p. 4) Wahabism did not really make itself felt, particularly in Bamako, until after the Second World War. As Kaba (1974) and Amselle (1977) have already shown, the spread of Wahabism to Bamako, the commercial crossroads between the Ivory Coast and Senegal, is due to two major factors: first, the increase in the number of pilgrims to Mecca in the last thirty years, and second, the return of the first West African graduates in about 1945 from the Al-Azhar University in Cairo.

Pilgrimage to Mecca was made much easier from 1935 onwards when the French colonial administration adopted a favourable attitude towards it. In addition to this the advent of air travel in 1950 allowed a growing number of Muslims, especially the merchants, to go to Mecca and meet other West Africans who had already accepted Wahabism (Triaud, 1983).

Likewise, since the graduates of Al-Azhar chose Bamako rather than Kankan as the centre for their proselytising activities, it became one of the principal homes of Wahabism in West Africa.[1]

From the time the graduates arrived in 1945, many Muslims who were attracted by the prestige that Al-Azhar had conferred upon them came to visit and enquire about Islam. Since the graduates were not able to obtain places in the colonial educational system because of the nature of their qualifications, they decided to take up preaching and organise conferences for debates with the marabouts[2] whom they easily out-classed thanks to the far superior nature of their Islamic learning.

Since 1945, Wahabism has attracted more and more sympathisers, in spite of the anti-Wahabi pogrom of 1957 and the closure by Modibo Keita's government of the Islamic Cultural Union (UCM) which had been founded in 1953 to bring together into one group all the Islamic reformers. In 1970, the Military Committee of National Liberation (CMLN) authorised the reconstitution of the Islamic Cultural Union and gave it land in the Hamdallaye ward for the construction of a centre and a mosque. At about that time the movement had three mosques under its control: one at Bajalan II, one at Badalabugu and one at Jikoroni. It also had a school (*medersa*) with 300 pupils at Niarela and controlled the Franco-Arab school at Ntomikorobugu (with 500 pupils).

In 1971 the CMLN suppressed the UCM which, according to the CMLN, was threatening the stability of the government (Kaba, 1974, p. 264 n.16). Today the Malian Muslims have regrouped themselves within the Malian Association for the Unity and Progress of Islam (AMUPI). This association was created by the authorities in 1981 to control the expansion of Wahabism and to prevent events happening in Mali similar to those which had ended in bloodshed in Northern Nigeria. At present the association is under the leadership of Oumar Ly, former government official, who is said to be a Tijani (member of one of the Sufi orders or brotherhoods which exist in Mali), and has ramifications in each area and each village.

In spite of this, Wahabism continues to grow and today the movement controls three large educational institutions. Laji Cheikna Yattabari, who was in charge of the school (*medersa*) of Niarela (300 pupils) is now the head of the Islamic Institute which has 1500 students, of whom 300 are girls, and 25 teachers. The second most important institution, the Narou Joliba Islamic Institute of Badalabugu, is in the charge of Amadou Kansai. It has several hundred students and has contacts in several quarters of Bamako (Hamdallaye, Niamakoro, Jikoroni and Daudabugu) as well as at Koulikoro. The third, the Khaled ben Abdul Aziz Institute opened in September 1983, is in the charge of Laji Baba Cissé, the Mali representative of the Amerian insurance company, the St Paul and Fire Insurance Co. He is also the external relations secretary of the AMUPI (Malian Association for the Unity and Progress of Islam). He has also bought several houses in Bajalan I which he has demolished, and on the site of which he has had built an imposing looking building.

The growth in the number of mosques is impressive. While the movement controlled only three mosques in 1970, in 1983 it controlled nine. That does not include the private mosques of three merchants which are near their shops: Yakuba Guindo (Malimag), Sheikh Ibrahima Ture (The Store of a Thousand and One Marvels), and Laji Tenemakan Dunbiya (co-owner of the Wonder Battery factory). As we have already stated, Wahabism first emerged among the merchants and until recently recruited its members from among them. Thus in 1970 almost all Wahabis were merchants and the pupils who went to their schools were nearly all their children. In the last ten years the situation has changed appreciably and today the movement increasingly includes intellectuals, minor officials, peasants and others.

First of all I shall try to set out the reasons why the Bamako merchants joined the Wahabi movement; then I shall try to look at the changing pattern of recruitment to the movement in relation to the economic, social and ideological crises which affect Mali today.

REASONS FOR THE MEMBERSHIP OF THE MERCHANTS

During the period following the Second World War, the Bamako merchants occupied only an inferior position in Bamako society in spite of their wealth and the prestige which they gained from going on pilgrimage to Mecca.

In political life, they played only a secondary role because they often came from lowly origins and rarely spoke French with any fluency. In the Islamic community where the proud title of Hajji should have given them high status, they were overshadowed by the marabouts and imams, for whom, furthermore, the merchants, were a chosen clientele. Like all the inhabitants of the Sudanese capital the merchants would go to the marabouts to be healed when sick, for success or faithfulness in love, and for prosperity in business. But the merchants would perhaps visit the marabouts more frequently than other inhabitants of Bamako, because of the speculative nature of their business affairs and of the inducements that made up their wealth. In order to succeed in their commercial enterprises, they would often spend very large sums of money in their consultations with the marabouts. They in return would make available ingenious treasures to 'sell' to a clientele which they knew to be financially well placed, in the form of sacrifices and amulets which they claimed to be infallible. This situation, where the merchants were always giving out money without ever receiving a tangible profit for their efforts, could only last while there was no alternative offered by their religion. As soon as an ideology appeared which would challenge the powers of the marabouts yet would allow the merchants to remain within the legitimate bounds of Islam, they were going to take it up in earnest.

THE ANTI-MARABOUT AND 'BOURGEOIS' ASPECT OF WAHABISM

Wahabism appeared from the beginning as an anti-marabout and anti-brotherhood doctrine. Article 3 of the statutes of the Islamic Cultural Union specifies that 'the Association aims to fight by appropriate means against the shameful exploitation of charlatans, fanaticism and superstition, in a word to purify Islam by getting rid of all corrupt influences and practices'.

They were aiming here particularly at 'mixing' (*shirk*),[3] innovation (*bida'a*) and Sufism, especially in the form of the cult of saints, all of which feature prominently in the brotherhood type of Islam found in West Africa.

In contrast to the *musherkin* (mixers), the Wahabis, who, incidentally, reject the title and make themselves out to be simply Sunnis, defend the doctrine of the Oneness of God.[4] At the same time they eagerly show up the marabouts to be individualists, exploiters, lazy, immoral and ignorant. Marabout practice is seen from a perspective which recalls the rationalist criticism of religion, as a technique to condition and manipulate the masses, as an 'opium of the people'.

The immorality of the marabouts is equally singled out by the reformists who insist that the imams and heads of Quranic schools often have more than four wives and frequently run after women.

According to the Wahabis the marabouts are obviously ignorant since many of them cannot correspond in Arabic, nor can they translate a text from Arabic into French. They also relate this ignorance to the essentially oral character of pre-reformist West African Islam.

These violent attacks aimed at the Muslim establishment had to find an echo among the Bamako merchants. The latter were tired of paying for individual 'hypocrites' and revellers who denied them access to the summit of the Muslim community, and who taught nothing useful to their children.

In contrast to the perverted marabouts the Wahabis presented themselves as followers of a pure and hardened form of Islam. They stressed that Islam was opposed to idleness and that a man could not live by religious performance alone. Wahabism therefore appeared as a work ethic, which in the West African context gave it the characteristics of a bourgeois ideology. Wahabism in effect totally rejected West African social structures that upheld inequality such as distinctions of caste and class inherited from the pre-colonial period.

For the reformers, all Muslims were equal whether they were chiefs, clients or slaves and so all must work. And these ideas were readily accepted by the Bamako merchants.[5]

By becoming Wahabis the merchants were able to reject the aristocratic ideology which kept them in a predetermined category. It allowed them to fight on their own ground, that is to say on the basis of social status founded upon wealth, without questioning the foundation upon which this wealth was made.[6] The model of the ideal man put forward by the Wahabis was that of the Muslim worker. If the Muslim succeeded in accumulating some wealth as a result of his labour, he had every reason to rejoice since 'a man cannot give alms without first owning some money'. We shall see below that this model of the Muslim worker has inspired certain merchants to formulate a sort of Afro-Arab theory in the informal sector, aimed at reducing urban unemployment which lies at the heart of the economic crisis that is affecting Mali at present.

Over and above an ideology which seemed to be 'made to measure' for the Bamako merchants, the propagators of Wahabism proposed to their clientele a system of instruction for their children. In contrast to the marabouts who were happy to teach them the Quran by heart, the Wahabis made available to their supporters a more elaborate form of instruction in Arabic. The Quranic High School, the first *medersa* founded by the Wahabis in 1950, offered in the first year a number of subjects including an introduction to the Quran, the study of Arabic, writing, arithmetic and grammar. In the second year these same subjects were continued and others were added, such as theology and the biography of the Prophet.

Today instruction offered in the *medersas* of Bamako is very elaborate. Thus, at the Islamic Institute (under the direction of Laji Cheikna Yattabari) pupils begin at the age of seven years and then follow for the next eight years courses in history, geography, physics, Arabic vocabulary and grammar and jurisprudence (*fiqh*).[7] They also study commentaries on the Quran and the Hadiths. The teachers are all from Mali except one Senegalese and one Somali, and most of them are former pupils of the school. The first three years of instruction are conducted exclusively in Arabic after which teaching is partly in French. At the end of this part of their schooling pupils can go and study in Arab countries. At present fifty students have been sent to Medina (Saudi Arabia), twenty-five to Cairo, ten to Libya and five to Algeria. Among those who studied at Medina a few have decided to teach in African countries under the auspices of the Saudis. They have never returned to Mali.

At the Narou Joliba Islamic Institute (under the direction of Amadou Kansai) the pupils who have completed the first part of their course in the branches of the Institute in the urban quarter come to Badalabugu to follow the second part of their course. The teachers are mostly from Mali but there are also Iraqis who give courses in Arabic and mathematics. The pupils continue their studies up to the DEF (Diplôme d'Études Fondamentales) in Arabic (equivalent to GCE 'O' level) and then begin their introduction to French in their final year. As in the former establishment, they can get scholarships for further studies in Iraq, Saudi Arabia, Egypt and Kuwait at the end of the second part of their course.

At present only two students are in the process of returning to Bamako; the first is about to return while the second is looking for a teaching post in higher education in Mali.

The founders of Wahabism intended this type of modern instruction in Arabic not only to rid the students of all impurities found in African Islam by means of direct access to texts, but also to enable them to become skilled in writing and arithmetic, both of which were directly useful for trade.[8] In the meantime, it was contrary to the aims of the colonial administration since it was given in Arabic. It implied the denial of the French presence and was orientated towards another cultural and political world, that is to say the Arab world whose virulent form of (Nasserite) nationalism continued to cause concern to the West.

THE NATIONALIST AND PRO-ARAB ASPECT OF WAHABISM

The students of Al-Azhar who came from West Africa were influenced by the reform movement that appeared in Egypt towards the end of the nineteenth century and which had taken on a nationalist flavour. At the university they met students who had been won over to the anti-Western ideas of the Muslim Brotherhood.

On their return to French West Africa they were unable to find positions in the French colonial educational system because they lacked knowledge of French, and so they turned against the French colonial authorities who denied them these positions and towards the

Arab countries which provided them with other attractive models of social organisation. This nationalist position also drove them to oppose the marabouts, whom they accused of being the faithful agents of the colonial authorities. The positions that were taken up struck a chord in the heart of the Bamako commercial community, whose accumulation of wealth was slowed down by French and Syrio-Lebanese merchants, some of whom were members of the United Sudanese Democractic African Assembly (USRDA).

In principle the Wahabi leaders were neutral in the rivalry between the pro-French Sudanese Progress Party (PSP) and the anti-colonial USRDA organisation, for they counted among their numbers both Fily Dabo Cissoko, leader of the PSP, and Mamadou Konaté, head of the USRDA. In fact it appears that the Wahabi intellectuals leaned towards the USRDA, whose more radical policies accorded well with their own ideology.

In spite of this it was difficult for the leaders of the reform movement to opt clearly for one or the other political party because of its social composition. Even though the Wahabis had among their ranks a majority of USRDA sympathisers – generally the under-privileged or the young (Kaba, 1974, p. 12) which came partly to the same thing – there was also a strong and very rich minority sympathetic to the PSP, consisting mainly of big merchants who financed much of the Wahabi movement, and without whom they could not therefore manage.

THE EVENTS OF MAY 1957

The fact remains that the government decided in 1957 to strike at the Wahabi movement and through it at the USRDA. It was believed that pro-USRDA feelings were taking hold within the movement and feared that it would become exclusive, and extremely radical, and so develop into a sort of Muslim wing of the USRDA. It was this that was behind the anti-Wahabi pogrom. The Wahabis demanded, with USRDA support, the construction of a mosque, the opening of a *medersa*, and the return of two of their leaders who had been expelled from French West Africa. This was virtually to put a match to a powder keg.

Without going in detail into the events of 1957 which have been related elsewhere (Kaba, 1974, pp. 202–18; Amselle, 1977, pp. 225–7), I merely note here that on the occasion of the pogrom tens if not hundreds of houses were destroyed by traditionalists, that is to say those who represented the interests of the colonial administration, the chief of the province and the marabouts. I should also note that the majority of these buildings belonged to members or sympathisers of the USRDA.

Shortly afterwards the leaders of the Wahabi movement, counting upon the support of the USRDA government, requested permission once more to open a *medersa* and to build a mosque, and to their great surprise they found that certain members of the government were opposed to them. This opposition reflected divergent interests between the leaders of the USRDA and those of the Wahabi movement that lay over and above their common struggle against colonialism.

The USRDA was controlled mainly by a small group of teachers. It represented basically the interests of officials and employees in the private sector and therefore of those who had passed through the French colonial education system, even though there were rich and influential merchants who financed its activities. The Wahabi movement, on the other hand, was controlled by those who were well-read in Arabic and were sworn to defend the claims of the Bamako merchants. As a result the USRDA had an interest in supporting the Wahabi movement as long as some of its members and sympathisers were faithful to it and the movement's ideology went along with its own policies.

On the other hand, the interests of these two movements in the final analysis were contradictory. The group that led the USRDA which would later form the nucleus of Mali bureaucracy hoped, consciously or not, to base its power upon keeping control of the learning it had inherited from its French colonisers.[9] The Wahabi leaders had a totally different cultural orientation. For them salvation could only come through drawing near to or even being incorporated politically within the Arab world and the Arabisation of Mali and West Africa generally.

This antagonism showed itself once more with reference to the teaching of French in the *medersas*, which Mali bureaucracy made obligatory. It resulted in the closure of Wahabi mosques, the state control of the *medersa* at Ntomikorobugu and the closure of the UCM by the Modibo Keita government, all of which sealed the political defeat of the merchant class and the triumph of the Malian state bourgeoisie.

Meanwhile the merchant bourgeoisie which continued to preserve its economic position and to extend its religious influence thanks to the development of Wahabism, began to work underground. This resulted in a *coup d'état* in November 1968. The military regime of Moussa Traoré was much more sympathetic towards the merchants and much more open towards Islam than its predecessors: it gave commerce a free rein and encouraged Islam. Today power in Mali remains as much in the hands of the merchants as of the marabouts.[10] For this reason the Military Committee of National Liberation at first authorised the reconstitution of the Islamic Cultural Movement (UCM), but finally outlawed it in 1971 and forced Muslims to join one common association, the Malian Association for the Unity and Progress of Islam (AMUPI).

Although it may be true to say that the Wahabis have made themselves felt as a force within the population of Bamako and even within Mali as a whole, or that the Mali government seeks to find favour with Saudi Arabia,[11] it is equally true to say that traditionalist forces, and notably the marabouts, are still powerful within the structures of the state.[12] It is well known in Mali that President Moussa Traoré and many of his ministers make use of the services of the more important marabouts to confirm their powers. It is this no doubt that explains in part why the Wahabis cannot speak openly and why they should be the object of violent reaction by other Malian Muslims, to which the recent ransacking of the Wahabi mosque at Joliba, a village situated some ten kilometres from Bamako is witness.

THE WAHABI MOVEMENT IN BAMAKO IN 1983

Until recently the Wahabi movement recruited mainly from the merchant classes. Today it recruits from other parts of the Bamako population. We saw above that the Wahabi movement had an ideology which seemed to be made to measure for the Bamako merchants because of its anti-marabout views, and its bourgeois, nationalist and pro-Arab perspectives. These perspectives in the Wahabi movement continue to be accepted by Bamako merchants and they certainly account for the strength of the movement in this social environment. However, in 1983 the political scene in Mali was vastly different from that which existed in colonial days. Power, as we have said, rested with the merchants and the marabouts, but nationalism, that is to say one of the aspects of Wahabi progressiveness, had evidently disappeared. The only thing that remained, from the point of view of what interests us here[13] was the 'bourgeois' aspect of the movement. Here Wahabism supplied certain merchants with an alternative social project to reduce urban unemployment, and this fitted in perfectly with the policy put in hand in Mali during the previous two years because of pressure from the International Monetary Fund and the World Bank (Amselle, 1983). According to Sheikh Ibrahima Ture,[14] proprietor of the Store of a Thousand and One Marvels, the Malian government was not able to provide work for the young people who came either from the state schools or the *medersas*. The only way to provide work for them was to develop commercial activities and crafts.

To this end he has rented a place from the government in which he has installed his shop, his personal mosque and a dormitory where his employees, who are at the same time his disciples, live. Apart from the older employees who are paid regularly, the others are paid amounts according to their 'courage' which vary from 40 000 to 100 000 Mali francs a month, and Sheikh Ibrahima Ture deducts from this each month a sum corresponding to the cost of their food. His pupils neither play, dance nor go to the cinema. If they were to break these rules they would be expelled. Sheikh Ibrahima Ture also has shops in the Niafunké and Mopti districts which are run by his disciples. At Bamako, he has set up some of his pupils as craftsmen (joiners and tailors).[15] In addition he has drawn up plans, with aid from Saudi Arabia, for the construction of a four to five-storey building which will accommodate a shop, a mosque, a dormitory for the pupils and a reading and lecture room. He is at present looking for land on which he can build his project.

One can see therefore that Wahabism provides a very favourable global framework for the pursuit of commercial activities. The master–pupil relationship and the monastic character of the commercial enterprise and craftsmanship guarantee the maintenance of order, the lack of competition and hence the payment of low wages. Many merchants therefore see in Wahabism an ideologial cover under which they can quietly go about their business. In the AMUPI these same merchants form part of a union with other Malian Muslims. Laji Baba Cissé is the one who is notably accused of having made use of his position as secretary to the external relations section of the AMUPI in order to get subsidies from Arab countries and to construct the building of the Institute which he now runs.

Another movement, which includes intellectuals influenced by Arab culture as well as groups formed in the West and even a former leader of the student movement during 1979–80, is opposed to any compromise with the rest of the Muslims. It wants to unite the *umma* (the Muslim Community) on the basis of the Quran and the Hadiths. The followers of this movement propose to open up Sunni Islam to science, which contradicts the position of the marabouts who have always denied, for instance, that man has landed on the moon. They postulate the complementary nature of science and Islam, which as the religion of the Prophet will give science a soul. Furthermore they give certain *surahs* (chapters) of the Quran a scientific interpretation and aim to produce by means of Islamic culture models which will rival Western science.[16] Owing to the fact that they have a favourable attitude to modernism, both in the scientific and in the social domains (for instance, the reduction of costs of the naming ceremony and of marriage) these intellectuals have had some success with the young people of Bamako.

Confronted by the moral, social and economic crises now hitting Mali which results in corruption, deprivation,[17] drug-taking and illegitimate births, the Sunni Muslims have looked for a solution. They try to convince the young not to seek refuge in the traditional past, in the glorious memory of great Sudanese empires of the Middle Ages, but to rearm themselves morally. They claim that their own exemplary behaviour of not smoking, not going to football matches, and especially of dressing simply, is a valuable example for the young.

For the moment there has not yet been any break between the Sunnis and the Mali government. It is true that the latter leans on the marabouts and discourages factional activities among Muslims. In the meantime it does not prevent the Wahabis from proselytising,[18] and maintains very correct relations with Arab countries, especially Saudi Arabia.

Muslim fundamentalism, of which Bamako Wahabism is but an example, could well represent a general feature of the process of the expansion of Islam. All new movements that want to establish themselves upon Islamic foundations seek to consign elements of the Islamic phase that preceded them to the darkness of paganism. For, as Godelier has rightly said (1972, p. 257), the evolution of religious thought is achieved by means of *denial* (denegation) and *transference* (transfert).

Appendix

Our appeal to Islamic youth throughout the world

Young Muslims throughout the world prepare yourselves for the defence of

Islam against those who want to transform or cut the throat of Islam. Let them know that a sword has appeared to cut their own throat. The enemies of Islam should know that they are trapped and will be destroyed and cannot escape.

Those who pride themselves as champions of Islam though they are not even in Islam are already known. All Muslims who do not follow the Sunna (practices) of the Prophet MUHAMMAD (Peace and blessings upon him) are followers of the devil Satan.

Sects multiply in Islam but the worst of those are the HAMADIA OF GHULAM Ahmad Kadjani[19] and the Shi'ites. It is the latter who have introduced a transformed Islam into Africa for the last thousand years and seek even now to upset our religion once more.[20] If KHOMEINI wishes to speak about Islam he should come out of Shi'ism for it is completely contrary to the Islam that the Prophet MUHAMMAD (Peace and blessings upon him) practised and taught. We have seen Shi'ism close up; we went to IRAN where we were allowed to see how the Shi'ites practise Islam. The followers of Hamadia and of Shi'ism should not set foot in MECCA just as an infidel (*kuffar*) is not allowed to set foot there.

The Saudi authorities do not have the right to allow into MECCA people who do not follow the tradition of the Prophet MUHAMMAD (Peace and blessings upon him), just as they should not allow an infidel from trampling upon the sacred Territory of MECCA. The defence of and respect for the sacred Territory are not the sole preserve of the Saudi Government; they are incumbent upon all Muslims whoever they are: King, Head of State, rich or poor; they should defend and protect these sacred places against all stains.

We speak of this today because it is our duty.

We are preparing ourselves to appeal to the whole world in a short while, if it pleases God, through responsible peoples, the Heads of Religions, Emperors, Kings, Heads of State, and the wise, to give you the most important information.

We ask the wise of the entire world in particular to be prepared for we will be submitting to them a questionnaire of a thousand questions, five hundred of which will be directed to the Pope, more than a hundred to Muslim wise men, and questions to scientists. The questions will be asked in parts, the first part being now attached to our message.

Here are some of them
1. It is said that in August 1531 a comet appeared over a town in a north-westerly direction. It was visible for fourteen days. What is the name of the town and in which country is it?
2. Today scientists prepare to meet up with Halley's Comet in May 1986. Four automatic probes will be launched from our planet; two Soviet probes will be launched in December 1984, one French probe GIOTTO will leave in July 1985 and will cross the path of the Comet on 7 May 1986 [sic], and the Japanese probe which will leave a month later will cross its path on 8 May 1986. Are you certain that the Comet will be at the rendezvous? For HALLEY himself made errors in his calculations

predicting it would be seen in 1758, but the Comet was not at the rendezvous.

We have to inform you that in about 1980 something similar to this long-tailed star visited Africa and left its trace. We have proof of it and witnesses have clearly described the long-tailed star which passed by a little village. Has the European interplanetary observatory seen this? We can tell you the month, the day and the hour. We invite you to come and verify this, bringing with you your instruments for establishing the facts. Is this a machine or a proper star?

3. Do beings invisible to the human eye exist? Do they have houses and even industrial buildings?
   — Can you prove that the moon is not inhabited?
   — Can you prove that Mars is not inhabited? (Because on earth men live with *jinns* and cannot see them. Man cannot see the angels which surround him.)

Young people of the whole world, Muslim or non-Muslim, now is beginning the age for the renaissance of Islam in the Sunna (practice) of the Prophet MUHAMMAD (Peace and blessings upon him). We invite you to join us and come to know Scientific-Islam.

OUR WISH IS THAT PEACE AND JUSTICE SHOULD REIGN
ON EARTH

THE RENAISSANCE OF ISLAM
BAMAKO, MALI, WEST AFRICA

Notes

This chapter is a slightly altered version of an article entitled 'Le Wahabisme à Bamako (1945–1985)', which appeared in the *Revue canadienne des études africaines* (vol. 19, no. 2 (1985) pp. 345–58, and was reprinted in B. Jewsiewicki and J. L. Triaud (eds), *Les défricheurs de l'Islam en Afrique occidentale/Islamic leaders in West Africa* (Québec: Safi/ACEA, 1985). I am grateful to Donald Taylor for translating the text.

1. Their choice of Bamako was no doubt premeditated. In fact a rapid glance at some of the towns of Mali shows that Wahabism took root easily as long as there was no *ulama* to prevent its spread. Such was the case at Bamako. Much of this was confirmed in conversations with Almami Malik Yattara and Muhammad Konaké, president of AMUPI for the region of Mopti (2 January 1984). For further details see Sanakoua (1985).
2. As Levtzion remarked in a conversation with me, the term 'marabout', which originated during the colonial period, is ambiguous. However, it

is better suited, to my mind, for referring to these unlettered Muslim diviners and magicians (*mori* or *karamoko* in the Bambara language) than the term *alim* (pl. *ulama*).

3. The notion of *shirk* must not be taken in an absolute sense. The *musherkin* is the one who mixes that which should be kept strictly apart (particularly mixing God with any other entity that may jeopardise his oneness). It is often used as a pejorative term against one's opponents. In a sense, however, we are all mixers.

4. In reality only those who are well versed in matters of religion categorically reject this title of Wahabi; others accept it more or less willingly. On the other hand, certain Wahabis (see Appendix) deny that other Wahabis are true Sunnis or Muslims. Other Muslims often accuse the Wahabis of hypocrisy, and suspect that they are only interested in the money which is distributed by Saudi Arabia. They also believe that the Wahabis follow practices that have nothing to do with Islam; for instance praying with their arms folded.

5. Many of the merchants were from low status groups, for example, Kooroko and Jawanbe.

6. 'Le Sunna défend notre fortune', said Abdoulaye Camara, the Imam of the Laji Tenemakan Dunbiya Mosque at Bamako (27 January 1983).

7. The attitude of some Sunnis towards *fiqh* (jurisprudence) is ambiguous, without going as far as to say that there exists a 'definite distrust' of it (Triaud, 1983). In an interview (7 January 1984) Modibo Sangaré remarked that 'in a general sense, the *fiqh* does not contradict the Hadiths'. Jurisprudence is taught in the *medersas*.

8. As we shall see, certain Wahabis believe that neither public schools in Mali nor the *medersas* enable the young to find work at the end of their studies.

9. This analysis is different from that of Kaba (1974, pp. 231–2), who insists upon the influence that Islam had upon Modibo Keita and in general on the USRDA. For those who knew the two periods, it is evident that the socialist regime was much more influenced by the laity than the military regime that followed it.

10. For a more complete analysis of Mali today see Amselle (1985).

11. After Senegal, Mali is the second country in non-Arab Africa to have received aid from Saudi Arabia (cf. Gresh, 1983, p. 73).

12. Interview with Modibo Sangaré (13 May 1983).

13. I leave aside such practices, which rightly or wrongly have been regarded as retrograde, such as the segregation of women, the veiling of women, the prohibition against shaking hands with a woman other than one's wife, and so on.

14. Interview, 30 April 1983.

15. Although the Wahabis claim to be anti-Sufi, they clearly carry out practices that are analagous to those found in the Sufi brotherhoods.

16. Interview with Sheikh Oumar Dembélé, (10 May 1983). See also Appendix.

17. I use here the actual terms employed by certain Wahabis.

18. See also Hamès (1980). During Ramazan 1983 all shops that sold alcoholic drinks in Bamako were closed by the Government because of pressure from the Wahabis. Some of them never reopened. The same

order was made for Ramazan 1984. In 1985, during the period of fasting, the Wahabis drove out all prostitutes from the Bakaribougou quarter with the tacit agreement of the authorities. A snack bar opposite the 'Thousand and One Marvels Store' was stoned. An Islamic tribunal was also set up at Kayes.

19. This refers to the Ahmaddiya. See Moreau (1982, pp. 280–2).
20. No doubt a reference to the Fatimids, the Shi'ite dynasty that conquered Ifriqiya (Tunisia) in 910 AD.

References

Amselle, J. -L. (1977), *Les négociants de la savanne* (Paris: Anthropos).

—— (1983), 'La politique de la Banque Mondiale au sud du Sahara', *Politique Africaine*, 10, pp. 113–18.

—— (1985), 'Socialisme, capitalisme et précapitalisme au Mali (1960–82)', in H. Bernstein and B. Campbell (eds), *Contradictions of Accumulation in Africa* (Beverley Hills: Sage).

Cuoq, J. (1975), *Receuil des sources arabes concernant l'Afrique occidentale du VIIIè au XVIè siècle (Bilad al-Sudan)* (Paris: CNRS).

Godelier, M. (1972), 'Marxisme, anthropologie et religion', in *Epistémologie et marxisme* (Paris: Union Générale d'Editions).

Gresh, A. (1983), 'L'Arabie Séoudite en Afrique non-arabe: puissance islamique ou relais de l'Occident', *Politique Africaine*, 10, pp. 55–74.

Hamès, C. (1980), 'Deux aspects du fondamentalisme islamique: Sa signification au Mali actuel et chez Ibn Taimiya', *Archives de Sciences Sociales des Religions*, 50, pp. 170–90.

Kaba, L. (1974), *The Wahhabiya: Islamic reform and politics in French West Africa* (Evanston, III: Northwestern University Press).

Laoust, H. (1983), *Les schismes dans l'islam* (Paris: Payot).

Levtzion, N. (1978), 'Islam in West African politics: Accomodation and tension between the ulama and the political authorities', *Cahiers d'Etudes Africaines*, 71, pp. 333–45.

Mahibou, S. M. and J. -L. Triaud (eds) (1983), *Voilà ce qui est arrivé, Bayan ma waqa'a de Al-Hagg'Umar al-Futi, Plaidoyer pour une guerre sainte en Afrique de l'Ouest au XIXè siècle* (Paris: CNRS).

Moreau, R. L. (1982), *Africains musulmans* (Paris: Presence Africaine, INADES).

Sanakoua, D. B. (1985), 'Les écoles coranique au Mali, problèmes actuels', *Revue Canadienne des Etudes Africaines*, 19, pp. 359–67.

Triaud, J. -L. (1983), *Abd al-Rahman l'africain (1908–1957) pionnier et précurseur du Wahabisme au Mali*. Paper presented to the seminar 'Les agents religieux islamiques en Afrique tropicale', at the Maison des Sciences de l'Homme, 15–17 December.

5 Rethinking Fundament- alism: the Readjustment of Jewish Society in the Modern World

Jonathan Webber

INTRODUCTION

'Fundamentalism' is sufficiently complex and ambiguous a concept as to make it an ideal cover-term in the ethnographic description and anthropological analysis of many of the inherent difficulties in accounting for patterns of traditional religious behaviour and self-identification in the modern world. The term is used in various senses, though principally to refer to a particular form or manifestation of Christianity and to a distinctive approach to the character of biblical literature. But the term may also be used of a mode of social organisation and tendency towards charismatic leadership, a self-perpetuating and self-enclosing group literature, style of oppositional discourse, social networks, boundary maintenance and world-view generally – such that the presence of a sufficient number of these characteristic elements would seem to provide a prima-facie case for the existence of the fundamentalist phenomenon and, thereby, a guide for its interpretation. Hence 'fundamentalism' is today spoken of amongst Muslims, Jews, Hindus and Sikhs (to name just a few of the religious groups being examined in this volume), and doubtless traces of fundamentalism will be claimed of a wider range of religions still. The term is rich enough – or, if you prefer, it is sufficiently complex or ambiguous – to offer scope for the identification of a new phenomenon (or possibly the new identification of an older phenomenon) and, as such, scope for the application of a useful heuristic category in the understanding of religious behaviour in the kind of modern world we live in today.

The juxtaposition of the term 'fundamentalism' with the term 'modern' as I have just used it, as indeed in the title of this paper, is deliberate. The word 'fundamentalism' itself is a recent coinage; it dates back no further than about a generation after the time when modernism became the international tendency in poetry, fiction, drama, music, painting, architecture and other arts of the West. And of course the ideological form of fundamentalism (that is, as opposed to any distinctive social characteristics that may be attached to it by anthropologists and others) largely came about as the self-conscious rejection of a modernism in theology that sought to take into account the results of biblical criticism, scientific discovery and the general conditions of modern culture. The legacy of this historical linkage of the two terms is still with us: it means, amongst other things, that the lines of battle have been drawn. Fundamentalism continues to occupy a good part of that cultural space where doubt is expressed over the relevance of modernism; or, to put it another way, this legacy means that the label 'fundamentalism' will tend to get pinned, willy-nilly, on to those who, in the sphere of religion, deem it fitting to reject modernism in some way or other. The way that the term seems to be used today, often as a catch-all pejorative expression to denote the religious beliefs or behaviour of those who are thought in some sense to have turned their backs on the wider cultural environment, means in effect that there is an indefinitely large number of elements that can be drawn upon for the definition, or partial definition, of the category.

It is, I think, not enough to say, as the Fontana *Dictionary of Modern Thought* (1977) suggests, that fundamentalism means the belief that the Bible possesses complete infallibility because every word in it is the Word of God. This is certainly the one specific issue that from the outset has seemed to stake out a minimum philosophical consistency in the use of the term; but it neither exhausts nor explains the actual use of the term. The infallibility of the Bible just happened to represent that point at which, when the term was introduced, any resistance to theological modernism could be expressed most effectively. Rather, for once, the *Shorter Oxford English Dictionary* has offered a more attractive definition: fundamentalism, it says, is the 'strict adherence to traditional orthodox tenets (e.g. the literal inerrancy of Scripture) held to be fundamental to the Christian faith: opposed to liberalism and modernism'. It is in that 'e.g.' and that opposition 'to liberalism and modernism' that one can glimpse the potential of the term and indeed its application, as we know, to issues far wider than the infallibility of the Bible and to religions far removed from the Christian sphere. What is of interest to the anthropologist is precisely that fundamentalism has found its way into the description of religions other than Christianity and also, even more interestingly, into the description, by members of these non-Christian religions themselves, of their own norms or deviations, as the case may be. Hence the complexity and ambiguity of the term, for modernism and perceptions of modernism will vary ethnographically from case to case, as will of course the respective fundamentalist responses.

In this chapter I am not proposing, therefore, to show how the evidence for fundamentalism in the Jewish case can be used for a general theory of the subject, although I hope that I have disposed of any preliminary objections that might be made to the use of the term in a non-Christian context. What I shall be looking for are the ideological structures that generate the reference to fundamentalism amongst the Jews and the particular circumstances that have given rise to their use of the category, whether it be seen as a 'response' to modernism or simply as a re-statement of traditional orthodox tenets which modernists classify as 'fundamentalist' so as to make their own position appear normative by contrast. In a sense, of course, any modernist rationalisation of religion will leave behind certain areas that cannot be accounted for, and this residual category – the parts, if you like, that the theory cannot reach – will be known by its own term, namely faith or superstition (depending on the critic's point of view); whilst the upholders of those elements within that residual category will receive the name of fundamentalists. Fundamentalists thus defined are certainly not without their representatives in modern Jewish society, and the way is thus left open for them to proclaim that the ultimate purpose and meaning of their religion is to be found precisely in those areas inaccessible to ordinary intellectual specula-tion – much perhaps as scholars often used to claim that the special quality of a particular language lay in its idioms, namely those linguistic forms whose meaning somehow resisted ordinary logical or traditional grammatical analysis.

The advantage of the case for what one might call the idiomatic definition of fundamentalism is that it suggests locating its character elsewhere than within itself, and specifically draws attention to the force of external categorisation in shaping its identity. Moreover there is good ethnographic evidence, as shall be indicated below, that the modernist challenge as defined in this way has been directly tackled by those fundamentalist Jewish groups who see it as their duty precisely to argue the case for religion in terms of its self-evident departure from the rationalist perspective. The drawback of the idiomatic definition, however, is that it is only a partial definition; in particular, it does not account for what may be peculiarly modern about fundamentalism, inasmuch as the stress in this theory is laid on rationalism as such. If fundamentalism means a withdrawal of some kind from the cultural experience of the modern world, the perceived need of those who voluntarily choose to associate themselves with a substantially different outlook may well lie in a sense of alienation from a whole host of things, not just rationalism. Modernity, says Peter Berger (1977, pp. 101–12), means a profound change in the temporal structure of human experience, a powerful shift from the past and present to the future as a primary orientation for imagination and activity; it also means that large areas of human life, previously considered to be dominated by fate, now come to be perceived as opportunities for choice, whether by the individual or by the group. One becomes aware of options, and the multiplication of options; one becomes seduced by the idea that things could be other than what they have been. This is, as Berger puts it, 'the turbulent dynamism of modernity, its deeply rooted thirst for innovation and revolution' (ibid., p. 108). Finally, the secularisation which modernisation inexorably brings in its train tends to lead to a frustration of deep human aspirations, in particular the aspiration to exist in a meaningful and ultimately hopeful cosmos; secularisation bypasses the provision of satisfactory ways of explaining and coping with the experiences of suffering and evil in ordinary human life. Indeed, as one may ask, is the modern conception of the individual a great step forward in the story of human self-realisation, as liberal thought since the Enlightenment has maintained, or is it, on the contrary, a dehumanising aberration, as it might appear to be in the perspective of many non-Western traditional cultures?

It is often to questions such as these that the contemporary Jewish fundamentalist likes to address himself, secure in the conviction that his orthodoxy contains within itself cogent answers. Jewish fundamentalism shares with its Christian counterpart, as James Barr (1977, p. 98) has described it, the tendency to proclaim a sense of certainty, the feeling of a secure reality. This is opposed to the doubts, hesitations, questionings and theorising typical not only of the modern humanities as practised at the university but of modern man's approach to religion also, characterised by the relativisation of knowledge, since without any divine sanction knowledge becomes a series of competitive systems. In its fundamentalist interpretation Judaism insists not upon the cultivation of an awareness of choice, or the multiplication of choice; far from it, the Torah ('teaching') and *halacha* ('the way') are held to pronounce fully reliable knowledge – this is how a rabbi's decision on a particular matter is to be understood, for it is certainly not to be taken, as a modernist would have it, merely as one out of many possible opinions. The laws and practices of Judaism, having been set out in the original divine revelation contained in the Bible, are treated by fundamentalists as enabling man to reach the highest possible spiritual level. To a very great extent, they expect the community to project itself back into the past, to be present in the past – as for instance in the domestic Passover ritual, which is a self-conscious re-enactment of the historical departure of the Israelites from the land of Egypt, a re-enactment which is held by definition to provide the participants at the ritual with a self-evident statement of its spiritual meaning and purpose.

There is ample scope, therefore, for the contemporary Jewish fundamentalist to assert a strong feeling of distance from the circumstances of modernity, not to mention of course the common tirades against the paganism of contemporary secular morality, for instance in the realm of sexual behaviour. The argument that I am leading up to is evidently one which is in sympathy with Barr's important suggestion that fundamentalism is to be best understood not as the product of a pre-scientific society, but, on the contrary, as a peculiarly modern phenomenon, drawing not only its primary stimulus but also its insights, points of reference and even its otherwise curious alliance with materialism, from certain distinctive features of the modern world (Barr, 1977, ch. 4). The very irreligiosity of the modern world even functions here as a benchmark: the Jewish reform movement, that in many ways paralleled and even predated Christian liberal theologies, has been motivated by the idea that outmoded conservative views are obnoxious to educated people, and it has attempted to provide a more refined, reasonable Judaism, less bound to the exact details of the tradition, in order to win intellectual respect. But today the secular rejection of Judaism has gone much further – even 'rational' forms of belief and practice are regarded as outmoded or absurd, with the result that all forms of practising Judaism are potentially tinged with the fundamentalist dye. In a context such as this the fundamentalist appeal to all Jews to return to the faith of their fathers paradoxically – and ironically – sounds more reasonable and appears even as a more rational survival strategy for assimilated Jews concerned with the longer-term threat to their identity posed by outbreaks of anti-Semitism. Barr, in noting a similar point in relation to Christian fundamentalists, suggests that the latter gain credibility and support in the modern world precisely because of its irreligiosity – one might, so to speak, as well be hanged for a sheep as for a lamb

(Barr, 1977, p. 102). In the Jewish context, for those preoccupied with anti-Semitism, such a line of thinking provides more than an echo.

The proposal, then, to treat contemporary Jewish fundamentalism not as a 'backward' form of 'primitive' thought or as some sort of fossilised survival from an earlier age, but rather as a religious form fully contextual with the modern world in which it moves, has a number of methodological advantages – but it also, as we shall now see, fits more closely with the ethnographic facts. The question of fundamentalism, and its role both in the armchair analysis and in the indigenous self-examination of matters such as ritual behaviour or ethnic identity, is in any case central to the discussion. The tension between fundamentalism and modernity lies at the very root of contemporary Jewish society, and it is virtually impossible to attempt a description of the latter without reference to such a tension. With the exception of the 1 700 000 Jews closeted in the Soviet Union, the great majority of the remaining 11½ million or so Jews scattered in very many (principally Western) countries across the globe[1] are themselves immigrants to those countries – of the first, second or third generation. Moreover, a very substantial proportion of these migrants were in fact practising double migration: that is to say, they were not merely moving from one country to another, they were often moving from a rural environment to an urban one, and indeed in very many cases from a traditional village environment to a highly modern urban metropolis or even megalopolis. Now, given such a history, the reconstitution of Jewish communities in these new contexts has clearly involved substantial readjustment in many aspects of traditional, social and cultural organisation, but perhaps the principal question remains this: how far has a fundamentalist definition of Jewish cultural goals, in terms for example of leadership, ritual or identity generally, interacted with or emerged from Jewish society's evident internal reconstruction on the basis of what one might call its encounter with modernity? Leaving aside for the time being, therefore, the general theoretical question of fundamentalism as a self-evident *universal* category in opposition to modernity (whether, for example, fundamentalists can be described comparatively between societies), what I wish to look at more closely is how the fundamentalist principle operates in, or is generated by, the readjustment process of Jewish society in the modern world. It is hoped that the data presented in this paper may in addition help to clarify some of the general considerations about fundamentalism that I have discussed thus far.

RETHINKING FUNDAMENTALISM

The modernist view of modern Jewish society

For the purpose of the discussion I have assumed up to now that there is no especial difficulty with the term 'fundamentalism' in the Jewish case, and I have even gone so far as to suggest that a tension between fundamentalism and modernity lies at the root of modern Jewish society. A closer inspection of the ethnographic material instantly reveals, however, that things are not quite so simple. In the first place there does not seem to be a word in Hebrew for fundamentalism or fundamentalist. This is not to say that the concept cannot be translated into Hebrew; it can, but only in rather cumbersome fashion (such as *hasid ha-emuna*, someone who is a follower or lover of faith, or *makpid be-ikkarim*, someone who is punctilious about matters of principle; and so on). The nearest one can apparently get to the term in Hebrew is *kenai*, which means a zealot, but this is a term of approbation inasmuch as it was used of the zealots at Massada who in the first century AD committed mass suicide rather than fall into the hands of the Romans. To the modern Israeli, sensing his country's continuing struggle for physical survival against the surrounding Arabs, such figures are in no way to be taken as the stereotype of the modern fundamentalist's sense of the religious struggle for spiritual survival, even though one could make out a perfectly good case that it might. When one looks at the Yiddish language the situation is a little more complex: there one finds a number of pejorative terms for religious Jews, such as *frumak* or *fanatiker*, as well as non-pejorative terms such as *religez* or *traditsyonel*. In addition, one comes across the term *shvarts* ('black', presumably referring to the traditionally black clothing worn by the Hasidim pietists of Eastern Europe), and this is used pejoratively by non-Hasidim, though not necessarily only by secular Jews; and also *haredish* (from a Hebrew word meaning someone who trembles, that is, before God), but this is used by religious Jews about themselves.[2]

In short, given that fundamentalism is in principle a category imposed from the outside rather than a self-descriptive category, and that it is understood pejoratively as the excessive adherence to tradition, it does not possess its direct translation in Judaism. Rather the linguistic evidence here confirms my previous argument, namely that fundamentalism is the creation, the categorial result, of modern ideological structures that have generated the concept in the process of interpreting and making sense of a much wider realm of social realities. In a phrase, Jewish fundamentalists are those who, to a modern assimilated Jew, appear to remain unassimilated or else claim a steadfast refusal to assimilate. In the Jewish context, fundamentalists represent a category rather than one specific group. Any Jew, Jewish community or Jewish ideology that cold-shoulders what a modernist would regard with rationalist conviction as the inevitably progressive nature of modern Western civilisation, but instead specifically looks backward either to the past itself or to earlier, pre-modern formulations of Judaism, would be likely to attract the label 'fundamentalist'.

In this sense, therefore, fundamentalism 'exists' in Judaism, but it is clearly not co-extensive in meaning with its referent in Christianity. Christian fundamentalists, narrowly defined, claim the inerrancy of the Bible; in the Jewish case such a claim is regarded as characteristic of the Karaites or the Samaritans, groups that incidentally still exist today, in very small numbers and with little or no wider influence.[3] Jewish fundamentalists, unlike these latter groups, claim the inerrancy not of the Bible but of the *halacha* (rabbinic law) – that is, they are to be defined as those who (unlike the Karaites or Samaritans) accept the leadership and authority of the long chain of rabbis who have made it their business to interpret the Bible and so to lead the community itself. The *halacha* is understood in this sense not as a historical development of Jewish law but, on the contrary, as the rabbinic amplification of the Torah itself, there being no other single formal authority over all Jews everywhere. The cultural space occupied by Jewish fundamentalism is thus *traditionally* not a sphere of oppositional discourse, as it may be in the Christian context, but rather the reverse – the self-defining embodiment of natural leadership and authority in the Jewish world. The traditional Jewish leadership had no need, therefore, to use the term 'fundamentalist' about itself; the whole traditional system was fundamentalist in that sense. The use of the term 'fundamentalist' today by modernist Jews is a signal of their challenge to the authority of that leadership and that system. By the very evocation of the term, modernists in effect signal that it is they who occupy the sphere of oppositional discourse. But a hundred years or more have passed by since the process of readjustment began – so the question is now whether, with the evolution of Jewish social change, the roles have today become reversed. Does fundamentalism still remain, so to speak, in the centre of the Jewish world, or is it to be understood as being at the constantly nagging, oppositional periphery?

The answer to this question lies squarely within an assessment of Jewish cultural assimilation, since this is the yardstick used to define the fundamentalist phenomenon or, indeed, that has actually generated it. How, then, does a modernist perceive the general process of the readjustment of Jewish society in the modern world? I can of course give only a schematic answer if I am not to spend the rest of this chapter on this really rather complex question. Leaving aside ideological developments in modern Jewish history, such as the emancipation and reform movements, perhaps the single most critical trigger of change and readjustment has been the steady disappearance, over the last 200 years, of Jewish social and political disabilities. Jews have, so to speak, moved out of the ghetto; and membership of a Jewish community is in most (though not all) countries entirely voluntary, instead of being imposed by the state. The social consequences that have flowed from this have varied considerably from country to country, but a few generalisations can usefully be made which for convenience I shall list under two main heads. Jews have become 'modern', or have readjusted to their new environments, by a movement outwards, that is, by becoming or attempting to become ordinary English or American or French citizens through immersing themselves, in various degrees, in the local secular culture and through adopting as their mother-tongue the local vernacular language. In this sense they have taken on an identity additional to their identity as Jews, a process incidentally which often leads to a good deal of confusion both amongst themselves and amongst their non-Jewish neighbours; in fact a preoccupation with the ethnic stereotyping of Jews by Gentiles (both the search for esteem and the fear of anti-Semitism, whether real or imagined) remains a distinctive feature of the sometimes quite tortuous process of modern Jewish self-definition. Broadly speaking, however, Jews consider themselves 'modern' to the degree that they have acculturated or assimilated into the wider secular or secularised culture, or even, for that matter, to the degree that they have participated or directly contributed to it. This outward movement of readjustment has been further supported by a variety of competing ideologies, such as the movements promoting enlightenment, religious reform, Yiddish socialism and of course the nationalist movement known as Zionism.

Jewish modernity possesses a second distinguishing characteristic, that of an inward change, namely the restructuring of the indigenous social institutions. If membership of the Jewish community is now voluntary, if Jews are free to join or not to join their local synagogue, to accept or not to accept the authority of their local rabbinical court (*Bet Din*), it means that they are now, in theory at least, free to develop new social mechanisms for the expression of group solidarity and perceptions of identity without being compelled to accept interference in these matters from the outside. The internal consequences that flow from what has become the individual decision to be 'Jewish' are today many and varied: the centrality of the synagogue, rabbi and Talmudical school has waned in favour of a whole host of sporting, recreational, philanthropic and cultural associations, the principal *raison d'être* of which lies in their exclusive recruitment of Jews as members rather than the pursuit of specifically Jewish aims or cultural goals. This means in effect that new areas of Jewish self-expresion and self-fulfilment have come into existence, in many cases even to replace the pursuit of traditional Jewish religious ideals, which – in the conspicuous absence of the unifying authority of *halacha* – have themselves fragmented institutionally into 'Orthodox', 'Reform', 'Liberal' and 'Conservative' denominations. The modern synagogue is now, so to speak, a community centre rather than a building invariably consecrated for divine worship or religious study. It goes without saying that very many religious practices that formerly defined Jewish identity have now been abandoned by the modern Jew, though at the same time it is clear that these newer forms of associational behaviour offer adequate scope for the maintenance of group solidarity and the formulation of group identity. Modernity in this sense, which rationalises religious practice even to the point where it may virtually disappear, makes it possible for agnostic and even atheist Jews to be very active in Jewish community life should they so wish, and indeed to see nothing particularly unusual about such participation despite their lack of religious commitment. The basis for the recruitment of membership has thus in effect been considerably broadened – hence the profound and widespread institutional diversification.

The brief description that I have just given is a reconstruction of the modernist's view of the process of readjustment in which, as it would no doubt be argued, there has come about a necessary re-allocation of cultural resources in response to the new circumstances of voluntary Jews living in a modern environment. From such a perspective emerges the residual category of 'fundamentalists', namely those Jews who – in defence of the effective loss of their erstwhile authority or monopoly of Jewish self-expression – either specifically reject the validity or cultural authenticity of the responses that have been made, by citing precedent or ideological objections of various kinds, or alternatively merely distance themselves from the often deeply-felt doubts and self-examinations of modernists struggling to come to terms with their new cultural solutions. Obviously there are elements here of the modernist's *need* for the existence of fundamentalists as a categorical reference-group against which the sincerity, complexity and creativity of their own cultural efforts can be measured; and accordingly fundamentalists will be characterised as hypocritical, simplistic and rigid.

The danger, of course, in the modernist's creation of such a category is that there remains the implication that perhaps the whole modernist edifice, built upon the perceived need to readjust the tradition for the sake of the higher good of group survival, might not have been necessary after all – given the fact, as modernists constantly assert, that Jewish fundamentalism is alive and well in the very modern world in which the supposed laws of history should predict their disappearance. Such a danger, however, is in practice mitigated by the contempt in which fundamentalists are held: presumably it is only through their intrinsic hypocrisy, simplicity and rigidity that they can cut themselves off from the modern world to the degree necessary for their own survival. Were they to discard these objectionable traits they would rapidly merge with the wider modernised Jewish society of today – and indeed modernists can point to just such a process; after all, their own parents or grandparents originally hailed from a traditional, pre-modern cultural background in the ghettos of Eastern Europe or the *mellahs* of the Arab world.

But who precisely are these Jewish fundamentalists? The point is, of course, that they are everywhere. Fundamentalism represents the notional past away from which the modernist bases the direction for his own cultural orientation. If he is to make progress, in such matters as dress, speech or cuisine, let alone in matters of religious ritual or biblical interpretation, the modernist must be constantly on his guard to avoid slipping into what might be sensed as a 'fundamentalist' approach. But here, again, a reference-group is needed, to substantiate the perception of a dichotomy or an alleged 'polarisation' of Jewish society. There is no *one* specific Jewish sect or denomination that is called by others as fundamentalist, any more than there is in the Christian world; Jewish fundamentalists are to be found in various institutional groupings, and supposedly work within them so as to ensure that they remain, so to speak, 'in line'. Yet certain Jewish groups are commonly identified as fundamentalist as such, notably, for example, the so-called 'ultra-orthodox' Neturei Karta Jews of Jerusalem – because of their well-known steadfast refusal to accept the legitimacy of the state of Israel (on the grounds that a Jewish state in the Holy Land is a religious and not a political category, and that it can be established only by the Messiah and not by human force of arms). The facts of modernist obsession with this really rather tiny group (numbering perhaps only a couple of thousand persons)[4] and its supposedly significant political influence carries all the signs of an interest in the existence of a reference-group against which the self-evident modernist acceptability in principle of a Jewish state can be the more easily made clear. Certainly there is very little evidence that the Neturei Karta pose any threat to the Israeli state in the real world.

'Ultra-orthodoxy', a somewhat politer label for fundamentalism but conveying much the same information with regard to the perceived division between modernists and 'the others', is attributed as a matter of routine to quite a number of Jewish groups, particularly the Hasidim, whose stubborn refusal to adopt modern Western dress is usually regarded by outsiders as a totally indefensible form of conservatism characteristic of a great deal more in their theological outlook. The physical distinctiveness of the Hasidim, coupled with their tendency to live close together in a manner reminiscent to modernists of the Eastern European ghetto, make them an ideal reference-group, particularly because there are sufficient pockets of Hasidim communities in various countries as to make them visible enough for the purposes of contrast and comparison. They are, indeed, to be found in quite a few major Western cities, such as New York, London, Paris, Antwerp, Melbourne and so on.

Moreover, this reference-group does share a number of attitudes typical of fundamentalism generally, as variously noted by Bruce, Caplan and other contributors to this volume: a tendency towards enthusiasm in prayer meetings, as contrasted with more 'decorous' liturgy found in other kinds of prayer houses; charismatic leadership; a certain cliquish self-righteousness; a good proportion of 'born-again' Jews (usually referred to as *baalei teshuvah*); and, at least in the particular case of one Hasidic group, known as Lubavitch Hasidim, a certain millenarianism together with a programme of religious (not political) outreach, often involving skilful use of the modern media (including bumper stickers declaring 'We want Moshiach [the Messiah] now', together with the prominent display of photographs of the charismatic leader, and international telephone hook-ups to his broadcast sermons). At the ideological level, furthermore, these fundamentalists tend to a rhetoric and polemic that has many of the hallmarks of an oppositional discourse: references, for example, to the 'lonely man of faith' (probably an allusion to Numbers, 23:9), the 'remnant of Israel' (*she'erit Israel* – Isaiah, 46:3; Micah, 2:12; and elsewhere), and an emphasis on belief in the tradition as based on *Torah min hashamayim* (literally, that 'the Bible [came] from heaven'). The use of the latter as a slogan is clearly reminiscent of institutionalised 'fundamentals of faith' and calls for the restoration of traditional authority so beloved of fundamentalists generally (see, for example, Taylor in this volume, Chapter 7). But much of this material in fact derives from more than a century of experience of rabbinical invective against modern Jewish reformists (for further details see Jacobs, 1984, pp. 229–31; Taylor (Chapter 7), also notes fundamentalism as a response to liberalism), and in this sense Jewish fundamentalism can be defined in historical terms – namely as the rump of traditional orthodoxy, now relegated as the result of the precipitate rise of Jewish modernism to an obscure, obscurantist corner of Jewish society.

Why, then, are modernists concerned about the category – if their battle for the control of a demographically defined normativism has already been fought, and won? One answer is that there are signs today of a substantial interest in a return to 'roots', in the context of which fundamentalist reference-groups offer a sense of authenticity that seems irresistible to the increasing number of modernist defectors (*baalei teshuvah*) to the traditionalist camp; a new threat, in other words, has appeared. Another answer, perhaps, is to be found in a threat deriving from the demographic evidence for a reversal: fundamentalist reference-groups are gaining in visibility in the Jewish world because of their high birth-rate and obviously high institutional commitment, as opposed to the very low birth-rate (less than the 2.1 minimum needed for demographic replacement; see Schmelz *et al.*, 1983, p. 2), high out-marriage rate and relatively poor institutional commitment of the assimilating modernist Jews.

A third answer is of a rather different kind, and one which brings the discussion back to the perceptual nature of the category. For reference-groups, important though they are, by no means exhaust the matter; they fill out the category, render it intelligible and lend it credibility for the description of those who are an object of scorn – but their existence in the real world does not in itself explain the crucial ethnographic fact that fundamentalism is treated in the Jewish context principally as a *relative* category, namely, relative to the speaker. This is because it leans for its importance not on those attributes of the fundamentalist phenomenon that can be suggested (as above) by the armchair observer, but rather on its capacity to rationalise or structure the otherwise highly complex series of ritual and cultural adaptations to be found within the established modernist forms of religious Judaism – of which four or five denominational distinctions are currently in use. Detailed native charts of the ethnographic subtleties underlying these distinctions are by no means common knowledge – far more clear-cut, and more widespread, is the perception of a binary principle, or sense of 'polarisation', between 'us', or 'our' denomination (who have gone to the trouble of making the proper rational adjustment to modern life) and 'fundamentalists' (who have not done so, because of their reliance on inherited certainties). *Any* position, in other words, that is more traditionalist, or closer to the *halacha*, than that of the person using the term is potentially 'fundamentalist', therefore ('Liberal' Judaism to a secularist, or 'Conservative' Judaism to a 'Liberal', and so on). This is why use of the pejorative term 'fundamentalist' often collocates with an attack on those who are 'obsessed with the minutiae of [traditional ritual] observance', although the group in question may be contemplating either only the most modest change to the *halacha*, or alternatively something much more substantial; the qualitative difference hardly matters, and certainly could not be read out of the reference.

Hence the comparative ease with which the label 'fundamentalist' finds itself pinned on to a range of groups and individuals who may in practice have little or nothing in common with each other. The value of the reference-group (in size perhaps 5 or 10 per cent of Jewish society) is that through their apparent rejection of the need for an ideology of modernity, they can be (correctly) designated as sociologically deviant; through the attribution of a pejorative label they can be held up as an example to others, *in any context*, not to follow in their ways. Or, to put it another way, Jewish society has become 'modern' precisely by ridding itself of its pre-modern authority structure, and in particular by shedding those 'fundamentalist' aspects of its traditional world-view which still in a sense pose a threat because they remain embodied in those deviant reference-groups. Fundamentalism remains, so to speak, lurking in the wings, constantly claiming authority and authenticity. But the Jewish readjustment to the modern world, in short, means in this view a rethinking of fundamentalism.

The readjustment of Jewish society in the modern world

What I wish to do in the rest of this chapter is to consider the adequacy of this argument, since the imposition of the binary principle evidently conceals other complexities. Let me therefore start the reconsideration at the place where it should logically begin, namely the counter argument from the fundamentalist position. This is obviously a notional position, given its relatively uninstitutionalised nature, but the main lines that can be proposed are, I think, reasonably clear.

The principal difficulty that the Jewish fundamentalist (as defined by acceptance of the total authority of the *halacha*, or membership in one of the modernists' reference-groups) would see in the modernist presentation is that it is not at all obvious that there is such a thing as modern Jewish society at all. It is no good saying that modern Jewish society consists of various sets of secularised versions of the society that preceded it. Traditional Jewish society bears no other definition except as one that was committed to a system intelligible only in terms of religious law and religious values as contained in *halacha;* *halacha* was the only legitimating principle underlying the total system. A secularised version of that kind of society, where the authority of *halacha* has been challenged, or at least where criteria other than those contained in the *halacha* have been imported as constituents of the system, is manifestly a contradiction in terms. In this sense, then, the modernist position is illogical, if not meaningless, as it makes a claim for both continuity and discontinuity at the same time. There is no fundamentalist objection to the reference to the modern world as such, since that is simply the name of the alien environment in which Jews happen to live today, but the idea that modernity is anything more than an illusion from a Jewish point of view, referring to anything more than mere surface realities, is a serious distortion of the nature of the Jewish world-view and it certainly cannot be used as its principal defining feature. Many of today's Jews may well be freethinkers of all kinds and may indeed choose to form their own quasi-religious associations – but that must have nothing to do with the social world of those who take great care to follow the details of the religious law as divinely ordained, for that is the only context in which it makes sense to speak of Jewish society. Modern Jewish society, as a thing apart, is therefore a contradiction in terms.

A position of this kind does not of course go very far in clarifying the general problem of Jewish readjustment in the modern world – unless, that is, we were ourselves to take it literally and propose that the modernist Jewish majority is itself to be understood as sociologically deviant (alienated, perhaps?). In fact traces of such a view are not difficult to find. Invited to write a Foreword to Gartner's historical study of the period of mass Jewish immigration to Britain between 1870 and 1914, the present British Chief Rabbi, Sir Immanuel Jakobovits, suggested that

> An influx swamping the original community on such a scale was bound to leave some indelible marks on the direction and content of Anglo-Jewish life. ...
>
> Nevertheless, what is astounding is the extent to which the principal features of the community and its institutions remained unaffected by the gigantic tide of newcomers. While it led to some marginal proliferation of synagogue organizations – and even these remained very confined in size and influence – the structure of the community withstood, and eventually almost completely absorbed, this tide. The Chief Rabbinate, the United Synagogue, the Board of Deputies, the Board of Guardians and even the chief provincial institutions emerged from this flood virtually unchanged.
>
> This remarkable phenomenon certainly testifies to the stability of Anglo-Jewry, and perhaps also to the oneness of the Jewish people. ...
>
> But the phenomenon also demonstrates the essentially conservative character of Jewish organizational life ...   (Jakobovits, 1960, pp. 1–2)

Despite an acknowledgement of certain changes 'in outlook and attitudes', the rabbi's emphasis on stability, as perceived through organisational continuity, is a significant pointer. The absence of an event here is critical.

A position of this kind, redrafting modern ('modernist') Jewish history, raises, however, a matter of considerable methodological interest that deserves some examination. Judaism is not a religion in the same sense as Christianity is a religion. The 'ism' of Judaism suggests a system, a system of law, philosophy and ethics – but the Jews are a people and a nation, *not* simply a voluntary group of believers in a religious creed, where the latter can be manipulated at will by fundamentalists and the 'others' (cf. the cases cited by Caplan in this volume, Chapter 8). There are thus two types of evidence in any case: the legal, jurisprudential, or normative, on the one hand; and the ethnographic, sociological, or behavioural, on the other. Nor are the two supposed to match each other. What defines the Jewish people is not the succession of adaptations to the numerous social and cultural environments in the various lands in which they have lived, but rather a notional adherence to the legal system of *halacha* that theoretically remains completely aloof from these environments. The *halacha* itself consists of detailed rules and regulations, originally presupposed as divine commands in the holy books of the Bible, that were in turn expanded exegetically as legal commentaries on the Bible (which are technically its oral traditions) by the contributors to the Talmud and later rabbinic works. The purpose of *halacha* is to specify how a divinely-prescribed guide to life can infuse spirituality, ever more widely and intensely, into day-to-day practical concerns. Thus the rules are supposed to generate behaviour; it is quite contrary to the theory of this system to suppose that it is behaviour that is responsible for the rules. What the modernist is today effectively proposing is that *halacha* should codify, and probably always did codify, Jewish social realities existing at a particular moment in historical time; whereas the fundamentalist is merely reiterating the traditional mode of explanation, namely that biblical commands are timeless and eternally valid. The fundamentalist does not perceive discontinuity at all, or if he does become aware of it he will shrug off its relevance or importance. However, the methodological value of the fundamentalist objection to the modernist's readjustment model of contemporary Jewish society is that it inexorably pulls the argument directly into the domain of *halacha*, which is of course the fundamentalist's home territory. But the categories supplied by *halacha* seem the only available truly 'Jewish' categories in any case; in this sense there is nothing particularly 'fundamentalist' about fundamentalism's emphasis on the general problem of *halacha*.

Let me take a simple example to illustrate the point. No matter how many Jews eat pork, the consumption of pork is still forbidden in the *halacha*; even if an entire Jewish community contained not a single Jew who abstained from eating pork or censured others for so doing, pork would still be forbidden. From an ethnographic point of view the anthropologist would be justified in claiming, in the latter case, that pork had in some sense become permitted, although he would also have to take into account the view that would most likely be held by members of such a community – that the law on this point embodied an authentic Jewish tradition but was out of touch with reality. But what if, as in fact is now quite common, Jews follow the dietary laws when they are in the confines of their own homes, but do not observe them when they are outside, say at a restaurant or when visiting Gentile friends? To account for a practice such as this the anthropologist might argue – and with some justification, I think – that the modernist Jew, in his readjustment to the world in which he lives, has in effect set up a new dichotomy, consisting of the domestic sphere, where he feels at liberty to express his Jewish identity in the traditional manner, versus the public domain, where he does not. And indeed there is other evidence of contemporary ritual behaviour to support such a proposition. Now the difficulty with such an analysis would be that such a dichotomy is unknown to the *halacha*, nor indeed is it likely that any modernist attempt to rewrite the *halacha* in the light of modern conditions would ever presume to incorporate such a novel distinction. What is more likely is that the modernist would simply perceive a historical trend, such as the steady decline of the observance of the dietary laws, and perhaps – in noting its continued observance in the home – add the recommendation that it should so continue, in the interests of codifying current social realities.

The fundamentalist, on the other hand, given his interest only in the actual observance of the religious law, would say that there was nothing particularly modern about keeping kosher at home, whatever his regrets might be that it was not followed outside. But the fundamentalist here is right, even though he is at the same time so very wrong; the single-mindedness of his approach to reality, his conviction that ultimately it is the rules of *halacha* that both generate and explain 'Jewish' behaviour, can here help to take the argument one stage further. For there is no reason to suppose in advance, as the modernist would have it, that the details of the readjustment process are by definition embedded in an ideology of modernity. It is far more likely that modernism remains in a state of tension with the fundamentalist *halacha* that it in fact continues to communicate with; the polarisation is not total; neither category is sealed off one from the other in energetically isolated enclosures. Rather, one is dealing here with a state of increased entropy, where both 'sides' so to speak are in collision with each other, and – no matter how much they would prefer to deny it – they are having some effect on *each other* in the process.

Putting this argument in strong form, the assertion here would be that the straight binary distinction that generated the category 'fundamentalism' in the first place is perhaps a little crude and may even be ethnographically unsound. Current Jewish social realities are, in this view, far more complex than can be explicated on the basis of such a distinction. The category of fundamentalism, far from helping the analysis forward, merely reproduces a polemic which, though surfacing as such from time to time, is by no means the key issue around which Jewish ideological structures that generate or interpret behaviour are in fact organised. To illustrate such a view two examples should, I think, suffice.

The first example concerns the attitude to modernity of fundamentalist Jews themselves. It seems, upon inspection, that their so-called fundamentalism reveals a greater degree of modernity, and readjustment to the conditions of the modern world, than is gained from dismissive modernist interpretations of their social life.[5] In the effort perhaps to discredit fundamentalist credentials, Barr specifically draws attention to the fundamentalist use of modern scientific views of the world in the context of biblical exegesis (1977, p. 93 ff.). Whereas a liberal would be content with eliciting the 'spirit' of a law or the general religious significance of a particular biblical passage, the fundamentalist, in arguing the case for the Bible's accurate representation of objective truth, sees nothing inherently inappropriate in showing how biblical material is in accord with science. His purpose is to show that events mentioned in the Bible are thus true events and in that sense are events in the real world and not just mythological products of the religious imagination. Now what the fundamentalist in effect is doing here is specifically to draw the criteria of modern science right into the heart of his traditional, supposedly anti-modern, territory. Perhaps his belief in 'science' as a category representing objective truth is naïve, but that is beside the point. The fact remains that the fundamentalist has extended and re-specified the purview of sacred knowledge, and has done so precisely with the effect of including material from that very modern world which he is supposed to have turned his back on. A useful illustration of the point can be found in the commentary to the Bible written by the late British Chief Rabbi, Dr J. H. Hertz, an author who drew approvingly from the results of archaeological research (which he cited extensively), but who at the same time was extremely clear on his fundamentalist objection to biblical criticism and modern source theory. Hertz's edition of the Pentateuch (1929–36) is incidentally still the standard text used for liturgical purposes in orthodox synagogues throughout Britain, the Commonwealth and the United States.

This extension or re-specification of the realm of the sacred, so as to include attributes of the modern world, seems the inevitable conclusion to be reached in the study of why, and how, the supposedly anti-modernist Hasidim have not only not disappeared in the megalopolises of the modern world but seem to thrive in them. Their opposition to the adoption of modern Western dress is merely, in this perspective, a convenient boundary device that is intended to mark them off not from the modern world as such (even though it might have this effect) but from other groups of Jews (including orthodox and even other 'ultra-orthodox' Jews); indeed, variations in styles of dress are used to distinguish different Hasidic groups from each other. No; a good deal of cultural energy is expended by Hasidim in finding ways of harnessing the economic structure of modern capitalism to their own advantage, in other words of investigating and responding to the circumstances of the modern world so that group members may take up new occupations and also be given guidance on the application of *halacha* in the use of modern technology.

Let me give one illustration of this, drawn from Solomon Poll's admirable ethnographic study (1969) of the Hasidim of Williamsburg, a district in Brooklyn. It was found that the ordinary use of refrigerators contravenes the *halacha* governing correct conduct on the Sabbath, inasmuch as the opening of the refrigerator door allows in warm air which will eventually cause the motor that cools the refrigerator to start up earlier than it would have done if the door had not been opened. (It should be added that the direct use of electricity is forbidden on the Sabbath; hence the difficulty with the motor.) To deal with this problem two solution were in theory possible: one was to withdraw from it altogether, to state in effect that this modern device cannot be used by a Jew at all, for the reason given; the other, which interestingly was the one adopted, was to find some way of reconciling the *halacha* with the technological advantage of using the modern refrigerator. An engineer was commissioned to devise a refrigerator whose motor would start up at regular intervals, rather than on the basis of thermostatic control; and indeed such a refrigerator now exists and is in common use amongst group members. However, the point at issue is this: the new refrigerator had to be produced, marketed, advertised, retailed and serviced (Poll, 1969, pp. 101–2). In other words it can be said that the effect of the application of *halacha* in this case was to transform a manufactured consumer product into a religious article, thereby to encourage a direct involvement in both new and existing areas of economic specialisation – an example, then, of the proposition that Jewish fundamentalism may in practice be quite deeply bound up with the issues raised by modernity. Certainly modernisation does not leave fundamentalism untouched.

I said above that I would offer two examples in support of the strong form of the argument that a binary distinction between modernity and fundamentalism should not be drawn too sharply. My second example, on which I shall be more brief, relates to another area entirely. Its purpose is to suggest that there may well be fundamentalist elements in one of the major preoccupations of modernist Jews – I refer to the question of Zionism.

Amongst assimilated diaspora Jews today a very considerable measure of the content of Jewish self-expression is directed towards the State of Israel, whether this be in the form of political or philanthropic activity on its behalf, the encouragement particularly of the young generation to go and settle in the country or at least to spend holidays there, the use of the synagogue/community centre for the promotion of selected items of Israeli culture such as folk dancing or cookery, or the study of the Modern Hebrew language. The range of such activities is immense. Quite a few observers have concluded that in a sociological definition of modern Judaism the orientation towards Israel has effectively toppled the erstwhile primacy of traditional Jewish ritual behaviour (see, for example, Neusner, 1981); indeed it is worth noting that the traditional liturgical pronunciation of Hebrew in use amongst Ashkenazi Jews (that is, Jews of European origin) has recently been replaced in modernist congregations by another pronunciation system deemed to be closer to that in use in Hebrew speech in Israel. And, significantly enough, such a change has not been introduced at all amongst fundamentalist Jews. The point I wish to make here is this: the nationalist re-evocation of the concept of the Promised Land amongst modernist Jews, though perfectly compatible with religious values and preoccupations as traditionally defined, is exceedingly odd in the context of a modernist ideology that would otherwise rid itself of obscure, irrational and mystical beliefs – but beliefs of this kind are precisely those that specify the overriding importance and truth of the ageless attachment of the Jewish people to the Land of Israel. And moreover, such beliefs rest squarely on a literal and fundamentalist reading of scripture and *halacha*, even down to the detailed specification of the borders of the country. From a fundamentalist perspective the picture of modern, freethinking Jews devoting themselves so obsessively to the working out of a part of the divine plan is indeed thought-provoking and raises many questions; interestingly enough, it has aroused the enthusiasm of Christian fundamentalists (see Barr, 1977, pp. 118–19), and indeed the potential fundamentalist connection with modern nationalism – through such images as territorial integrity explained on the basis of a divine donation of land, or the perfect primal state in some bygone age – has been described elsewhere in this volume. But the case of Israel draws attention to what one might call the reallocation of fundamentalism within Judaism. To the extent that Judaism, being scriptural religion, is probably bound to retain within itself a fundamentalist potential (as noted also by Nancy and Richard Tapper in this volume, Chapter 3), it could well be argued that however hard modernists may try to free themselves from the grip of scriptures, some form of fundamentalist intepretation may well manifest itself elsewhere within the cultural system.

Israeli experience itself confirms this: the fundamentalist literality of the claim of the Gush Emunim movement – on the basis of biblical evidence – that Jews have a sacred duty to settle the whole 'Land of Israel', including the militarily-occupied West Bank, is astounding. But perhaps the appearance of the Gush Emunim can be understood as the long-delayed but inevitable fundamentalist response to the secularist Zionist ambition to create a Jewish state in the land promised a very long time ago by God to the Jews but abandoned by them for nearly 2000 years. More to the point still is the extraordinary effect that the capture of Jordanian Jerusalem seems to have had on the ordinary Israeli population in 1967: very suddenly, and very powerfully, biblical messianic language came into use in order to comprehend the cosmic significance that the Jewish return to its holy places in the Holy City was felt to embody. The realities that the Bible describes were then felt, by the ordinary secularist citizen of Israel – and indeed the modernist diaspora Jew also – to have actually arrived.[6] There is certainly, in other words, a case for the fundamentalist penetration of modernism.

CONCLUSION

There is, then, a need to 'rethink' fundamentalism, given the evidence that the straight opposition between modernity and its opponent is not

quite so clear-cut as may at first be imagined. Of course, the examples I
have just given in support of the contention that the matter is more
fudged than may be expected are themselves controversial and open to
criticism: nationalism is not necessarily fundamentalist, despite a
certain convergence of ideas in the Jewish case, and modernisation
and modernity should also mean two quite different things, despite a
confusion between the two in native usage. Hertz, incidentally, was
not at all confused: in the Preface to his commentary he quotes the
rabbinic doctrine 'Accept the true from whatever source it come'
(1929–36, vol. I, p. vi); quite so, it is the truth he was interested in, not
the source. But one suspects that his clarity on this point is not always
shared by his readers.

The fudging of the boundary around the category 'fundamentalist'
in the Jewish context is an important clue: this category, like so many
others taken on recently from the vernacular languages and secular
cultures in which the Jews have absorbed themselves, does not quite
fit. There are multiple categories at work in the contemporary
modernist process of Jewish self-definition, and this has led to a
considerable lack of ideological clarity – indecision, for instance, on
what some would see as a straight choice between the desire to
assimilate, on the one hand, and the desire to retain a form of
autonomous group identity, on the other; or the variable use of
outsiders' definitions of Jews and Jewishness, however these may be
used; or even a theory of social context, to be used for specifying when
and how one's Jewishness is to be considered relevant. Fundamentalism is in this context a useful reference-point for a notional past in
which these vexing questions did not have to be posed, or for those
Jews of today who appear not to feel the need for posing them at all.
But it is useless to attempt actually to plot the behaviour or beliefs of
such fundamentalists on the ground,[7] because the moment such an
effort is made other considerations enter the picture, and the
supposedly monothematic character of this reference-group falls
away. Whatever its share in objective reality, fundamentalism as
thought of amongst Jews is a cultural preconception reflected on to
history and then explained in terms of chronological time.[8] Hence the
evident Jewish capacity to mobilise any set of ethnographic data to
prove its existence.

This suggestion, then, that fundamentalism is a historiographic
category should help us understand why it has come into use by
modernists at all – it raises those particular issues that topicalise
problems of identity, intra-Jewish boundary definitions and changing

patterns of leadership and authority, all of which are major preoccupations for Jews attempting to reconstitute their communities after the massive demographic and structural changes (not to mention the mass genocide)[9] that they have experienced in the twentieth century. The contemplation of such matters is a survival strategy in itself. The vagueness of the term, as it is actually used, barely matters.

A recent controversy in the Jewish press in England should serve here as a final example to illustrate this. The term fundamentalist surfaced in 1984 in the context of a serious scholarly study of *halacha* done from what the author, Rabbi Louis Jacobs, explicitly described as a 'non-fundamentalist' point of view – namely that *halacha* has developed over time, in response to changing social conditions (Jacobs, 1984, ch. 16). The idea was seized upon in a review published in the *Jewish Chronicle* (2 November 1984) by a traditionalist rabbi (Jonathan Sacks), who, predictably, declared that Jacobs's 'non-fundamentalist *halacha*' was either a contradiction in terms or alternatively a euphemism for declaring independence from the authority of *halacha*. In a reply (*Jewish Chronicle*, 16 November 1984) Jacobs first defended his use of the term 'fundamentalism' on the grounds that it was central to the debate, and then – a paragraph later – suggested that the term should be left aside, as he had used it only (as he put it) 'for convenient shorthand'. Barr's book on fundamentalism (1977) was cited by both Jacobs and Sacks, then abandoned as being irrelevant.

Shorthand for what? Fundamentalism seems to be functioning here as a keyword for an internal cultural debate (cf. Moeran, 1984), an area of contemplation, a category that is good to think with. For the feeling that the term is both 'central' and 'irrelevant' simultaneously is one that should not be passed by. If Jacobs's view is correct – namely that Judaism was never frozen, that the *halacha* always adapted itself, and that it should do so today, in explicit recognition of this – traditional Judaism is thus not fundamentalist, by the modernist's own definition. Modernists in effect are, ironically, taking the contemporary fundamentalist position too literally, for what is evidently at stake here is the degree of explicitness that should be involved in formulating a global comprehension of the system. What sustained the system traditionally, and provided a sense of continuity, was a myth that it rested on an intrinsically changeless scriptural text, the backward reference to which provided the basis for the articulation of the law at a given moment in time *as if* nothing had changed. It is in that 'as if' that the contemporary debate about the nature of fundamentalism generates difficulty. The modernist, concerned in principle not with the past but rather with the present-future, cannot perceive the viability of such a logic. Yet he cannot escape from his 'fundamentalist' inheritance entirely, much as he would try. And once such an awareness catches up with him, the question is how to classify it. The category itself is not inerrant; doubt and vagueness seem part of its definition.

In short, there is no reason to suppose that fundamentalism should be thought of as a self-evident category, let alone as a universal one. References to it may be incoherent or inconsistent, but that in a sense is just what is to be expected of a category that subsumes the distant, the past, the unknown, and the threatening within one's own tradition. Fundamentalism, in the Jewish case, is indeed a 'convenient shorthand', and it should be taken literally as no more than that. An understanding, then, of the inward aspect of the readjustment of Jewish society in the modern world means a rethinking of fundamentalism in more ways than one.

Notes

1. These figures, which some may see as controversial, are intended here as a rough guide. 'Accurate' Jewish population statistics are in any case difficult to accept at face value (because of technical problems in collecting data and in defining who is a Jew, for example); for an up-to-date account see Schmelz *et al.* (1983).
2. I am grateful to Dr N. S. Doniach and Dr Dovid Katz for advice on these linguistic points.
3. For an interesting recent study of three Karaite communities (in Turkey, Egypt and Israel), see Trevisan Semi (1984).
4. On the Neturei Karta see Marmorstein (1952, 1969).
5. A similar conclusion is reached by Heilman and Cohen (1986), in their discussion of traditional Jewish life in contemporary America; see also Friedman (1986).
6. For a description see Webber (1981).
7. A good illustration of this can be afforded by attempting to compare the details of Jewish and Christian 'fundamentalist' assertions. The traditional Jewish idea, for example, that the book of Deuteronomy was written by Moses (and not at a time many centuries after his death, as critics commonly suppose) seems 'fundamentalist' in non-fundamentalist Christian eyes, as being too plain a reading of the text. Yet Christian beliefs that Jesus was the son of God, or rose from the dead, also based on the surface reading of the text, are not so identified. Why is one reading

'fundamentalist', the other not? The answer, of course, is that the purpose of making an accusation of fundamentalism against Jews is to render a Christian view normative by contrast, *ipso facto*. But from an analytical perspective the point is that the empirical *details* of the fundamentalist accusation cannot be compared as propositions about the real world, since they function as constituents of categories within different systems and thus are relative to them (cf. also Barr, 1977, pp. 284–6).

8. The phrase I have used here leans on an (unpublished) formulation by Edwin Ardener in proposing a definition of the concept of 'event'.

9. The role of the Holocaust in relation to the issues discussed in this paper is a large and complex one. For some modernist Jews, the very fact of the mass murders rendered religious Judaism and a belief in God altogether meaningless, thereby strengthening their resolve to move away from the values they associated with fundamentalism. For others, the survival of fundamentalist Judaism seems, on the contrary, to be almost a religious duty ('not to allow Hitler posthumous victory', to quote the secular phrase sometimes encountered) – especially given the fact that a very high proportion of those who were murdered came not from modernist circles but from amongst the ultra-orthodox, notably the Hasidim. Hence, in part, the latter's high birth-rate nowadays, referred to above – to replenish the population stock, as it were. At any rate, a strengthening of piety has become characteristic of the religious Jewish response to persecution and massacre (as also after the Chmielnicki disasters of the seventeenth century, for example). At another level, contemporary modernist curiosity about traditional Jewish life in the context of the search for 'roots' has to some extent derived from an awareness (quickly turned to a romanticised nostalgia) of a world in Eastern Europe that vanished during the war, sentiments that are in turn not too far removed from an aggressive nationalist self-consciousness – ironically thus fed by a fundamentalism that by and large is very differently preoccupied.

References

Barr, J. (1977), *Fundamentalism* (London: SCM Press).

Berger, P. (1977), *Facing up to modernity: excursions in society, politics and religion* (Harmondsworth: Penguin Books).

Friedman, M. (1986) 'Haredim confront the modern city', *Studies in Contemporary Jewry*, 2, pp. 74–96.

Heilman, S. C. and S. M. Cohen (1986), 'Ritual variation among modern orthodox Jews in the United States', *Studies in Contemporary Jewry* 2, pp. 164–87.

Hertz, J. H. (ed.) (1929–36), *The pentateuch and haftorahs*, 5 vols (London: Oxford University Press).

Jacobs, L. (1984), *A tree of life: diversity, flexibility and creativity in Jewish law* (Oxford University Press (Littman Library))

Jakobovits, I. (1960), 'Preface', in Lloyd P. Gartner, *The Jewish immigrant in England, 1870–1914* (2nd ed.; London: Simon Publications).

Marmorstein, E. (1952), 'Religious opposition to nationalism in the Middle East', *International Affairs*, 28, pp. 344–59.

—— (1969), *Heaven at bay: the Jewish Kulturkampf in the Holy Land*, Middle Eastern Monographs, ed. A. Hourani, no. 10 (London: Oxford University Press).

Moeran, B. (1984), 'Individual, group and *seishin*: Japan's internal cultural debate', *Man* (N.S.), 19, pp. 252–66.

Neusner, J. (1981), *Stranger at home: 'the Holocaust', Zionism, and American Judaism* (Chicago and London: University of Chicago Press).

Poll, S. (1969), *The Hasidic community of Williamsburg: a study in the sociology of religion* (New York: Schocken Books). First published in 1962.

Schmelz, U. O., P. Glikson and S. J. Gould (eds) (1983), *Studies in Jewish demography: survey for 1972–1980* (New York: KTAV [for the Institute of Contemporary Jewry, the Hebrew University, Jerusalem, and the Institute of Jewish Affairs, London]).

Trevisan Semi, E. (1984), *Gli ebrei caraiti tra etnia e religione* (Roma: Carucci).

Webber, J. (1981), 'Resacralization of the Holy City: the capture of Jerusalem in 1967', *RAIN*, no. 47, pp. 6–10.

6 The *Khalsa* Resurrected: Sikh Fundamentalism in the Punjab

Angela Dietrich

INTRODUCTION

The concept of Sikh 'fundamentalism' may, to anyone with even a cursory knowledge of Sikhism, seem a contradiction in terms, since this religion is generally characterised by tolerance and a marked absense of rigidity and 'orthodoxy'. In the present discussion, Sikh fundamentalism is traced back to the formation of the religio-military brotherhood of the *khalsa* at the turn of the eighteenth century. In particular it will be shown how the *khalsa* tradition has been kept alive and embodied through popular charismatic religious leaders, and how a mass fundamentalist movement arises whenever the coherence and integrity of the Sikh community is seen to be threatened by dominant, hostile forces. In this sense, Sikh fundamentalism can be said to comprise a repository of a specific cultural-cum-religious tradition, an important aspect of which is the ethnically determined value of honour and retribution, emanating from the culture of the majority peasant community. It will be argued that this value, which is linked to the notion of equality, is decisive in the process of ensuring identity maintenance through the medium of fundamentalism.

The phenomenon of fundamentalism has increased in significance in the modern era due to the imputed growth of the threat of cultural disintegration. It has assumed a new relevance mainly because of contradictions fostered by the subsequent integration of the peasantry, inheritors of a proud tradition which included Sikh sovereignty, into a modern state and bureaucratic system implying increased dependence on the central government. The peasant proprietor emerged as the chief supporter of the most recent upsurge of fundamentalism, a militant accompaniment to the agitation led by the Akali Dal party for the achievement of greater autonomy for the Punjab.[1]

THE EVOLUTION OF THE KHALSA

Comprising the final stage of the religious institutionalisation of Sikhism, the creation in 1699 of the *khalsa panth* – 'the path of the elect' – represented the infusion of fundamentalist ideology into what was an essentially anti-ritualistic, mystic doctrine. Since the persecution of the Sikhs by the then ruling power had increased, it was deemed necessary to militarise the formerly pacific villagers through a spiritually sanctioned medium. Thus, a specific set of symbols and code of conduct was employed to instil a willingness and ability to fight for their rights if need be, through recourse to arms, even in the face of seemingly insurmountable odds. Sacrifice became a key notion in *khalsa* ideology, exemplified through the last in line of ten religious preceptors, Guru Gobind Singh, who sacrificed his entire family for the sake of upholding the honour of the oppressed. The concept of honour, central to the value system of the Jat peasantry who formed the majority of converts to Sikhism, became universalised through the religion, linked to that of retribution for atrocities perpetrated on members of the *panth*, the community of the faithful.

Membership of this religio-military brotherhood was never deemed compulsory, particularly in view of the spirit of Sikh doctrine as articulated through the holy book, with its emphasis on interiority of belief and outward adjustment to reality. Throughout its history, only that part of the community professing greater religious fervour chose to undergo the specific initiation rite into the order of the *khalsa*. An initiate is thereby obligated to keep the 'five Ks',[2] recite daily five prayers taken from the scripture, abstain from intoxicants, including tobacco, and agree to overcome the 'five sins' (sexual excess, pride, attachment, anger and jealousy). The major injunction however, concerns the pledge to dedicate one's property, intellect and even life to uphold the honour of the oppressed, the dignity and integrity of the community.'

Before his death in 1708 Guru Gobind Singh invested religio-political authority in the Guru Granth, the Sikh scripture, and in the collectivity of believers, the Guru Panth. The latter, in particular, led to the formation of a fundamentalist movement, the dynamic force behind territorial liberation of the Punjab in the mid-eighteenth century, entailing redistribution of land amongst the peasantry. These egalitarian precepts fostered by fundamentalism were, however, undermined when half a century later, a Sikh empire was founded which, according to Khushwant Singh, became the most powerful

state in Asia (1977, p. 3). In the wake of empire formation the
principle of Guru Panth was superceded by Guru Granth (McLeod,
1976, p. 50).

THE SIKH TEMPLE AND ITS LIBERATION

Guru Granth Sahib (scripture) forms the focal point of worship in the
Sikh temple or *gurdwara*, the 'door to the Guru'. Upon entering the
building with covered head and bare feet, the first act of supplication is
to the holy book located at the back. A collection box is situated in
front of the scripture and donations are voluntary. However,
according to religious precepts, one should give one-tenth of one's
material or non-material resources (time, effort spent) to support the
temple, or in a wider sense, the community. The donations are utilised
not only to sustain a congregational form of worship but also to feed
the poor and needy in the free communal kitchen attached to the
temple. This constitutes an important precept of Sikhism – *seva*
('selfless service') – and all are welcome to serve others and dine there
regardless of creed or caste, on the basis of general commensality in
defiance of caste regulations. The temple became an important
community centre for the development of Sikh culture, where the
Punjabi script (*Guru-mukhi*) devised by the Sikh Gurus, martial arts
and hymn singing were taught by volunteers. Temples have served as
forts for security and still today there are often rest house facilities
attached to the building. With annexation of the Punjab by the British
in the mid-nineteenth century the temple, and especially the Golden
Temple at Amritsar, became the focal point for the articulation of Sikh
identity. A strong tradition developed of protecting this main seat of
Sikhism, which included the Akal Takhat (Timeless Throne) facing
the Golden Temple, from desecration and destruction, and of
avenging attacks by hostile forces.

During the period of the Sikh empire religious institutions of all
communities were well endowed with landholdings and other
facilities. With the Punjab's annexation, landholdings attached to the
temples became even more valuable due to the extension of the system
of canal irrigation. By the turn of the present century, temple
custodians (*mahants*) were able, under British law, to attach the
properties to themselves.[3] In addition, they incorporated Hindu idols
in the temples to attract a wider circle of potential donors. Even the
head priest of the Golden Temple introduced Hinduised practices into

the holiest of holies by, for example, not allowing scheduled castes to enter along with other worshippers (Khushwant Singh, 1977, p. 196).

In the wake of the upsurge of revivalism in the Punjab during this period, the Sikh elite became aware of the necessity of organising themselves in order to rid their historical shrines of non-*panthic* forces. As indicated by Jones, the Sikhs as the smallest of the three communiites in the Punjab were slowest to articulate their community interests. In contrast, the Arya Samaj movement of Hindu revivalism harbouring strongly chauvinistic overtones, paved the way for that community's ascendance, a process entailing the denigration of the religions and cultures of the other groups (Jones, 1976, p. 22). Not only did the Hindus deny the separate nature of the Sikh religion but they also lent their support to anti-Sikh forces like the temple managers. Recourse to the courts was not sufficient, as the Sikh reformers discovered, since the mangers' alleged 'private property' was protected. With the goal of deposing these managers and bringing the temples under *panthic* control, while simultaneously asserting the separate and distinctive nature of Sikhism and the community, a committee of temple management organised according to parliamentary precepts was formed in 1920.

The Shiromani Gurdwara Prabandhak Committee (known by its initials SGPC) was headed by members of the Sikh aristocracy; however, the actual initiative to 'liberate' the temples was spearheaded by the masses. Towards this aim, a semi-military corps of volunteers calling themselves the Akali Dal – the army of the immortals – evolved a particular agitational style termed *morcha* (literally 'entrenchment'). According to Nayar this entails largely non-violent direct confrontation with the authorities, often organised and directed from within the temple. It consists mainly in sending out *jathas* (groups of initiates) to break the law and fill the jails (Nayar, 1966, p. 234). This movement of temple liberation was fundamentalist in spirit in view of the sacrifices made in terms of loss of life, property and position, and of the prison sentences served. The Akalis were composed largely of initiates into the *khalsa panth*, who, inspired by the symbols and ideology, did not waver from their resolve to adhere to non-violent resistance in conformity with Gandhi's *satyagraha* movement, awakening world-wide admiration and sympathy for their cause. However, although the Akalis were in the forefront of the movement, there is some speculation that its success was ensured by recourse to greater militancy on the part of small groups of sympathisers. Those styled Babbar Akalis, many of whom were former members of a communist-inspired nationalist group, the Ghadrites, avenged what were perceived as the atrocities perpetrated by the authorities on the peaceful activists. As indicated by Mohinder Singh, the Babbars increased the Akali's bargaining power *vis-à-vis* the government through terrorising the bureaucratic machinery and its supporters (1981, p. 125).

That the Shiromani Akali Dal had emerged as the leading Sikh political party is not only due to its role in temple and national liberation: it is also a uniquely Sikh party in the sense that it was founded on a basic premise in Sikhism of the unity between religion and politics. Moreover, its organisation is *panthic* in that it is supported by the entire community: the SGPC which controls the temple donations of Sikhs resident in India and all over the world, uses these to fund its missionary, educational and welfare institutions as well as the Akali Dal. The party has preserved its original form of organisation and agitational tactics which also involve the community to a significant degree. It has a far-flung network of local party workers who set up Akali Dal branches everywhere, even outside the country. The heads of the two organisations, SGPC and the Akali Dal, carry equal weight in Sikh politics and religious affairs.

SIKH AUTONOMY DEMANDS AND THE EMERGENCE OF FUNDAMENTALISM

In the framework of independent India, Akali campaigns for the greater articulation of Sikh identity represent the chief means through which this small minority (1.9 per cent of the population) can resist absorption. This has become increasingly difficult under conditions of 'democracy' entailing majority rule and without the safeguards which the British had introduced to secure minority rights. In addition, the intensification of centralisation has had the effect of subverting regional cultures, a process encouraged by the Congress (I)'s policy of undermining elected non-Congress state governments. Moreover, the Punjab is the state most subject to centralised control (Dalip Singh, 1981, p. 36). A particular grievance of the Sikhs in this regard concerns the fact that river water and irrigation headworks are regulated by the centre, which has diverted a portion of the Punjab's rivers to other states, with the result that its farms lack sufficient water for irrigation. Furthermore, the centre has not issued permits for large-scale industry in the Punjab (claiming as its reason the state's sensitive border position next to Pakistan), which has resulted in inequitable economic growth. Possibly due to its leading agro-economic position in India, the Punjab has the smallest allocation of government funds for development, and capital reinvestment in the state is not condoned by the centre. Young people in particular have been frustrated by this, since there are not enough jobs for them in the non-agricultural sector and the preferred jobs to be had, for example, in the police force and in the field of education are seen to be available mainly through connections, bribes, and so on. This has also meant a continuing necessity for migration.

Opportunities in a traditionally highly prestigious field of employment, the defence forces, have also been severely curtailed due to the introduction of a quota system giving equal representation to all sectors of society in the defence forces, regardless of merit, historical or other factors. This has meant the reduction of the Sikh contingent from over 33 per cent in 1947 to less than 1.3 per cent today, to accord with their proportion of the population (Satindra Singh, 1980, p. 10). However, it disregards the argument that the Sikhs made proportionally far greater sacrifices for the freedom struggle than any other sector of the population: over 80 per cent of those killed or imprisoned for life were Sikhs (Duggal, n.d., p. 18). These factors, coupled with others like the centre's reluctance to declare the regional language, Punjabi, as the official state language (as it had done in every other state of the union) due to the Hindu revivalist opposition to the demand, caused the Sikhs to feel that their very existence as a respected people with a separate cultural and religious dispensation, was threatened. Punjabi Suba (the state's reorganisation along linguistic lines giving it a narrow Sikh majority) was acceded in 1966, but only after 15 years of arduous agitation on the part of the Sikh masses under Akali Dal leadership. However, this and the other grievances engendered an abiding 'minority psychosis', as the following statement by Sirdar Kapur Singh testifies to:

Deliberate and persistent efforts are being made to disintegrate and dissolve the *khalsa* ever since the country has gained freedom. Under the guise of democracy, secularism and the false theory of 'one nation' subtle schemes and sinister policies are being pursued with the aim of first disintegrating the *khalsa* into individual Sikhs and then debasing the individual Sikhs into secular, unrelated citizens so that they just make good cannon-fodder, good chowkidars of banks and business establishments owned by others, and good chauffeurs for expensive limousines of industrial magnates of a united Indian nation and thus they are deprived of their history-making potential and dynamism.   (Gur Rattan Pal Singh, 1979, pp. 116–17)

Kapur Singh helped formulate the Anandpur Sahib Resolution in 1973, encompassing Sikh demands for greater state autonomy, deemed more suited to India's multi-ethnic social and cultural make-up. The Akali Dal has made this resolution its political platform and has launched agitations for its realisation.

In the course of the discussion it has been shown that, throughout Sikh history, fundamentalism has arisen whenever the dominant power threatened the community with what it conceived as its imminent extinction as a distinct entity separate from the Hindus. Under these circumstances, a fundamentalist movement initiated by a charismatically charged leadership acted to motivate the Sikhs to a militant defence of the *panth*. In the mid-1970s such a threat arose again in the form of a particular heretical sect which, as the Sikhs were led to believe, was charged by the central government with the mission of dividing and demoralising the community. Although Sikh frustrations focused on this particular sect, their cause must be seen to have been wider, encompassing the Akali leadership and its increasing impotence in remedying Sikh grievances linked as indicated, to problems posed by the process of modernisation.

In the late 1960s the Green Revolution in agriculture had the effect of bringing about prosperity, but at the price of increasing dependence on the central government to supply the technology needed and widening the gap between those who could benefit from this revolution and those who, more noticably, were seen to lag behind. In the mid-1970s the terms of trade improved for industry to the detriment of agriculture, causing a crisis in the Punjab which affected the smaller landholder most adversely.[4] Due to its increasingly vacillating and compromising stance the Akali Dal was perceived as colluding with the richer landholders and the wealthier urban Sikhs in the interest of maintaining its position, while pacifying the masses with the achievement of minor concessions. The conflagration which developed with the heretical sect referred to above acted to expose what were seen as nefarious designs of the Akali Dal and of the central government, and was instrumental in paving the way for a fundamentalist revival. This revival was spearheaded by Bhindranwale Jatha, characterised by a strong *khalsa* tradition and headed by a succession of religious leaders (*sants*) with a reputation for fighting against what they regarded as injustice in every sphere – political, social and moral.

SANTISM AND THE NIRANKARI CHALLENGE

According to Sikh tradition, it is not enough to be merely a *sant*, a spiritually advanced personality empowered to guide others in the proper means of worshipping God as articulated through the divine name, *nam*. The ideal rather corresponds to the image of *sant-sepoi*, a saint who also fights to uphold righteousness. On this basis, Sikh *sants* have taken a leading role in the promotion of social and political movements and in keeping the fundamentalist spirit alive.[5] They have also been instrumental in the perpetuation of Sikh cultural, moral and religious traditions. For example, *sants* have become prominent for their community service rendered through the erection of temples (often at inaccessible and desolate places), educational and welfare institutions. Once they have gained some renown, *sants* often found their own *jathas*, groups of young men whom they train to become itinerant preachers, readers of the scripture, hymn singers and successors. Their own missionary activity is focused on initiating Sikhs into the *khalsa*, by recounting its historical significance, elucidating its principles and the contemporary relevance of keeping the 'five Ks'.

A significant focal point of their missionary work is in the field of combating drug (mainly opium) and alcohol abuse, to which Sikhs as hard workers and fighters are particularly prone. As the increased prosperity of the Punjab has also contributed to the prevalence of these addictions, *sants* have been faced with an ever greater challenge in weaning people away from intoxicants and encouraging them to become morally regenerated individuals, proud inheritors of the *khalsa* tradition. The government has had a vested interest in suppressing these *sants* due to the considerable hold they often exercise over the masses. It must be noted that Sikhs, especially ruralites, traditionally harbour distrust for officials and government authority and thus have tended to place greater confidence in charismatic, 'natural' leaders emanating out of their own ranks, rather than through an election system which, they allege, entails manipulation and corruption.

Bhindranwale Jatha,[6] under a succession of leaders since the turn of the present century, has achieved renown for encouraging Sikh revivalism and fighting against injustice. Sant Kartar Singh Khalsa, in conjunction with the Akali Dal, was a leading force of opposition to Mrs Gandhi's Emergency (1975–77). Once the Emergency was lifted, the *sant* helped the Akali Dal to win the Punjab state elections in return for the party's solemn assurance that it would continue to stand up fearlessly against oppression, for the defence of Sikhism and the community. Another cause espoused by this leader of Bhindranwale Jatha was the combating of anti-*khalsa* forces. The sect referred to above, which was considered especially pernicious in its undermining of Sikh tenets, institutions and even the ten Sikh Gurus, was that of the Sant Nirankaris (the prefix differentiating it from the actual Nirankaris, descendents of turn-of-the-century Sikh revivalists, not considered offensive). Its most insidious aspect was the fact that it was being openly patronised by the central government, as part of a 'divide and rule' policy to thwart *panthic* unity necessary in the fight for autonomy and Sikh rights. Due to what was felt to be the increasing virulence of the Sant Nirankari guru's anti-Sikh propaganda, in which he was also supported by militant Hindu organisations and the Arya Samaj vernacular press, Sant Kartar Singh called upon the Sikhs to take up arms in the defence of their faith.

Upon the latter's death in 1977, Jarnail Singh Khalsa was appointed his successor. Besides the leadership of the organisation, however, Jarnail Singh, the son of Jat Sikh farmers, inherited the conflict with the Sant Nirankaris. Although several of the Nirankari guru's meetings were broken up, the sect's right to 'religious freedom' was protected by the central government. In recognition of this fact and, particularly, of the reluctance shown by the Akali state government to counter the sect's activities – despite the fact that it had only achieved electoral support on the basis of such a pledge – fundamentalist Sikhs took this duty upon themselves.

In April 1978, on the anniversary of the *khalsa's* foundation, a group of several dozen prominent Sikhs belonging to different fundamentalist groups were incited by Sant Jarnail Singh to disperse a gathering which had been called by the Sant Nirankari guru in Amritsar. A White Paper entitled 'They Massacre Sikhs' issued by the SGPC, reported that the Sikhs who had joined the *jatha* were unarmed:

> They were stopped at a distance of about 200 yards away from their venue for a period that proved sufficient for a para-military platoon, armed with lethal weapons, guns, revolvers, acid-filled bottles and mechanical propellents for shooting poison-tipped arrows, to emerge from the Sikh-baiter's gathering and take up positions

behind a row of motor trucks already lined on one side. The Sikh protesters had, in the meantime, been persuaded by police officers on duty into believing that steps were being taken to stop further provocations to Sikh religious sentiments. Then, the voice of the Chief of these Sikh-baiters was heard outside through the elaborate sound-system set up within their enclosure saying: 'These Sikhs think they can stop us from freely carrying out our programme. Let them know today how mistaken they are. Time has come to be active for those who have come here for this job.' At this stage a para-military platoon advanced towards the Sikh protesters who, in the meantime, had been joined by many more men, to make a concerted attack on the Sikhs with bullets, acid-bottles and poisoned arrows. The police on duty hurled tear-gas bombs against unarmed Sikhs, ostensibly to disperse them, but converting them into sitting ducks for their hunters and shikaris... A dozen and a half Sikhs lay dead on the spot riddled with bullets. Over 40 Sikhs received serious injuries... (Gur Rattan Pal Singh, 1979, pp. 332–3)

The 60 Nirankaris brought to trial in the case were let off, together with their guru. Despite the fact that the entire *panth* was enraged about the incident, the Akali state ministry, under pressure from its coalition partner, the Janata party, did not take effective measures against the activities of the Sant Nirankaris, which continued as before. The sect's places of worship, which the Akalis had succeeded in closing, were again reopened (apparently at the behest of the centre), leading to further Sikh–Nirankari clashes, and resulting in more deaths, especially at the hands of the police assigned to protect the Nirankaris.

In compliance with an edict issued from the main seat of religion and politics, the Akal Takhat (Timeless Throne), debarring Sikhs from entertaining any relations with Sant Nirankaris and to 'counter their influence by any justifiable means', members of fundamentalist groups launched a 'holy war' against the sect's members. Particularly active was a newly formed fundamentalist group calling itself 'Babbar Khalsa', after the militant wing of the Akali temple reformers. Like their namesakes, they were dedicated to avenging the deaths of those killed in the defence of the faith.

The sporadic murders of Hindus and Nirankaris gave the authorities the excuse for launching a massive campaign against initiated Sikhs of all shades. There is, however, an allegation that the Congress itself instigated at least some of the murders of Hindus, making it appear that fundamentalists, who were being dubbed 'extremists' and 'terrorists' committed them. Particularly when the centre dissolved the state assembly in 1980 under the pretext that the Akalis were incapable of controlling the situation and imposed President's rule in the Punjab, many people suspected the central government of having created the law and order problem in the first place to rid itself of the popularly elected state government. This allegation tallies with the theory that the centre encouraged fundamentalism (through, for example, the support and encouragement of the Sant Nirankaris), as a force to counter the Akalis by discrediting them and thereby preventing their re-election.

THE *KHALSA* RESURRECTED

In 1982, having confined himself to the Golden Temple premises due to mounting police harassment, Sant Jarnail Singh launched the 'holy war' agitation for the achievement of full state autonomy. All Akali leaders including the *sant* took a vow at the Akal Takhat not to relent until all demands included in the resolution for autonomy were fully met by the government. The momentum of the 'holy war' *morcha*, 30 000 having volunteered to give themselves up peacefully for arrest in the first month alone, attests to its popularity amongst the Sikh masses due to the infusion of fundamentalism into the autonomy movement. During its course, casualties resulted from the often brutal means employed by the authorities to suppress the agitation. This acted to escalate the movement and inspired all the various fundamentalist groups to join in and new militant wings to be created. A major force was composed of the Sikh youth under the leadership of Bhai Amrik Singh, son of the previous head of Bhindranwale Jatha, organised in the All-India Sikh Student's Federation (AISSF). This religio-political organisation was mainly devoted to raising the consciousness of the youth and intelligentsia and to the propagation of Sikh cultural and religious demands. For example, the introduction of legislation underlining the separate nature of the Sikh community and religion was advocated along with the declaration of Amritsar as a 'holy city'.

Recurrent themes in fundamentalist preaching were the necessity of re-establishing the unity of the *panth* on a corporate, egalitarian basis; the importance of espousing *khalsa* ideology and donning the 'five Ks' towards this aim and in the interest of combating anti-*panthic* forces existing not only in the dominant community but more significantly perhaps, within their own, especially in its leadership; and the imperative of re-establishing a relation of equality between the Sikh minority and Hindu ruling majority necessary for the Sikhs to regain their dignity and integrity. As suggested by Pettigrew, the ethos of retribution which is a Jat cultural value, acts to uphold and articulate equality (1975, p. 58).

Fundamentalist ideology was formulated which could serve to reform existing institutions. For example, it was critical of the electoral system in India, entailing as it does manipulation and corruption. This system was deemed particularly inappropriate for Sikh religious bodies since it encouraged people to affiliate to these institutions primarily as a means to enter politics (Gobinder Singh, 1982, p. 219). The fundamentalist critique extended to what were considered other signs of the degeneration of tradition and morals. Besides an almost fanatical rejection of intoxicants and meat consumption (the latter is not strictly forbidden according to the mainstream interpretation of Sikh precepts), media such as film, television and radio which were regarded as spreading anti-Sikh feelings and manipulating people's consciousness in other ways, were criticised. The modern education system, especially the governmental one, was considered implicitly questionable for the same reason; by contrast, Bhindranwale Jatha was dubbed a 'mobile university' capable of teaching people most of what, in fundamentalist opinion, they really needed to know.

The escalation of events culminating in the invasion of the Golden Temple in June 1984 must be viewed in light of the following developments. Fundamentalism, which the centre had allegedly originally encouraged to crush the Akali Dal and thereby thwart the autonomy movement, became a 'frankenstein' threatening to create the unity necessary to achieve Sikh demands. The government's tactics of discrediting the fundamentalists, through launching a vilification campaign against Sant Bhindranwale and inciting the Akalis to oppose him by making the latter fear for their own positions, back-fired. The *sant* became more popular the greater his victimisation and that of his followers, so the Akalis dared not criticise him openly for fear of loosing their own increasingly tenuous hold on the masses. The government's installation of President's rule in Punjab with the attendant curtailment of civil liberties, although designed to stem the tide of violence, had the opposite effect. Politically, its policy of isolating and splitting the Akali Dal also proved counter-productive, since it only acted to radicalise the movement further. The government then sought to resolve the resulting heightening of communalism through the invasion of the Golden Temple (see Editorial in *Economic and Political Weekly*, 6 October 1984).

That the Akal Takhat (Timeless Throne) happened to be the main target of the attack is, on a symbolic level, not coincidental, considering what it represents. Through its destruction, perhaps the government thought it could demolish the very principle of the unity of religion and politics. In the process, no doubt, it nearly succeeded in rooting out fundamentalism in the Punjab through having killed its major proponents.[7] However, Sikh history has shown that fundamentalism as a force cannot be completely vanquished; it arises, phoenix-like, in response to oppression. In this light, should Sikh aspirations for greater autonomy and self-determination continue to be thwarted, the movement will doubtlessly experience a revival in due course.

CONCLUSION

Sikh fundamentalism arose as part of an ideological process of community formation, especially in having constituted a militant response of the peasantry and village menials to oppression perpetrated by a foreign (non-Sikh) ruling power and its collaborators (large landlords, money-lenders, and so on). Notably, during the half century of Sikh rule in Punjab, there was no indication of a fundamentalist resurgence (despite the stated deviation from *khalsa* precepts), a factor further corroborating this thesis. It can be concluded that fundamentalism was a religiously legitimated affirmation of a distinct Sikh identity, striving to maintain its integrity in the face of dominant, antagonistic forces.

In terms of the historical dialectic outlined by Sharpe (1983), and referred to by Taylor in this volume (Chapter 7), it can be postulated that Sikh fundamentalism originated from a concerted rejection of the old religious authority, a process culminating in the creation of the *khalsa panth*, the blueprint for subsequent movements. One of these, which emerged as a reaction against colonialism, preceded the second phase, characterised by a moderate, or in Sharpe's term, liberal, form of religiosity in the wake of the Akali movement, finally embodied through the establishment of religio-political institutionalisation in the post-colonial era. This 'mainstream' form of religious organisation and bureaucratisation significantly sought to contain tendencies towards *khalsa* fundamentalism. The latter had started to manifest itself as a result of the religio-political establishment's compromising stand which was due in part to constraints imposed by the outer framework of co-existence in a modern nation-state founded on Western, secular precepts.

This most recent form of fundamentalism, concurrent with Sharpe's scheme, can be seen to have come about as a reaction against this trend of increasing compromise, both religious and political, and accordingly aimed for a restoration of what fundamentalists propagated as the 'ultimate authority' – a revival of the ideals and institutions of the *khalsa*. In this regard, it has been shown how the extremism of the fundamentalist movement, in a fashion similar to that of the Tamil community outlined by Taylor (in Chapter 7), was determined by the law enforcement authorities' repression in having countered what was purported to be a largely peaceful movement with excessive violence. However, once ignited, the militant flame became difficult to extinguish, especially since fundamentalism as propagated by the movement's charismatic head, amplified a value deeply rooted in the Sikh psyche and in the egalitarian ethnic and *khalsa* tradition, that of honour calling for resort to retribution.

Of special interest to social scientists in the cross-cultural analysis of contemporary religious fundamentalism is its significance for the process of social transformation in Third World societies. The populist dimension becomes manifest especially in fundamentalism's critique of or reaction to modernism and secularism as postulated by some of the contributors to this volume who espouse Barr's thesis that it constitutes a specifically 'modern' phenomenon (1977, p. 173). In this sense, as illustrated by the Sikh case, it emerges as a vehicle of world-view reconstruction, the content of which features the following: a nostalgic longing for oneness or unity as opposed to the reality of social divisiveness and contradictions characterising modern Sikh society; a desire to resurrect the coherence and vitality of a distinct cultural tradition, severely afflicted by processes of alienation and impending disintegration felt most strongly by young people, the main proponents of fundamentalism; and an attempted realisation of a vision of a society completely egalitarian in nature according to *khalsa* tradition, whose only hierarchy refers to those values or attributes assumed universally accessible, given the adherence to a fundamentalist interpretation of religious precepts and norms. The most salient of these, in the case of the Sikh fundamentalists, appears to be demonstrable willingness to sacrifice for the sake of the re-creation of a spiritually sanctified social order, to counter the threat of cultural and social absorption or annihilation, real or imagined, of the Sikh minority by a dominant majority and ruling power.

Notes

1. The interpretation and data presented results from field work conducted in Punjab during 1982–3. Discussions with fundamentalist members of Bhindranwale Jatha and the All-India Sikh Student's Federation (AISSF) and their sympathisers were particularly illuminating in this regard.
2. The 'five Ks' characterise pious Sikhs to this day: *kes*, uncut hair, signifies an attitude of renunciation; *kanga*, the comb, a symbol of restraint, in conjunction with *kes* implies that mysticism is only justified when mediated by social responsibility; *kara*, the steel bangle doubles as a weapon of defence and a reminder of being 'handcuffed' to the service of God and man; *kirpan*, a dagger, is also a weapon of defence of honour; *kachera*, undershorts, signify modesty and restraint of passion. To further instil bravery and equality, the caste or clan appellation was substituted by the term *Singh*, lion, for a man and *Kaur*, prince, for a woman, underlining her equality.
3. By the eighteenth century, the management of temples devolved on these custodians because, not being 'proper' Sikhs, they did not generally carry the five Ks and thus could evade persecution.
4. During this period, 24 per cent of small and 31 per cent of marginal farmers fell below the poverty line. This was in contrast to the richer landholders who could be expected to continue to earn at the same rate of return as in the early 1970s (Gill and Singhal 1984, pp. 1728–9).
5. One example is the Namdhari leader, Baba Ram Singh, who sought to revive the *Sant Khalsa* in order to drive out the British and restore Sikh rule on an egalitarian, non-feudal basis. Another prominent *sant* was Bhai Sahib Randhir Singh, founder of the Akhand Kirtani Jatha – even today one of the most prominent fundamentalist groups – who served virtually a life sentence for his role in the Ghadr nationalist movement. *Sants* have also involved themselves in mainstream politics: the movement for a linguistic state in the Punjab was led by two *sants* and more recently, the presidency of the Akali Dal was filled by Sant Longowal until his assassination in 1985. Nesbitt observes that Sikh politicians, no matter what their affiliation, depend to a crucial extent for their power upon *sants* (1985, p. 76).
6. The actual institution associated with the *jatha*, forming the basis for its importance, is Damdami Taksal, which has been controlled by a succession of Bhindranwale *sants* since the turn of the present century.

Damdami Taksal represents the most renowned missionary institution of its kind in Sikh tradition as it was founded by the tenth Sikh Guru personally, to guard against scriptural falsifications and distorted renditions of the *khalsa* tradition which threatened then as now to undermine Sikh tradition.

7. For a description of the action by Indian army troops during the invasion of the Golden Temple in June 1984, see Pettigrew (1984).

References

Barr, J. (1977), *Fundamentalism* (London: SCM Press).

Dalip Singh (1981), *Dynamics of Punjab Politics* (Delhi: Macmillan India)

Duggal, D. S. (n.d.), *Sikh Quom da Shandar Virsa* (Sikh History Research Board, Amritsar: SGPC).

Gill, S. S. and K. C. Singhal (1984), 'Response to Development Crisis of Agriculture', *Economic and Political Weekly*, XIX, pp. 1728–32.

Gobinder Singh (1982), *Religion and Politics in Punjab: A Case Study of the SGPC*, Chandigarh, PhD Thesis, Punjab University (unpublished).

Gur Rattan Pal Singh (1979), *The Illustrated History of the Sikhs (1947–78)* (Chandigarh: Akal Printamatics)

Jones, K. W. (1976), *Arya Dharm: Hindu Consciousness in 19th-Century Punjab* (Berkeley and Los Angeles: University of California Press).

Khushwant Singh (1977), *A History of the Sikhs* (vol. 2) (Delhi: Oxford University Press).

McLeod, W. H. (1976), *The Evolution of the Sikh Community* (Oxford: Clarendon Press).

Mohinder Singh (1981), *The Akali Movement* (Delhi: Macmillan India).

Nayar, B. R. (1966), *Minority Politics in the Punjab* (New Jersey: Princeton University Press).

Nesbitt, E. (1985), 'The Nanaksar Movement', *Religion* 15, 67–79.

Pettigrew, J. (1975), *Robber Noblemen* (London: Routledge & Kegan Paul).

Pettigrew J. (1984), 'Take not Arms against thy Sovereign: the present Punjab Crisis and the storming of the Golden Temple', *South Asia Research*, 4, pp. 102–23.

Satindra Singh (1980), 'Khalistan: the Politics of Passion. *The Overseas Hindustan Times*, XXVII (16 October), pp. 9–11.

Sharpe, E. (1983), *Understanding Religion* (London: Duckworth).

7 Incipient Fundamentalism: Religion and Politics among Sri Lankan Hindus in Britain

Donald Taylor

In this chapter I put forward the thesis that one of the conditions for the emergence of a fundamentalist sect is a shift in members' compliance with authority from that legitimated on traditional grounds to that legitimated on charismatic grounds. Members of a fundamentalist sect are those who accept the charismatic authority of a leader who, in turn, draws upon religious teaching that has been legitimated on traditional grounds.

The chapter falls into three parts. In the first I shall clarify what I have said above by discussing a view put forward about fundamentalism by Eric Sharpe, a comparative religionist, in his book *Understanding Religion* (1983). In the second part, I sketch in the Sri Lankan background to Hindu migrations to Britain. In the third part I explain why a group of Sri Lankan Hindus in Britain, who showed marked tendencies towards fundamentalism, failed to develop into a sect. This chapter, therefore, is about incipient fundamentalism.

Let me sketch out Sharpe's thesis. There comes a time in the history of most societies when the traditionally accepted ultimate authority is challenged; this may occur at times of peaceful contact, or war, or colonialisation. In Europe, this has occurred through the process of secularisation. There are three phases of this process and they are not necessarily consecutive. The first is that of *rejection*, the second *adaptation*, and the third *reaction*.

In the first phase, rejection, the old ways and the old authority are rejected and there is a desire to adopt the new authority. As an example, Sharpe quotes from Jawaharlal Nehru's *Discovery of India*:

> We have got to get rid of that narrowing religious outlook, that obsession with the supernatural and metaphysical speculations, that loosening of the mind's discipline in religious ceremonial and mystical emotionalism, which comes in the way of our understanding ourselves and the world. (Nehru, 1956, p. 552ff.)

Sharpe comments: 'Clearly in this case, "science" is being put forward as a counter-authority to religion, and one may perhaps be tempted to conclude that *homo religiosus* is simply moving sideways and exchanging one type of priesthood for another' (1983, p. 117).

In the second phase, adaptation, efforts are made to adapt the old authority to the new, and this involves a restatement of beliefs and an attempt at reconciliation. Sharpe suggests that it is during this phase that the 'liberal' position emerges.

It is during the third or reaction phase, according to Sharpe, that fundamentalism occurs. He says that fundamentalists are those 'who claim to be representing the true faith, but who are in most cases restating a position in extreme polemical terms over against those who have rejected it and those who have tried to adapt it' (1983, p. 119).

He goes on to widen the meaning of the word fundamentalism by stating:

> If we use the term 'fundamentalism' to refer, not to a particular school of thought in Protestant Christianity, but to the utterly uncompromising adherence to any formulated (usually scriptural) tradition, then it may be claimed without too much exaggeration that fundamentalism always emerges in response to a previously existing liberalism. It is, in other words, as much a product of the secularisation process as is the liberalism it attempts to abolish.
>
> (Sharpe, 1983, p. 120)

After giving us that definition, Sharpe goes on to make three observations about fundamentalism. The first is that authority is a key word in the process; second that the process includes the emergence of minority groups; and third that it is not confined to the West. I shall comment on these three observations later, but first I want to discuss some points about Sharpe's use of the word, which will clarify further our understanding of it.

As noted above, Sharpe indicates that he means the word to refer to a historical process. According to Sharpe, fundamentalism emerges as one of the effects of the secularisation process.[1] From this we can conclude that fundamentalism must have first occurred in Western societies, for it was in these societies that secularisation first appeared. Therefore it is a relatively modern phenomenon and is often linked with liberalism and modernity. Indeed, although Sharpe seems to be suggesting that it occurs at any time in history as a result of 'the utterly uncompromising adherence to any formulated (usually scriptural) tradition' (1983, p. 120), he does seem to suggest that it cannot be separated from liberalism, and that liberalism is part of the secularisation process which itself is a comparatively modern phenomenon.

But even though Sharpe restricts the word to the modern period, he does not seem to restrict it to secularisation alone. For he acknowledges that fundamentalism can emerge during times of social change, as a result of conquest or even colonialisation. However, if we look closely at the way in which he uses it, saying that it generally emerges after 'an attempt to adapt the old authority to the new', we will see that something like the process of secularisation is not far from his mind. For if we take secularisation to mean the process whereby traditional religion loses its social significance, then it is possible to identify periods during the comparatively recent colonial period of European expansion which have had precisely the same effect. However, to equate colonialism with secularisation is not possible, and Sharpe does not do so. What he is referring to is a colonial period during which attempts are made to adapt to the ways of the colonial power, after which comes a period of fundamentalism.

Perhaps an example from India might clarify the matter. It could be said that the great Indian reformist Ram Mohun Roy who at the beginning of the nineteenth century formed the Brahmo Samaj attempted to adapt the tenets of traditional Hinduism to the rationalism of the new masters.[2] This could be regarded as the stage of liberalism. But by the end of the nineteenth century a reaction had set in and an uncompromising Hindu stance was taken by Ananda Saraswati when he formed the Arya Samaj, which cared neither for the foreigner nor for his salvation. This surely was the fundamentalist stage, but India could hardly have been called a secular society at the time.

Thus there seems to be an ambiguity in Sharpe's position. On the one hand, he seems to want to tie the term to secularisation, of which he sees liberalism as an essential component. On the other hand, he wants to say that it occurs under colonial rule, especially where there is adaptation of the old authority to the new. But such colonialism cannot easily be equated with secularisation. What seems to be the link is the notion of liberalism which can be interpreted in a variety of ways. Thus if we say that fundamentalism seems to occur after a period of liberalism (in the sense of freeing oneself perceptually from traditional beliefs and practices), and that liberalism can occur both during the process of secularisation and adaptation to colonial rule, then I think we shall be getting near to what Sharpe has in mind. The result of all this of course is to regard fundamentalism as being in opposition to liberalism (hence permissiveness), modernity, and Westernism (as perceived by those who have come under the domination of the Western powers).

It must be noted too that the word 'fundamentalist' is not often used as a self-designation. It is a term more usually applied by a third party, and though some groups may acknowledge that they are fundamentalists, they would only do so if pressed. Certainly no Hindu would call himself a fundamentalist. The word does not exist in the Indian languages and circumlocutions have to be used (see also Webber, this volume, Chapter 5). Thus when I use the term about Hindu Sri Lankans in Britain, it is a term that I am applying as a third party. Needless to say, in no way do I use it pejoratively.

Finally I return to the three observations which Sharpe makes about fundamentalism. He first of all notes that authority is a key word in the process, since he takes fundamentalism to refer to a restoration of that which has been challenged by an appeal to ultimate authority, whether this is perceived to reside in a scripture or a person who is in a special relationship with ultimate reality. What Sharpe seems to be referring to is a combination of what Weber (1968, p. 215) called traditional authority (appeal to scripture) and charismatic authority (appeal to a person).[3] This seems to be reasonable enough. For when customs and norms legitimated by traditional authority are perceived to be under threat, then it is not surprising to find that an appeal to restore and reinforce these same norms should be legitimated on charismatic grounds. I shall return to this question of authority once I have discussed Sharpe's other two observations.

The second of Sharpe's observations is that fundamentalism involves the emergence of minority groups. What Sharpe seems to have in mind here is the emergence of sects as the term was used by Troeltsch (1931). According to him a sect is a group that has splintered off from the main body of the Church so that it is always in opposition to the Church and to society. That Sharpe has this meaning of minority group in mind is confirmed by his further description of them. Sects 'have rejected the dominant values of secular society and the compromises of the major religious bodies in the face of these values' (1983, p. 120). But his use of this typology of sect and Church is problematic and has been rejected by a number of sociologists. Perhaps the most widely accepted typology today is that put forward by Bryan Wilson (1975).

Wilson uses neither doctrine nor organisation as the classifying principle for his typology, but 'response to the world'. In doing so he identifies seven different types of sects or new religious movements. All perceive evil to be located in the world, but not all reject the values of the world, nor do all reject the compromises the major religious bodies have made with the world. Some are not at all concerned with the major religious bodies, and others have not developed from the major religious bodies at all, but have done so from being cults, for example, the Church of Scientology (see Wallis, 1977). Thus whereas all fundamentalist groups may be sects (in Wilson's meaning of the word), not all sects are necessarily fundamentalist (in Sharpe's meaning of the word).

However, even the above proposition needs to be clarified, especially with reference to the meanings of the terms 'group' and 'sect'. Whereas a group may consist of individuals who pursue a common interest or goal, it does not necessarily have the same degree of permanence as a sect. Most of the sects that Wilson describes (1975) seem to have survived the death of their leader and to have continued to exist in the succeeding generation of followers. Sects therefore seem to be more like corporate bodies, existing independently of their members.

If we ask how a fundamentalist group becomes a sect, Wallis seems to give us the outline of an answer in his discussion of the transformation of cults into sects. The essential feature seems to be the centralisation of authority, especially charismatic authority (1977, p. 17). It takes place as a deliberate move by a cult leader who makes claims that are legitimated on charismatic grounds. It would appear therefore that a similar process takes place in the transformation of a fundamentalist group into a sect. The fundamentalist leader, while interpreting the situation in traditional terms, requires his interpretation to be accepted on charismatic grounds.

It is at this point that I return to the question of authority in the emergence of a fundamentalist sect. The leader may have a charismatic personality, but as long as the grounds for accepting his teaching are largely traditional the group will not transform itself into a sect. Once, however, there is a shift from traditional to charismatic grounds, there is every chance of the group becoming a fundamentalist sect. There must therefore be the right mix of traditional and charismatic authority for this to occur. What the right mix is will depend upon the circumstances.

Finally, when considering fundamentalism in the context of minority groups we have also to consider the relationship between a fundamentalist group and a faction (Nicholas, 1965). Since I regard a fundamentalist group as one that exists within a corporate body such as a Church, then it could also be regarded as a factional group, in opposition to other rival factions within the body. However once the group has emerged to become a corporate body on its own, that is to say a sect, then it can no longer be regarded as a factional group. On the contrary it must now be seen as another body competing with (and often in opposition to) the main religious body from which it has broken away.

Sharpe's third observation that fundamentalism need not be confined to the West, has been covered by what I have already said. In a society that has been affected by either secularisation or rapid social change involving an attempt to supplant the older traditional authority by a different one, and which results in a form of liberalism, it is possible for fundamentalism to emerge. And such conditions are not confined to Western societies.

Let me now state in a summary form what I see as the main characteristics of fundamentalism. I suggest that there are five.

(1) *The perception of a challenge to an accepted ultimate authority*
I use the phrase 'ultimate authority' because I wish to underline the fact that the perception is primarily a religious one. The perception of course is not a private one, but rather socially acknowledged and often attributed to a leader. The acceptance of the leader and of the leader's perception is usually made on charismatic grounds, that is to say on non-rational, often emotive grounds. In this sense we can call the leader a charismatic one, because of his/her ability to interpret the situation and to rouse people to accept it.

(2) *The decision that there can be no compromise with the perceived challenge*

(3) *Reaffirmation of the ultimacy of the challenged authority*
This is accompanied by a claim of undeniable access to that authority either through reference to scripture or through a person who stands in a special relation to that authority. Here we have the inter-relationship

between traditional and charismatic authority. The charismatic leader appeals to traditional authority in order to refute the challenge.

(4) *The recognition of standing in opposition to those who challenge or those who are believed to have compromised*
This suggests the development of a minority consciousness which is always in oppostion to a perceived majority whether that majority is a numerical majority or not. I give two examples, the first of which refers to the Sinhalese Buddhists of Sri Lanka. They are in the majority numerically. But they act as if they perceive themselves in opposition to the Hindu Tamils not only of Sri Lanka but also of South India. Thus the Tamils are perceived as the majority even though they are numerically in a minority in Sri Lanka. My second example refers to the Shi'ite Muslims, especially in Iran. Though in a majority in Iran itself, they regard themselves as a minority in opposition to the Western world and to Sunnis.

(5) *The use of political means in order to further their interests*
Thus, although fundamentalists begin as religious interest groups, they can take on the function of political pressure groups, or at least make use of political structures in order to achieve their ends.

This also raises the question of the relationship between fundamentalism and nationalism. The Tappers in this volume (Chapter 3) seem to suggest that fundamentalism and nationalism are parallel phenomena in states where the dominant religion is of Semitic origin. They also try to show how the secular nationalism of Turkey can be expressed in terms of the four characteristics of Barr's model of Protestant fundamentalism.

My own position is not very different, but I make a clear distinction between nationalism and fundamentalism since nationalism does not necessarily have to be legitimated by an ultimate authority as in the case of fundamentalism. Thus I am suggesting that these two spheres are interdependent of one another. I shall try to show how the politician in one instance has drawn upon fundamentalist sentiments to further political (nationalist) ends, and how fundamentalists in another instance have drawn upon political (nationalist) sentiments to further fundamentalist ends (see also Bruce in this volume, Chapter 9).

Let me now summarise my position from the foregoing discussion. The problem of fundamentalism is viewed from two perspectives: first the emergence of fundamentalist sects within a historical context, and second, the substantive characteristics of fundamentalism whether a sect has emerged or not.[4]

With regard to the emergence of fundamentalist sects, this has occurred during stages of secularisation in Western societies and in reaction to liberalism. In some other societies sects have emerged during colonialism, again in reaction to liberalism or Westernism. With regard to the main characteristics of fundamentalism there seem to be five that are important. Thus a group can have these characteristics and so be called fundamentalist, but although it may form around a charismatic leader it does not necessarily become a fundamentalist sect until there is a shift of emphasis of legitimating authority from traditional to charismatic grounds. Until it does so it remains an instance of incipient fundamentalism.

This brings me now to the end of my discussion about fundamentalism. In the light of Sharpe's thesis, I now want to move on to the ethnographic context of the fundamentalist sect that failed to emerge among Hindu Sri Lankans in Britain.

Nationalism among Hindu Sri Lankans is a recent phenomenon. Today it takes the form of the demand for a separate state consisting of what Tamils call their 'traditional' homelands in the north and east of the country. This state is to be called Tamil Eelam. To understand why this is so we have to go back to a period just prior to Independence in 1948.[5]

Tamils and Sinhalese regarded themselves as equal partners in the struggle against British rule. A Ceylon National Congress was formed in 1919 to which both Tamils and Sinhalese belonged. But very soon after that the Tamils left and formed their own Tamil Congress. As events proceeded towards Independence the Tamils realised that they were numerically in a minority, and made attempts to safeguard their customs and language. The British took very little heed of all this and believed that, politically, ethnic or communal voting would not take place. Just before Independence the Ceylon National Congress became the United National Party and with the collaboration of the Tamil Congress won the election that eventually took them to Independence in 1948. From that moment things did not go well for the Tamils.

Within a year the United National Party deprived the 900 000 Tamil plantation workers known as Indian Tamils of their citizenship. These were the Tamils who had come to Ceylon under British rule in order to work on the plantations, and were also considered by the Ceylon Tamils to be different from themselves. Consequently the Ceylon Tamils made no protest at the time against this action, a decision which many of them have come to regret.

At this point a form of Buddhist fundamentalism began to emerge which was immediately seized upon by some Sinhalese politicians. It had been developing for some time, especially among the Buddhist clergy who were reacting to the British presence on the island. The arrival of the British in the nineteenth century and the cession to them of the Kandyan kingdom in 1815 had resulted in the clergy's loss of royal patronage. This was undoubtedly a challenge to their understanding of ultimate authority. The situation was exacerbated by the presence of Christian missions and the encroachment of Christian schools. They were also annoyed by the British Government's practice of renting out liquor licences from which many Sinhalese made vast profits at the expense of what they saw as the 'social evil' of drunkenness and immoral living. Attempts had been made at reform and revival before, but none of these had been successful at the national level, though there were some results in the regions.[6] But the Buddhist clergy were not defeated. They turned to their chronicle of the founding of Buddhism in Ceylon, the *Mahavamsa*.[7] From this three myths became very popular and spread rapidly. They were, first, that the Sinhalese are Aryans, originating from a place in North India called Sinhapura (which cannot be identified today). Their forefathers arrived in Ceylon in 584 BC, the year that the Buddha died and achieved the state of Nirvana. The second is that the Buddha himself visited Ceylon on three occasions during his lifetime. The third is that the Buddha said that Ceylon would be the home of Buddhism and that the Sinhalese would be the guardians of Buddhism. These myths took hold among the majority of Sinhalese, especially the small planters and petty bourgoisie.

What I have been describing has at least four of the five characteristics which I have ascribed to fundamentalism, and so I take it to be an incipient form of it. The groups of Buddhist clergy who were associated with these movements were all led by charismatic types of individuals, each legitimating their claims upon traditional grounds.[8] The fifth characteristic of political manoeuvre emerged once the political scene allowed it to happen.

It was Solomon Bandaranaike, the minister for local government in the United National Party, who sensed the groundswell of discontent among the majority of Sinhalese once the political promises made at the time of Independence began to evaporate. He sensed too, the political potential of the fundamentalist movement that was gathering momentum through the activity of the Buddhist clergy. He then broke away from the United National Party and formed his own party, the Sri Lanka Freedom Party.

To gain power he drew upon the fundamentalist sentiments of the Buddhist clergy, which he presented in terms of Sinhalese ethnicity. In return he was fully supported by the Buddhist clergy and their leaders. He emphasised that Sri Lanka was for the Sinhalese, who were the guardians of Buddhism, and that they should do everything to protect Buddhism against the encroachment of others. He also said that it was a disgrace that the language of government continued to be English, and that once his party was elected to power he would pass a Bill which would make Sinhala the only language of government and of the courts. The Sri Lanka Freedom Party won a resounding victory at the polls in 1956, and Bandaranaike pledged to carry out his election promises.

The United National Party felt itself to be in a difficult position. It had great plans to run the island's economy on the same capitalist lines that had been introduced by the British. After all many of the party's leaders had acquired their wealth in such a system, and believed that an intensification of capitalism would create wealth for the majority of the people as well. However, in spite of efforts to introduce thoroughgoing capitalism, the economy seemed to reproduce itself as it had been during colonial days and the numbers of small planters persisted.[9] Yet it was amongst the small planters that the sentiments of Buddhist fundamentalism and Sinhalese ethnicity had taken the greatest hold. Very soon after Independence the party lost Tamil support, and so had to turn more and more to the Sinhalese small planter and others. Yet the more the party did so, the more it had to accept the demands of the Buddhist clergy. And the more it did this the more it reinforced Sinhalese Buddhist ethnocentricity and the further away it was from forming a truly nationalist government or even forming a true nation state.

The United National Party lost power to Bandaranaike's Sri Lanka Freedom Party in 1956, and from then until 1970 was intermittently in and out of office, and from 1970 to 1977 was completely out of office. In 1977 it regained power once more and remains the ruling power to this day. However, it can hardly be called a national party in the strict sense of the word, for it is primarily a Sinhalese party that will tolerate the Tamils only as a minority to whom some concessions might have to be made.

The Tamils had been willing at first to co-operate with the United National Party, but when the Indian Tamils were made stateless and deprived of their citizenship and right to vote, they became alarmed. So in 1949 a new Tamil party was formed called the Federal Party. The founder of the party, Mr Chelvanayakam, a Christian Tamil and a lawyer, wanted autonomous regional government for the Tamils, with a central federal government at the head of a unified state. The model which he had in mind was Switzerland.

However, both the United National Party and the Sri Lanka Freedom Party were opposed to the idea of the Tamils having their own autonomous regional government, for two reasons. The first was that it would virtually divide Ceylon into two nations. And the second was that such a move would leave the door open to India, and it was believed Ceylon would be flooded in no time with Tamils from India. This would mean that the Sinhalese would become a minority in their own land, and their religion would be in danger of being overwhelmed, to disappear for ever.

Thus the two Sinhalese parties blocked the demands of the Federal Party at every turn. When the latter was not able to get its own way by parliamentary means it resorted to extra-parliamentary action in the form of civil disobedience. The model which they drew upon was that used by Gandhi against the British in India. But the demonstrations of civil disobedience were greeted with violence from the authorities, which in turn bred violence from the demonstrators.

When the parliamentary appeal for federation failed, the Federal Party decided to reform itself. In 1972 it joined forces with the Indian plantation Tamils who were now organised along semi-Marxist lines as the Ceylon Workers Congress. These two merged and became the Tamil United Liberation Front, which now openly demanded the formation of a separate state for the Tamils as the only way of achieving their human rights. The opportunity came in 1977 for them to put their demands to the electorate, and at the General Election that year they received about 70 per cent support from the Tamil areas where they had candidates.

Neither the Federal Party nor the Tamil United Liberation Front were committed to violence. They sought and do still claim to seek a political solution to the problems between the Sinhalese and the Tamils. But violence did break out, first in the form of anti-Tamil riots (1956, 1958, 1961, 1974) and then in the form of reaction to that violence from Tamil youths. Many of these youths had been students on demonstrations at first, then because of anti-Tamil and police harrassment of Tamil areas, they began to form vigilante patrols. This soon escalated into armed violence against the security forces by those who called themselves the Tamil New Tigers (formed in 1972). By 1976 the latter were pressing for the formation of a new Tamil state to be called Tamil Eelam, and they regrouped themselves under the name of Liberation Tigers of Tamil Eelam. The United National Party government eventually responded to these demands by outlawing both the Liberation Tigers and the Tamil United Liberation Front. This meant that the latter's members of parliament were virtually deprived of their seats. They also passed the Prevention of Terrorism Act which almost makes every Tamil a 'terrorist' by definition. Since then there have occurred the most hideous anti-Tamil riots and massacres (1982 and 1983) which have been followed by retaliatory violence on the part of the Liberation Tigers and other Tamil organisations. This sequence of events continues to this day.

Much more could be said about the situation in Sri Lanka, but I must now address myself to the question of fundamentalism. I have suggested that fundamentalist groups emerged under the charismatic leadership of a number of Buddhist abbots before and around the time of Independence in 1948. That these groups were fundamentalist (in the sense that I am using the term) there can be no doubt. They perceived their understanding of ultimate authority, the Buddha's teaching, as challenged, even though denied by the Tamils and others. They reaffirmed the teaching of the Buddha, especially by means of their interpretation of their scriptures, the *Mahavamsa*. They also perceived themselves in a minority, overwhelmed by the majority Tamil Hindus. In addition they felt themselves alienated from their own politicans, who at that time were mostly Westernised and not necessarily Buddhist, and who hardly spoke Sinhalese.

But these groups did not have any political clout until mobilised by Solomon Bandaranaike and his Sri Lanka Freedom Party. Bandaranaike used their fundamentalist sentiments to arouse feelings of ethnicity, especially among the small planters and petty bourgeoisie who also felt themselves under threat. He therefore clothed his political message in fundamentalist Buddhist dress, and thereby gained the support of both the fundamentalist Buddhist clergy and the small planters. We saw that this strategy gained him the 1956 elections.

Here we have a clear example of the politician drawing upon fundamentalist sentiments in order to achieve political (nationalist) ends. We have now to ask whether there was a Hindu fundamentalist reaction at this time. The answer seems to be that there was not. I am suggesting three reasons for this, though there may be more.

First, the threat was perceived by the Sri Lankan Tamils as political and not as challenging their view of ultimate authority. Second, Tamils are fragmented into Indian, Ceylon, Christian and Muslim Tamils and so their response was also fragmented. I have tried to show how the Ceylon Tamils did not join forces politically with the Indian plantation Tamils until 1972, some fifteen years after Independence, during which time most of the Indian plantation Tamils had been disfranchised and deprived of their citizenship. Third, the political threat and the threat of violence forced the Tamils to close ranks. But they saw themselves as defending Tamil culture and the Tamil language, rather than Hinduism or any religion.

So there seems to have been no alliance between Tamil politicians and Tamil fundamentalists during this period. It is when we turn to Britain, however, that we find what I shall call an incipient fundamentalism emerging among a very small minority of Tamils.

It was the developing political situation in Sri Lanka that forced many Hindu Tamils to come to Britain. Today the Tamils say that they number 35 000. The majority of them arrived in the early 1960s. Many were professional people – doctors, engineers, lawyers, administrators and teachers. Most of them had left Sri Lanka because of the Sinhala Only Language Act of 1956. Unwilling to learn Sinhala, they preferred to emigrate rather than to remain in the country and face unemployment or a life on their family lands.

Most of those who came to Britain were supporters of the Federal Party's policies when they arrived. After their departure from Sri Lanka the Federal Party ceased to exist and merged to form the Tamil United Liberation Front. This latter party, as I indicated, does not demand federation but separation. There is therefore a split among Tamils in Britain between the older Federal Party view that advocates the possibility of co-operation with the Sinhalese government on the basis of autonomous rule within one nation state, and the more militant view that advocates the formation of a separate nation state as the only answer to Tamil survival. At present the incessant violence against Tamils in Sri Lanka has forced those in Britain to close ranks and gloss over these divisions. But they do exist even though one hears very little about them.

From the point of view of religion, the Hindu Tamils brought with them their own form of Hinduism, especially the worship of the Hindu deity Siva (sometimes pronounced and spelt Sivam by the Tamils). The formulated tradition of Saivism is known as Saiva Siddhanta and is expressed in a number of canonical texts (one set of which is called the Agamas) which are held to be as sacred as the Vedas. The first immigrants used to meet in one another's homes where their traditional rituals were performed. However, there were no Brahmin priests from Sri Lanka at that time in Britain, so these rituals had to be performed by the most ardent devotees. One such devotee, Mr X, had already studied under a teacher in South India, and though not a Brahmin considered himself entitled to perform them.

As time went on and the number of devotees increased, the weekly rituals could no longer be held in private homes and a hall was hired for the purpose. In 1966 Mr X and his supporters formed an association to further the interests of his group, with the hope of eventually building a South Indian style temple to the deity Siva in London.

In the meantime Mr X had acquired an image (*vikragam*) to which the appropriate rituals were being performed by him. This image and another associated with him and his supporters later became the subject of controversy, which came about in the following manner. By 1974 many Tamils believed that the time had come to form a trust and so embark upon the building of their proposed temple. A site was found and work slowly began on its construction. In the meantime, many felt that the time had come to instal a new image and to cease using the one belonging to Mr X, even though the temple was nowhere near completion. So a new image was ordered from sculptors in South India. Mr X however, cancelled the order. Many were upset, but finally the matter blew over, and a new image was installed temporarily in the temple, while Mr X kept his own image at home, where he continued to perform rituals for his small supporting group.

Before going on to indicate the existence of incipient fundamentalism in what had occurred, let me continue with an account of other episodes in Mr X's attempt to introduce and maintain pure Saiva Siddhanta worship in the temple.

Mr X tried to ensure that only Tamil-speaking Saivite Hindus should become members of the temple congregation. He asked all members to make a credal statement about belief in and devotion to Siva. But most of the other members refused to do so on the grounds that they had never done such a thing in Sri Lanka and were not prepared to do so now. Mr X withdrew his request, but his intention had been to keep the temple exclusively Tamil for the worship of Siva. He wanted to exclude other Hindus lest they tried to introduce non-Saiva Siddhanta practices and therefore less 'pure' forms of worship.

Eventually Mr X and his supporters saw that they were being isolated from the others so he adopted a number of strategies. One such strategy was to get a number of politically active supporters of the nationalist cause to be on a temple committee and then to announce his moral support for the national struggle for freedom in Sri Lanka. This had a twofold effect. On the one hand, he gained the confidence of the committee, since no Hindu Tamil felt that he could go against him on such an issue. On the other hand, divergent views between those who had backed the old Federal Party calling for regional autonomy and a federated state and those who backed the Tamil United Liberation Front and its call for a separate nation-state began to be quietly voiced. The majority did not want what they saw as a political matter being dragged into what they considered to be a purely religious affair. However, Mr X managed to keep control over the committee, and the matter eventually blew over.

Let me now consider these events in the light of the five characteristics of fundamentalism which I previously noted. In the first place Mr X believed that Saiva Siddhanta as an ultimate authority was being challenged. It was the subtle challenge of those features that I have called secularisation, Westernism, liberalism and permissiveness, and it was his personal judgement of what was happening that was accepted by a small group.

Second, as an ardent devotee of Saiva Siddhanta, he could not compromise in any way, and gathered around him his supporters. This was made much easier by the immigrant situation in which Sri Lankans found themselves. As happened with most immigrants from the Indian subcontinent, they turned to their religion for mutual support. Thus there was nothing peculiar in the fact that a small group should gather around him in order to continue their religious practices. Perhaps what singled them out was their determination not to compromise in any way with the perceived challenge. The determination of course took a religious form rather than the rejection of any economic advantages they might have experienced in having become immigrants.

Third, the group went about to reaffirm its belief in the ultimate authority of their tradition by an appeal to their scriptures. For instance the secretary of the executive wrote:

Saiva Siddhantam [*sic*] is the quintessence of Hindu philosophy which names the supreme God as 'SHIVAM' in preference to any other name. Saivism has maintained the ancient Dravidian ritual forms and practices which leads one to realisation of Dharma. The most important event in Saivite history started with Thirumalai's Thirumantiram, a complete treatise in Agamic saivism which established saivism in South India where it continues as the major faith. Saivism is a pure and fully independent religion carrying within itself the eternal truths of religious growth.[10]

The appeal to a treatise which is said to be part of the Saivite Agamas is implicit in the above passage.

Fourth, Mr X's request that members should make obeisance to Siva not only by going through a public ritual but also by making a credal statement to that effect, isolated him and his supporters from other Saivite devotees. Indeed, Mr X was willing to oppose both other 'liberal' Saivites and other Hindus generally. In doing so he realised he was in a minority, but he was certain that he was right and seemed to be heading for a split with the majority of the temple congregation and his executive committee.

Fifth and finally, Mr X had to come to a compromise in order to retain his control. He did this by drawing upon the nationalist (hence political) sentiments of his followers. At the same time, differing views about the solution to the Tamil problem in Sri Lanka were re-activated, and some members left the temple for other places of worship. Here we have a clear example of a fundamentalist using political sentiments to achieve fundamentalist ends.

Mr X and his supporters, however, never became a truly fundamentalist sect. The pressures of the immigrant situation were too strong to allow a split of this nature to occur. Thus all the strategies adopted by him and his supporters never developed into a fundamentalist sect as such. What we have is incipient fundamentalism and not the fully fledged type at all.

When we look at the events in the light of Sharpe's thesis, all the elements of the process seem to be there as well: secularisation, challenge, threatened adaptation and liberalism, Westernism and modernity. All seemed set for the emergence of such a sect. We have to ask why it did not happen. The answer is not simple. First, Mr X was never able to base his authority on charismatic grounds. Though he had a charismatic personality his authority was constricted to tradition. Thus, though he tried to introduce innovations to the tradition (for instance by insisting upon performing rituals, though he himself was not a Brahmin, and by requiring members to make credal statements) he never got wholehearted support from his followers. Second, Mr X's supporters never saw themselves as the nucleus of a sect. They were willing to follow him in a factional dispute but sectarianism was out of the question. Furthermore the factional dispute did nothing to shift the basis of their compliance from traditional to charismatic authority. But perhaps the most important condition that prevented the emergence of their fundamentalism into a fundamentalist sect was the immigration situation. There was urgent need for solidarity, and this was mainly achieved by accepting the traditional authority of their religion. They preferred to comply with the traditional authority of a temple and its management rather than with the charismatic authority of a strong personality.

Thus, though all the conditions seemed to be there for fundamentalism to emerge, they were never there in the right proportion and with the right intensity for the incipient fundamentalism to develop into a properly defined fundamentalist sect.

Notes

The fieldwork on which this chapter is based was carried out in 1982 by means of a grant from the Emslie Horniman Trust, to the trustees of which I extend my thanks.

1. See Berger (1973, p. 113), who defines secularisation as 'the process by which sectors of society and culture are removed from the domination of religious institutions and symbols'. Wilson (1966) has a similar definition.
2. For the work of Ram Mohum Roy (d. 1839) and the Brahmo Samaj see Joshi (1975).
3. Weber distinguishes between three types of authority: traditional, charismatic and legal rational. Traditional authority rests on an established belief in the sanctity of immemorial traditions and the legitimacy of those exercising authority under them. Charismatic authority rests on devotion to the exceptional sanctity, heroism, or exemplary character of an individual person, and on the normative patterns revealed or ordained by him. Legal rational authority rests on a belief in the legality of enacted rules and the right of those elevated to authority under such rules to issue such commands.
4. As a result of these observations it would seem that the word 'fundamentalist' has a range of meanings. As an adjective it can qualify either group or sect. When qualifying a group it seems to have a weaker meaning than when it qualifies a sect. This weak and strong sense can be extended to the noun 'fundamentalist'. Individuals are sometimes called fundamentalists though they do not belong to a group or a sect.

5. My sources for this historical sketch are de Silva (1977), Jupp (1978), Ponambalam (1983), Jayawardena (1984).
6. Anagarika Dharmapala led a reformist movement at the beginning of this century. His reform was mainly ethical and directed against the intrusion of the Christian missions.
7. The *Mahavamsa* is one of the Buddhist chronicles of Ceylon written in Pali during the sixth century AD.
8. The charismatic leaders of the Buddhist clergy are mostly Buddhist abbots. Buddharakita, abbot of the monastery at Kelaniya, for instance, was the secretary of the Eksath Bikku Peramuna that was behind much of the agitation for the sole use of Sinhala.
9. For a discussion of this feature of Third World 'capitalism' see Kahn (1978).
10. The quotation is from a programme for a concert given in 1978 by the Britannia Hindu Temple Trust with S. S. Govindarajan as principal artist. The programme itself is not dated.

References

Berger, P. L. (1973), *The Social Reality of Religion* (Harmondsworth: Penguin University Books).

Jayawardena, K. (1984), 'Class formation and communalism', *Race and class*, xxvi, pp. 51–62.

Joshi, V. C. (1975), *Rammohun Roy and the process of Modernisation in India* (New Delhi: Vikas).

Jupp, J. (1978), *Sri Lanka: Third World Democracy* (London: Frank Cass).

Kahn, J. (1978), 'Marxist anthropology and peasant economies: a study of the social structure of underdevelopment' In J. Clammer (ed.), *The New Economic Anthropology* (London: Macmillan).

Nehru, J. (1956), *Discovery of India* (London: Meridian).

Nicholas, R. W. (1965), 'Factions: a Comparative analysis', in M. Banton (ed.), *Political Systems and the Distribution of Power*, ASA Monograph, no. 2 (London: Tavistock)

Ponambalam, S. (1983), *Sri Lanka: the National Question and the Tamil Liberation Struggle* (London: Zed).

Sharpe, E. J. (1983), *Understanding Religion* (London: Duckworth).

de Silva, K. M. (1977), *Sri Lanka: a Survey* (London: Hurst).

Troeltsch, E. (1931), *The Social Teaching of the Christian Churches* (transl. O. Wyon) (New York: Macmillan)

Wallis, R. (1977), *The Road to Total Freedom: A Sociological Analysis of Scientology* (New York: Columbia University Press).

Weber, M. (1968), *Economy and Society* (vol. i) (eds G. Roth and C. Wittich) (New York: Bedminster).

Wilson, B. R. (1966), *Religion in Secular Society* (London: Watts).

—— (1975), *Magic and the Millenium* (St Albans: Granada).

8 Fundamentalism as Counter-culture: Protestants in Urban South India

Lionel Caplan

INTRODUCTION

The term 'fundamentalism' is said to have first seen the light of day in 1920 when the editor of a prominent Baptist paper, alarmed at what he saw as the 'havoc' wrought by 'rationalism' and 'worldliness' in American Protestant churches, coined the term and defined fundamentalists as 'those ready to do battle royal for the Fundamentals of Protestantism' (Sandeen, 1970, p. 246; also Marsden, 1980, p. 159).[1] These fundamentals have from time to time been reiterated by the orthodox Protestant churches. In 1910, for example, the northern Presbyterian General Assembly adopted a declaration of Essential Doctrines: (i) Biblical inerrancy; (ii) Virgin Birth of Jesus Christ; (iii) His substitutionary atonement; (iv) His bodily resurrection; and (v) the factuality or authenticity of miracles. Richard Niebuhr, in the *Encyclopaedia of the Social Sciences* (1937), listed these same beliefs as the 'five points of fundamentalism'. It is worth noting, however, that in some proclamations of the core doctrines prior to 1910 the Second Coming was included, and Sandeen insists that earlier fundamentalists showed 'no particular preference for five rather than fourteen, nine, or seven articles' (1970, p. xiv). So the basic fundamentals themselves are periodically re-constituted – the 'sacred history' re-constructed (Sami Zubaida in this volume, Chapter 2). More importantly for our present purposes, the 'essentials' may also be re-formulated in as much as in certain periods and contexts some doctrines are left unstressed, while others are elaborated.

In this chapter, I want especially to concentrate on the significance of 'miracles' in the two main varieties of Protestant fundamentalism which can be identified in Madras city, the capital of the state of Tamil Nadu in south India, and the locus of my study. One variety is the legacy of the 'Evangelical Awakening' in Europe, which gathered strength during the last twenty years of the eighteenth century. Like the Pietism movement a century earlier, it concentrated on the salvation of the individual, and on a personal relationship with the saviour. Its authoritative source was the Bible, regarded as inerrant, and interpreted literally (Neill, 1964, p. 227; Sharpe, 1965, p. 25). To both the pietists and evengelicals in India, Hinduism was not only 'idolatry', but a 'false religion', and the encounter between Christianity and Hinduism was seen as a simple conflict between good and evil. Evangelicals, pressing in the House of Commons for the inclusion of a clause in the 1813 Charter Act of the East India Company allowing more open access on the part of missionaries to the sub-continent, stepped up their attacks on Hinduism to prove that India was in ever greater need of Christianity. Despite considerable differences of theology and ritual among the many denominations represented in the mission field, there was a common basis of evangelicalism and a sharing of the view that there could be no meeting point with non-Christian religions, which had to be 'attacked, destroyed and replaced by ... Christianity' (David, 1983, p. 88).

In the early part of the present century this consensus was challenged by the growth of liberal theology which took account of Darwinian ideas, countenanced biblical criticism, and sought to 'socialise' Christianity, to make it more responsive to social concerns. In south India the missionaries who introduced this social gospel also urged a more tolerant and accommodative attitude towards Hinduism, which, while still regarded as a lower stage in the evolution of human religious forms, was no longer seen as the road to perdition. As Marsden remarks, 'the suggestion ... that God revealed himself in non-Christian cultures had profound implications for missionary programmes' (1980, p. 167). The social gospel became the preferred discourse of intellectuals and theologians within the missionary fold, and subsequently among the dominant sections of the indigenous Protestant church and community.

By contrast, the prevalent religious orientation of ordinary Protestants remained (and still is) much closer to the conservative evangelicalism of the nineteenth-century missionaries. Emphasis is placed on scriptural infallibility, Bible-centred sermons, piety, prayer and persistent evangelisation of Hindus. Most ordinary members of the Protestant community, in other words, favour a form of religiosity which Barr (1977) identifies as 'fundamentalist'. Moreover, a crystallisation of this consciousness arose around the intense hostility to the liberalism or 'modernism' of the ecclesiastical and secular elites, seen as opposed to the 'true' gospel. Religious distinctions have thus become associated with the local hierarchy of power.

A different variety of fundamentalism found in Madras subscribes to the doctrine of conservative evangelicalism, but places even greater stress on the significance of the Holy Spirit, and the 'gifts' it confers. Crucial among these is the gift of healing and so the performance and authenticity of miracles. This kind of fundamentalism first reached south India in the early years of this century when a few – mainly Pentecostal – emissaries from the West attempted to make converts and begin small congregations, though with only minimal success. By the 1930s barely a handful of such sectarian groups had established themselves in Madras. It is not until the late 1960s that we can detect a substantial expansion of their presence in the city. Today there are probably hundreds of small and large congregations propagating such a view of Christianity, and while they still embrace only a small minority of Protestants in the city, their influence has reached deep into the orthodox churches. Though the great majority of Protestants still retain their memberships in these orthodox congregations and continue to worship, marry and be buried there, they are increasingly persuaded by fundamentalist ideas and practices. This occurs principally through their participation in a variety of rites at which charismatic prophets claiming miraculous gifts through the power of the Holy Spirit offer assistance to those who, in one way or another are, and/or believe themselves to be, the victims of affliction. The persons most attracted to this form of Christianity are those who, by virtually every measure, are located far from the centres of power and privilege. It is this kind of fundamentalism with which the present discussion is primarily concerned.

The recent fundamentalist efflorescence is not unrelated to the increasing emphasis on international evangelism by mainly US-based organisations. The worldwide growth of 'liberation theology', and the recent coalitions between fundamentalist and 'New Right' groups in the United States have certainly encouraged this activity. Fundamentalists now devote more personnel and resources to the 'winning of souls' than the orthodox Protestant churches which had for so long monopolised the international mission field. Not to put too fine a point on it, US-inspired fundamentalism has spread with American overseas influence in much the same way as early missionary Christianity spread with colonialism.

But whatever the global political significance of this expansion, it must also be understood in the context of indigenous social and cultural circumstances. The narrative which follows attempts to unravel the various strands in this story. It first examines the urban Protestant context in which these religious developments have occurred. It then outlines the beliefs and observances of fundamentalists who have recently entered Madras, and considers the ritual contexts in which ordinary people are 'addressed' by these discursive practices. Finally, the fundamentalist challenge to orthodoxy is discussed, as are the ways in which such forms of religiosity can constitute a popular opposition to the dominant 'power bloc' (Hall, 1981) and the authoritative status of its culture.

PROTESTANTISM IN SOUTH INDIA

The Western missionary presence in India was intimately connected with the expansion of the Anglo-Indian empire. To concentrate their limited resources, and preserve some measure of harmony among the various organisations, each mission tended to focus its efforts in a limited number of areas. While the larger urban centres were regarded as common property, the rules of 'comity' required that one mission should respect and refrain from entering the field of labour of another. Denominational affiliation for the average convert was therefore not so much a matter of personal choice or conviction, but of the missions' territorial claims.

As they became more mobile, Protestants found themselves living, working and worshipping alongside persons of other mission backgrounds. In the course of time a number of developments, not least the rise of nationalism, further mitigated, blurred and even abolished the lines separating the different denominations. In 1908 Presbyterian and Congregational churches were brought together in the South India United Church (SIUC), and in 1947, the year of India's Independence, the Church of South India (CSI) federated the SIUC, Anglicans and Methodists. With well over one and a half million adherents, or just under a third of all Protestants in India, it is today the largest Protestant body in the country. While there were inevitable compromises of dogma and liturgy in the course of negotiating the amalgamation, the outcome was recognisably Western and orthodox Protestant: synods and dioceses, a hierocratic order including episcopally ordained bishops, a selected and trained male clergy, formal rites of (child) baptism, marriage and death, as well as agreed procedures for all other ritual occasions. My own fieldwork in Madras was mainly among members of this united church – the CSI.

While the early denominational communities were more or less homogeneous in terms of socio-economic criteria, by the late nineteenth century some differentiation was already apparent. This was occasioned, in part, by the limited benefits which the missions were able to offer, and the unevenness of their availability to adepts. Inequalities of education, skills and opportunities therefore arose within and between mission congregations. The gradual expansion of administration, commerce and industry in south India intensified these differences as Christians from the rural areas as well as smaller urban places began migrating to metropolitan centres like Madras city.

With the dramatic growth of industry and infrastructure in and around the city during the Second World War and even more so after 1947, this migration reached significant proportions. A minority of migrants came to acquire advanced educational qualifications, to pursue professional careers, or to assume senior positions vacated by Europeans at the time of Independence or created in the wake of post-Independence expansion and industrialisation. The majority, however, entered the capital to meet the demand for skilled and semi-skilled workers in newly established concerns, for teachers in the expanding school system, for clerks and assistants in the burgeoning administration and commercial sector. Many also came to establish or attach themselves to the innumerable petty enterprises of the 'informal sector' which arose in its shadow.

But the numbers of migrants more than outstripped the pace of growth, and as economic expansion halted – indeed was reversed in the 1960s – the situation for those at the lower levels of the occupational order grew increasingly difficult. Their prospects now seem, if anything, less bright than in the past; their material conditions have, and are felt to have, deteriorated. The missionary institutions (now part of the indigenous church) which had once provided education, training and employment to a fairly wide cross-section of the Protestant population, can no longer meet the overwhelming demands made on them, and have become the preserve of the well-to-do, who seek to intensify their hold on recently-won privileges in the educational and occupational fields. Social arteries have considerably hardened; mobility has become a thing of the past.

Not surprisingly, the dominant voice in the church is that of the new middle class, which provides both its ecclesiastical and lay leadership. In addition to its formal religious concerns, the church has responsibility for the operation of a variety of educational, medical and other social service institutions. The proper functioning of these enterprises relies to a large extent on lay persons voluntarily contributing their time, knowledge and experience. Because of their special managerial skills and professional qualifications, their wide contacts built up over many years, and because only the better-off can contribute their time in this way, the lay leadership tends to be drawn from those belonging to the dominant segment within the community. Many of these elites worship, moreover, in a handful of grandiose churches built by and for Europeans during the colonial period, where rites are still conducted in English. By contrast, Protestants among the lower class – who attend mainly Tamil churches – do not possess the qualifications and previous work experience to be invited to assume positions of responsibility in these organisations. Nor do they possess the kinds of resources – contacts, finances, personal transport – which would enable them effectively to donate their services even if called upon to do so.

The CSI leadership, like that of the other main Protestant churches in Madras, has a strong commitment to the 'social gospel'. This is a direct legacy of the dominant liberal theological emphasis within missionary circles which gained the ascendant in the early twentieth century, and especially during the run-up to Independence. By the 1930s, writes one opponent of this tendency, modernism had spread 'like cancer' through Christian colleges and high schools, sowing 'unbelief in the word of God' and turning denominational churches into 'moral and spiritual graveyards' (Daniel, 1980, pp. 89–90). In the context of contemporary south India the social gospel means a concern for economic development (as defined by regional and national governments) as well as for the alleviation of individual poverty and hardship. The CSI originates and/or participates in, among other things, programmes for the relief of drought-stricken regions, the improvement of water resources in rural areas, the provision of agricultural extension services, industrial and craft training, the betterment of urban slum sanitation, and the building of low-cost housing in the city. Kurien remarks that 'they are the *avant-gardes* of the modern age and of the social gospel of the church', and have won for the latter 'a certain respectability in this land' (1981, p. 4). Funds are also directed to a host of welfare enterprises which, though run by

Christian organisations, benefit the poor irrespective of religious affiliation.[2]

One obvious corollary of this kind of intense engagement with the 'world' is that relationships to persons of other faiths are conceived in a more positive light. The ecumenical tendency finds expression in a greater readiness to acknowledge a common Dravidian culture with Tamils and other south Indians irrespective of religious affiliation and to acknowledge the need for co-existence with other faiths. The CSI's Bishop in Madras writes of 'spirituality in other religions', and the need to learn from them, even to incorporate certain of their qualities, for example, 'devotionalism' (*bhakti*), and to find Christ 'in the lives of men and women of other Faiths'. He calls for dialogue which will 'lead ... to knowledge of other religions which is so lacking in the Indian Christian community' (Clarke, 1980, pp. 95–8).[3] Such views are frequently heard from the pulpits of elite congregations, and are widely shared by those, mainly within the dominant class, who are regularly engaged in welfare and development activities as part of their commitment to the social gospel.

While there is recognition of the obligation of Christians to spread the message of the gospel, it is regarded as most effectively communicated by the example of 'social work', and therefore implicit rather than explicit. People in the congregations of the well-to-do, I was told by a leading member of one, 'are not very much in favour of standing on the pavement and preaching to people'. Another related how, during a hospital visit, he and several other members of his congregation were appalled and embarrassed when one of their number refused to distribute the light magazines they had collected and brought along. 'He felt that these sick people should be given evangelical literature, so that they would see the error of their ways before it was too late.' This kind of 'vulgar evangelism' is not thought suitable for members of elite congregations.

The vast majority of Protestants – those outside the tiny power bloc – neither benefit from these welfare programmes, nor take any part in their planning and execution. It would not be accurate to relate a weak commitment to the social gospel among ordinary Protestants entirely to their own material circumstances. Liberal doctrines now, as in the past, are seen to threaten the pietism which, for the better part of two centuries, has formed the core of popular south Indian Protestantism. It is frequently suggested that the price of the social gospel is the neglect of people's 'spiritual needs', that it replaces 'salvation through faith' by 'salvation through social concern', as one lay preacher phrased it. The social ministry is misguided, it is said, because 'people will only agree to follow Christ if they get something in return'.

Even those who are not totally opposed to welfare efforts on behalf of the less fortunate are convinced, nevertheless, that these should be accompanied by intense evangelism, so that people of other faiths can be brought to see the 'light of Christian truth'. The missionaries are thought to have arrived at a perfect balance between their social concerns and their promulgation of the Christian message. But the social gospel, it is protested, has come to mean 'giving without preaching the word of God'. One man who had been involved for a short time in a development project sponsored by an inter-denominational organisation linked to the World Council of Churches, complained bitterly that

the agencies do not allow us to proclaim that these programmes come from a spirit of Christian charity; so they are bereft of the love of Christ. Social welfare is divorced from evangelism ... if we insist on tying our giving to preaching our religious views, these agencies refuse to have anything to do with us.

The reference is to a policy meant, in part, to take account of the Indian government's extreme suspicions of the motives underlying Christian aid, but one which also reflects liberal Protestant respect for the sensitivities of people of other faiths, and, as already noted, a less aggressive and overt approach to evangelism (see also Clarke, 1980, pp. 96–7).

In brief, then, it is not simply that the conservative evangelicalism –what Barr (1977) would label 'fundamentalism' – of the early missionaries has been overtaken by the social gospel favoured by those who now dominate the structures and shape the discourses of the church. It is also that the beliefs and practices of ordinary people have for some years been effectively demoted, left behind in the wake of a confident, modernist, development-orientated ecclesiastical whirlwind. Those so excluded from the exercise of influence within the church as within society, and denied the authenticity of their own religious preferences by the dominant segment within the church and community, are precisely those most attracted to and by the new fundamentalism.

MIRACULOUS FUNDAMENTALISM

The fundamentalist sects which have entered Madras recently insist on the centrality of the Bible, on piety, prayer and worship, in Protestant life. They inveigh against the 'infidels of modernism'. They are indifferent if not opposed to inter-faith dialogues and ecumenism, social and political activity on behalf of the poor, church involvement in development programmes, and the whole paraphernalia of social action. They are therefore very much in tune with the kinds of views and practices favoured by most Protestants outside the dominant class, as well as having much in common with the earlier conservative evangelical, pre-modernist tendency within the missionary fold.

But what seems even more to account for the attraction of the new fundamentalist movement is its stress on the authenticity of miracles – one of the 'essential' doctrines of Christianity which has all but disappeared from Western Protestant orthodoxy. It refers to and stems from the Biblical episode when on the occasion of Pentecost the Holy Spirit descended on the original Christian community with the charismata. The fundamentalist claim is that the gifts of the Holy Spirit – tongues, prophecy and healing, among others – were not meant for the early Christians alone, as the mainline Protestant view would have it, but are immanent in every period, if people are but ready to receive them. Moreover, they assert that the devil and all his legions are still abroad in the world and, if anything, Christ is needed as never before to save people from these malignant powers. One hears on fundamentalist platforms or reads in its press that 'hundreds of thousands of people in India are under the influence of demons' (Sargunam, 1974, p. 130). Or, as one statistically-minded young man told me, 75 per cent of all hospital cases in Madras are due to possession by spirits. Here, fundamentalists are in tune with popular theodicies: that the sources of human affliction may be located in occult evil forces.

Sorcery (*suniam*), for example, is popularly thought to account for various kinds of misfortune – by Hindus and Christians alike. The human agents responsible are the *suniakaran*, sorcerers who are thought to have access to secret knowledge and mystical powers which they employ on behalf of paying clients. The persons who are thought to engage the services of such experts for harmful ends bear personal grudges against the intended victims or their close kin. Thus, rejected suitors, clerks who fail to obtain promotion against less experienced colleagues, dissatisfied heirs, unsuccessful job applicants, or political rivals, may turn their anger and frustration against those whom they feel are responsible for their misfortunes.

Sorcery in its aggressive aspect implies a variety of ritual techniques to inflict harm, including the utterance of spells or their inscription on copper plates, which are then buried in the victim's house or place of work. Sorcerers also perform contagious or associative magic. The latter may include the making of clay figures or dolls (*bomai*) as likenesses of the intended prey, on which all manner of simulated injury may be inflicted to produce a similar effect on the human subjects. These practitioners are associated with graveyards, where they are said to obtain the skulls of eldest children (especially sons) who have died young, from which to prepare their pernicious medicines (*mai*). They are also assumed to control a number of spirits whom they can despatch to bring a variety of afflictions to their victims. Some are simply poltergeists, impish and clown-like, creating havoc wherever they go – causing stones to fall around houses, food to turn to excrement, dishes to fall off shelves or people out of their beds. Most superhuman assistants of the *suniakaran*, however, are portrayed as considerably more malign, and their principal means of attacking victims is through possession. These are the evil spirits known in Madras, as in Tamil Nadu generally, as *peey*. Further, the most malignant of these *peey* operate outside human control, in an entirely capricious and destructive manner (see Caplan, 1985).

Fundamentalists do not deny the reality of such (evil) forces which, by intention or otherwise, bring adversity. In this respect, they provide a strong contrast with the orthodox churches and their missionary predecessors. In south India, as in virtually every part of the missionised world, Protestant evangelists long ago turned their backs on such concerns. The essential Christian doctrine of belief in the authenticity of miracles was suspended. Whereas Hindus had resort to a variety of deities and ritual specialists to protect them, the missionaries refuted and eliminated the agencies by means of which converts to Protestantism and their descendants sought protection from these dangerous powers (see Wilson, 1973; Norman, 1981). They discredited popular beliefs in the existence of evil spirits and the efficacy of magic and sorcery, and any practices which acknowledged such forces were condemned.

Protestants looked in vain to their missionaries and later their indigenous clergy for a satisfactory response to these popular conceptions of affliction, and so were denied the authenticity of such forms of knowledge. These were ridiculed, explained away and disqualified by ecclesiastics who had long since rejected their own thaumaturgical legacy. Thus, the Anglican Bishop of Tinnevelly (in Tamil Nadu), reporting on the widespread belief in the activities of demons, assured a meeting of the Anthropological Society of Bombay in 1886 that he had 'never yet had an opportunity of being present where symptoms, that seemed to me to be incapable of being explained by natural causes, were exhibited ... and this has been the experience, so far as I have heard, of all English and American missionaries' (Caldwell, 1886, pp. 96–9). In Europe, by the seventeenth century, the devil had been severely downgraded. It was not the growing scientific community, moreover, but the church itself which was keen to extirpate magical practices which were thought 'superstitious' (see Hill, 1983; Macfarlane, 1985). By the era of Protestant expansion throughout what we now call the Third World, belief in the contemporary factuality of miracles had virtually disappeared from orthodox Protestantism. Neither in their own theological education, nor in that given to indigenous candidates for the ministry were those aspects of Christian tradition seriously considered. CSI clergymen with whom I discussed these questions could recall no occasion during their training or subsequently as ordained pastors when issues of this kind were even raised within orthodox circles.

Fundamentalist doctrine confirms the existence of evil forces, thereby providing evidence both of satanic influences in the world, and the power of the Holy Spirit to defeat them. These themes emerge time and again in the various contexts where people meet to 'hear the word of God' as they put it. I want to dwell for a moment on such contexts, for they constitute an important site within which Protestants belonging to the main churches are addressed by fundamentalist discourses.

CELLS AND CRUSADES

The existence of 'prayer cells' is a widespread phenomenon in the Protestant world, and they are certainly evident in Madras. These informal groups, usually composed of persons who feel that Sunday worship alone is insufficient, constitute a self-selected religious elite, who meet regularly in each other's homes to pray, read the Bible, give 'witness' to their faith, and so on. Members of the CSI churches situated in the neighbourhoods of the lower class now take part in numerous rites organised by and around cell leaders with fundamentalist leanings. These attract not only adherents of different CSI congregations, but persons belonging to other orthodox denominations as well as to diffeent sectarian groups.

Such gatherings do not follow a precise pattern, but almost certainly include gospel songs, and a 'strong message', as the Bible-based, heavily didactic and exhortative sermon is termed. There is ample scope for individual expression and enthusiasm, through impromptu prayer, Bible readings, exegesis, and personal testimonials. Considerable time is also given to the detailed submission by participants of their personal problems. While women are preponderant among attenders, and certainly among those volunteering problems for the group's attention and concern, it is not only their own individual difficulties which they present, but their husbands' and children's as well. Generally, these are dealt with by a patient and sympathetic hearing, and collective prayer. Persons whose wishes have been fulfilled, or whose troubles resolved, 'witness' to the Lord's grace and, more especially, to the power of the Holy Spirit.

Those who organise and lead such groups invariably claim one or more gifts of the Holy Spirit, and almost certainly the gift of healing. This involves the ability to diagnose the causes of affliction – which can mean anything from infertility to cancer, from unemployment to examination failure – and to prescribe suitable remedies, which may include intensive fasting and prayer, or the imbibing of substances blessed in the name of Jesus. They also deal with the effects wrought by a plethora of maleficent human and superhuman agents who are identified as the sources of misfortune.

A few charismatic prophets earn a reputation beyond their own congregations, and attract followings from outside their immediate neighbourhoods. The more miraculous their achievements, the wider their notoriety. Some develop 'specialisations', that is, they become known for dealing effectively with particular kinds of problem: certain prophets in Madras are thought to have a singular gift for finding lost property, identifying thieves, exorcising spirits or even predicting whether a particular marriage proposal is likely to lead to a happy and successful union. Those who achieve supra-local fame do so because they are seen to stand above the innumerable local healers in terms of their charismatic powers. They are also acknowledged to be strong orators, able to hold an audience for (sometimes) hours at a time, to present the word of God in a compelling and convincing way.

There are a handful of prophets whose reputations extend throughout the city and even beyond, in certain cases to other parts of the world (for example, south east Asia, Sri Lanka) where there are large numbers of Tamil-speakers. Though the core of their adherents may be found in a particular congregation, their popularity ensures a much more widely based support. Some in fact do not have an established congregation at all, and are therefore not closely associated with any particular sectarian organisation, though the ideology they foster is no less fundamentalist.

The attainment of this level of recognition requires a strong public persona, one which is not simply established in the context of regular interaction with, and validated in terms of experiences within, a small group of followers. The achievement of such a status seems to require evidence of a special and ongoing relationship with the divine. Because such prophets are removed to a very great extent from those who seek their assistance, their links with the supernatural must be reiterated continually. The biographies of these prophets, which become public knowledge through print as well as by word of mouth, emphasise not only the acquisition of charismata, but the dramatic circumstances in which these are obtained. The literature they issue recounts the life histories of the prophets, with special emphasis on miraculous events. What is also stressed is the contrast between their lives before and after receiving the Holy Spirit. In the period immediately prior to this experience these prophets portray themselves as being at the brink of spiritual if not physical death. (In the case of one prophet, the official biography has her actually summoned back from the dead). They write and speak of being plagued by incurable illness, long and hopeless unemployment, in a state of total despair and near suicide, and frequently engaged in a life full of 'sin' (drinking, smoking, cinema-going, and political activity). Conversion and the Holy Spirit changes their lives totally and brings them into regular contact with Jesus, who thereafter guides them in all their undertakings, and channels his power (*vellamai*) through them. Their reported struggles with satanic forces are hair-raising in the extreme, taking on mythic dimensions, and their victories all the more amazing for it.

The main contexts within which the public encounters these popular prophets are 'crusades' or 'conventions'. These take the form of open meetings which may extend over a period of several days, and which can attract thousands. Each evening includes entertainment by gospel singers, sermons by lesser personalities, and to crown the evening, the appearance of the prophet, who gives his or her 'message', and concludes with a healing session. At these gatherings, God is said to give them sight of the malignant forces at large in the audience, and the drama of the occasion seldom fails to produce cures and converts, demonstrating again and again the power of the Holy Spirit (and of course, of the prophet). There is usually a hierarchy of assistants on hand, trained by the prophet, to deal with those individuals who may, while attending a meeting, undergo such an experience.[4]

The most successful prophets travel throughout the south, and increasingly to other parts of Asia, where the local Tamil communities organise crusades. The best-known charismatic in south India has established an organisation to produce and distribute his sermons and songs on tapes, using sophisticated electronic equipment imported from Japan and the west. It deals with upwards of 500 letters daily (usually asking for help and advice), produces a monthly magazine, and runs a 24-hour a day telephone service which, in reply to the supplicant's stated problem, plays an appropriate recording of the prophet's voice.

THE CHALLENGE OF CHARISMA

Charisma, as Weber (1964) pointed out, challenges orthodoxy. As Msgr Cauchon, the Bishop of Beauvais in Shaw's *Saint Joan* puts it: 'The church's accumulated wisdom and knowledge and experience, its council of learned, venerable pious men, are thrust into the kennel by every ignorant labourer or dairymaid whom the devil can puff up with the monstrous self-conceit of being directly inspired from heaven...' (Shaw, 1946, p. 95). Few topics have been as vigorously debated in the sociological literature as charisma. Weber applied the term to leaders whose authority rests upon the recognition in him, by his followers, of 'supernatural, superhuman, or at least specifically exceptional powers or qualities ... regarded as of divine origin...' (1964, pp. 358–9). He understood charisma as non-institutional, even anti-institutional: the prophet is seen as the ideal opponent of hierocratic institutions.[5] While Berger (1963), Worsley (1970), Kiernan (1982) and others have challenged and qualified certain of Weber's views and emphases, his general statement still has a wide credibility, and can certainly be applied to the situation I have been describing.

In the Madras Protestant context the charismatic prophet threatens to undermine ecclesiastical structures based on an authoritative, episcopally ordained ministry. The majority of those who are members of the CSI readily compare their priests – 'the bishop's employees', as I have often heard them called – with the prophets who are, in their view, especially chosen by God to do his work. An explicit contrast is drawn between the kinds of knowledge invested in these two figures. Protestants from the orthodox churches who flock in their hundreds and thousands to hear the word of God from the prophets frequently stress how awesome are the insights conferred by the Holy Spirit as against the insignificance of the formal theological training undergone by their own priesthood. They are quick to note that no education, birth (caste) or gender qualifications are necessary for divine selection, not even a Christian commitment. Indeed, if any particular set of qualities appears to count more than anything else, it is – as the public biographies of the prophets suggest – poverty, unhappiness, despair, even a life of sin and godlessness. The appropriation of prophecy by the disprivileged and the dominated within the Protestant community is evident. The strong representation of women among the category of charismatics also illustrates the careful separation made between these two forms of knowledge. The acceptance of a male monopoly within the orthodox clergy contrasts sharply with the gender blindness exhibited by those who seek prophetic inspiration or assistance. The very people who submit themselves to and sing the praises of a female charismatic might oppose, with equal ardour, the ordination of women in the church.

In so far as the gifts of the Holy Spirit – especially those which bestow miraculous competences – remain outside the control of the institutional churches, they constitute an insidious threat to the dominant element within the Protestant fold. The miracle is, after all, a manifestation of power on the part of individuals who are not fitted by their place in the social order, nor designated by human authority, to hold and exercise it. Gilsenan notes how, in a different (Muslim) context, the miracle becomes a 'weapon or refuge of the dominated, an essential part of the discourse, hopes, expectancies and creations of the poor' (1982, p. 77). It is no surprise that Christian miracles have for so many centuries been denied by the orthodox churches through being consigned to the age of Christ and the Apostles.

The European missionaries and their indigenous successors in the mainline churches have all along been hostile to the beliefs held by the majority of people – Christian and Hindu alike – regarding the aetiology of affliction, as well as to the fundamentalists and their thaumaturgical solutions to these problems. Until quite recently those found associating with the handful of fundamentalist groups in the city were threatened with excommunication. The post-Independence ecumenical church has been generally contemptuous of the fundamentalist enterprise. Prophets have been constantly ridiculed, stigmatised, denied CSI pulpits, or even the use of church grounds for their meetings. The dominant elements within the Protestant community speak disdainfully of their less-privileged co-religionists who 'chase miracles'. The well-educated, well-to-do, well-connected and well-employed on the whole regard fundamentalist views as the 'superstitions' of the ignorant. The Protestant middle class does not see popular beliefs about affliction as a coherent and authentic system of knowledge. It is, rather, a regrettable, if understandable, failure due mainly to ignorance on the part of the uneducated masses, to comprehend and accept a religious world-view based, like their own, on 'rationality'. They see this 'superstition' as clear evidence of irrational thinking. Popular notions about misfortune therefore constitute the people who hold them as backward and subordinate.

DISCUSSION AND CONCLUSION

In the context of a Christian population characterised for several decades by growing economic and social divisions, the privileged minority has, through its control of ecclesiastical structures, effectively determined what was to be the dominant theological emphasis. The social gospel, which the early twentieth-century missionaries introduced to south India, has remained the principal doctrine in the post-Independence indigenous church, and the favoured discourse of the dominant section within the community. But for the majority of ordinary Protestants, to whom this gospel has no appeal, it is a precept which is simply 'unconvincing, despite [its] authoritative source and stamp' (Turton, 1984, p. 64). For some years they have pursued a sober, exclusive, devout and pietistic Bible-based faith, one, moreover, which maintains a firm trust in the literal truth of scripture, and refuses to compromise with those who have not accepted its message. This is the legacy of their nineteenth-century conservative evangelical missionary forebears, a kind of religiosity which Barr (1977) would regard as 'fundamentalist'.

During the last two decades there has been a dramatic explosion of interest in charismatic forms of Christianity, in south India as in many parts of the Third World. This 'new fundamentalism' has, in large part, been encouraged and funded by American organisations, and may be seen as part of a global Cold War strategy. The spread of such ideas and practices in Madras, however, has also coincided with a large-scale influx of migrants, rapid industrial growth followed soon after by stagnation and retrenchment, and the consequent sharpening of class polarisation within the Protestant community as within the city's population at large. While remaining firmly planted in the CSI, those belonging to the congregations of the lower class increasingly participate in the prayer cells organised by local evangelists and healers, where enthusiasm, emotion and direct communication with the divine prevail in place of the liturgical coolness and priestly mediations of the orthodox congregations. They also flock to the crusades of the popular prophets who claim to heal with the power of the Holy Spirit.

Protestant fundamentalism in urban south India, therefore, must first of all be seen as a historical category, in the sense that it has emerged in the context of particular social and political circumstances, though this is not to suggest that it can or should be explained entirely by them. It is defined, moreover, in terms of its opposite: the reformism and modernism of liberal theology and its social gospel, which are seen to challenge Biblical veracity in the most profound way. Scripturalism, however, is not all of a kind, and does not necessarily imply exegetical uniformity. An emphasis on different Biblical doctrines by conservative evangelicals, on the one hand, and those who stress the charismata, on the other, identifies quite distinct varieties of fundamentalism. The charismatics accommodate the principle tenets of conservative evangelicalism, but revive and focus on a particular 'essential' of Protestant dogma, namely the authenticity of Christian miracles. This canon has obvious affinities with widely-held popular ideas – among both Christians and Hindus – concerning the nature of affliction, and the means of dealing with it.

Certain of these 'fundamentals', it might be noted, appear to contradict, or, at any rate, sit uneasily alongside one another. For example, a predisposition to perceive the 'world', the mundane experiences of everyday life, as a domain set apart from and potentially contaminating to the spiritual domain, confronts an outlook which differentiates little between the domains, so that many human and superhuman agents (for example, sorcerers and *peey*) continually cross the dividing line and partake of both. The Bible, as Hollenweger points out, 'does not speak in terms of a sphere of nature, governed by natural laws, and a sphere of the Spirit, governed by supernatural laws...' (1972, p. 373). Again, while one set of views may be seen as an ideology demanding acceptance of personal responsibility for adversity – its 'interiorisation' (Taylor, 1985) – the other displaces helplessness in the face of suffering by projecting it on to external mystical beings. But the contradiction is never resolved, because it is not perceived as such and because it does not and is not allowed to emerge so starkly. This is itself partly attributable to the constant negation of popular ideas and practices relating to affliction on the part first of missionaries and later the indigenous church and community leadership.

The manner in which certain kinds of knowledge are disqualified by being labelled 'superstitious' or 'irrational' encourages us to move away from a primary concern with core doctrines towards a more careful consideration of how 'truth' is produced and contended for. In the context we have been considering the emergence and popularity of charismatic forms of Christianity cannot be adequately understood without taking into account the exercise of and resistance to power, which concerns appropriate religious views and observances no less than scarce jobs and control of property. While there can never be a wholly autonomous popular knowledge which 'lies outside the field of force of the relations of cultural power and domination' (Hall, 1981, p. 232), there are cultural (including religious) formations which may be seen to represent the perceptions, outlooks and ways of acting upon the world of those excluded from circles of privilege. The popular version may emerge as a somewhat mediated rendering of the dominant mode, which is how we might see the strongly pietistic, conservative evangelical Protestantism brought to south India by the European missionaries, and which still largely characterises the religious predilections of the majority in post-independence Madras. Or, it can express the more authentic experience of the disprivileged majority, which is how I would interpret the new fundamentalism. This movement is frequently portrayed by its proponents, I think accurately, as a counter-theology, or, in the wider sense, a counter-culture. It represents an instance of what Foucault terms an 'insurrection of subjugated knowledges' – popular knowledges which have been muted and downgraded – and through whose reappearance 'criticism performs its work' (1980, pp. 81–2). After all, it accords with and authenticates widely-held theodicies, and offers true believers a way of confronting and overcoming the affliction in their lives. While radical theologians and Christian activists may, with some justice, see the movement as an American-inspired attempt to *defuse* popular protest, paradoxically, in the local context, it may be read as a form of resistance to the dominant minority and the dominant theology within the church and community.

Notes

The fieldwork on which this chapter is based was supported by the School of Oriental and African Studies, to which I here express my gratitude. I am also indebted to Pat Caplan, who read and offered many helpful comments on an earlier draft.

1. Bruce, in this volume (Chapter 9) offers a slightly different version of the 'origins' of the term.
2. To its critics in the church's radical wing, the social gospel is a form of institutional philanthropy which does not seriously challenge the existing social hierarchy.
3. In 1980, Protestant leaders in Madras met with representatives of the Tamil Nadu branch of the RSS, a militant Hindu organisation, to hear and examine 'the impressions and grievances [of] influential Hindus concerning the work and life of the Christian Church in India' (*Christian Focus*, 15 July 1980).
4. The evangelical potential of this demonstration is overtly acknowledged in fundamentalist writings and statements. 'The people who blame most sickness on evil powers', writes one historian of Pentecostalism,

   do not find any difficulty in believing that [the Christian] God is the One who has the supernatural power and that He can and will help sick people. Divine healing campaigns will attract many people ... [and] when people get healing ... some of them accept Christ as their personal saviour. The divine healing ministry has helped the growth of the Pentecostal churches all over the world. (George, 1975, p. 54)

5. This opposition is, of course, not confined to the Judeo-Christian context. Berreman (1964) noted the distinction in Hindu villages between the Brahmin, a religious conservative, operating within prescribed textual and traditional constraints, and the shaman, who plays a more creative and innovatory role.

References

Barr, J. (1977), *Fundamentalism* (London: SCM Press).
Berger, P. (1963), 'Charisma and religious innovation: the social location of Israelite prophecy', *Amer. Soc. Rev.*, 28, pp. 940–50.
Berreman, G. D. (1964), 'Brahmins and shamans in Pahari religion', *J. Asian. Stud.*, 23, pp. 53–69.

Caldwell, R. (1886), 'On demonolatry in southern India', *Journ. Anth. Soc. Bombay,*, 2, pp. 91–105.

Caplan, L. (1985), 'The popular culture of evil in urban south India', in D. J. Parkin (ed.), *The Anthropology of Evil* (Oxford: Basil Blackwell).

Clarke, S. (1980), *Let the Indian Church be Indian* (Madras: Christian Literature Society).

Daniel, J. (1980), *Another Daniel* (Madras: The Laymen's Evangelical Fellowship).

David, I. (1983), *God's Messengers: Reformed Church in America Missionaries in South India, 1839–1938*, Doctor of Theology Thesis, Lutheran School of Theology, Chicago.

Foucault, M. (1980), *Power/Knowledge: Selected Interviews and other Writings 1972–1977* (ed. C. Gordon) (Brighton: Harvester).

George, T. C. (1975), *The Growth of Pentecostal Churches in South India*, M. A. thesis in Missiology, Fuller Theological Seminary, California.

Gilsenan, M. (1982), *Recognizing Islam: an Anthropologist's Introduction* (London: Croom Helm).

Hall, S. (1981), 'Notes on deconstructing "the popular"', in R. Samuel (ed.) *People's History and Socialist Theory* (London: Routledge & Kegan Paul).

Hill, C. (1983), 'Science and magic in seventeenth-century England', in R. Samuel and G. Stedman Jones (eds), *Culture, Ideology, and Politics* (London: Routledge & Kegan Paul).

Hollenweger, W. J. (1972), *The Pentecostals* (London: SCM Press).

Kiernan, J. P. (1982), 'Authority and enthusiasm: the organization of religious experience in Zulu Zionist churches', in J. Davis (ed.), *Religious Organization and Religious Experience* (London: Academic).

Kurien, G. (1981), *Mission and Proclamation: the Church in India Today and other pieces* (Madras: Christian Literature Society).

Macfarlane, A. (1985), 'The root of all evil', in D. J. Parkin (ed.) *The Anthropology of Evil* (Oxford: Basil Blackwell).

Marsden, G. (1980), *Fundamentalism and American Culture: the Shaping of Twentieth-century Evangelicalism 1870–1925* (Oxford University Press).

Neill, S. (1964), *A History of Christian Missions* (London: Penguin).

Niebuhr, H. R. (1937), 'Fundamentalism', *Encycl. Soc. Sc.*, 6, pp. 526–7.

Norman, E. (1981), Christianity in the Southern Hemisphere: the Churches in Latin America and South Africa (Oxford: Clarendon).

Sandeen, E. (1970), *The Roots of Fundamentalism: British and American Millenarianism 1800–1930* (London: University of Chicago Press).

Sargunam, E. (1974), *Multiplying Churches in Modern India* (Madras: Evangelical Church of India).

Sharpe, E. (1965), *Not to Destroy but to Fulfil: the Contribution of J. N. Farquhar to Protestant Missionary Thought in India before 1914* (Uppsala: Gleerup).

Shaw, B. (1946), *Saint Joan* (London: Penguin).

Taylor, D. (1985) 'Theological thoughts about evil', in D. J. Parkin (ed.), *The Anthropology of Evil* (Oxford: Basil Blackwell).

Turton, A. (1984), 'Limits of ideological domination and the formation of social consciousness', in A. Turton and S. Tanabe (eds), *History and Peasant Consciousness in South East Asia* (Osaka: National Museum of Ethnology).

Weber, M. (1964), *The Theory of Social and Economic Organization* (London: Collier-Macmillan).

Wilson, B. (1973), *Magic and the Millenium* (London: Paladin).

Worsley, P. (1970), *The Trumpet Shall Sound: a Study of 'Cargo Cults' in Melanesia* (London: Paladin).

9 The Moral Majority: the Politics of Fundamentalism in Secular Society
Steve Bruce

INTRODUCTION

The features of a social movement which will be isolated for description and explanation must obviously represent the more general interests of the analyst. In this account of the new Christian right (NCR) in America I will identify some general problems confronting any movement which seeks to reintroduce the sacred into the political culture of a largely secular society.[1] I will briefly describe the formation of the socio-religious culture of the United States and then show what forces have led to the recent politicisation of American fundamentalists before going on to argue that the very structure which permitted fundamentalism to survive and flourish in certain regions now creates major motivational problems for the political interventions of the NCR.[2]

FORMAL SECULARISATION AND REGIONAL RELIGIOSITY

The United States of America was once a Protestant country: 'colonial religion generally derived from the tenets of the Protestant Reformation' (Carroll and Noble, 1982, p. 62). Many of the settlers were self-consciously Protestant, having moved to the new country so that they could practise their dissenting religion without hindrance. Those who did not see themselves as persecuted saints were nevertheless from Protestant cultures. As late as 1830 only some 300 000 people (about 3 per cent of the population) were Roman Catholic (ibid., p. 179). That most early Americans were not Roman Catholic did not, however, produce a homogenous religious culture, as the diverse ethnic origins of the settlers were reproduced on American soil:

> The tendency to form ethnic enclaves, which was the natural consequence of group migration and of the economic and geographical forces that determined routes of settlement, was especially marked among the Germans and the Scotch–Irish ... [T]he most striking instance of this was in Pennsylvania where German and Scotch–Irish settlers lived in communities as completely isolated from each other as they were from English-speaking communities ... As a result there were such contrasts in language, religion, customs, architecture and agricultural methods between the two regions that they could plausibly be compared with neighbouring states in central Europe. (M. A. Jones, 1960, p. 49)

The establishment of a federal decentralised system of government had a lot to do with the experience of colonial status and a desire to avoid heavy-handed rule, but it also provided a way of accommodating the diversity of the early American people. In the regions in which they were strong, each religio-ethnic group could maintain its own culture and society with little regard for what others did elsewhere.

In the period from 1685 to 1795, ethnic discord resulted from competition between various groups of early settlers. From the 1830s one sees a different sort of conflict with the long-established settlers uniting as 'native Americans' in opposition to the great waves of Roman Catholic migration from Ireland and Southern Europe. Many 'nativists' doubted the loyalty of Catholics: while they owed their primary allegiance to the Pope of Rome could they be good Americans? Anti-immigrant sentiment was channelled into a number of political movements. In the 1850s the American (or 'Know Nothing') Party wanted restrictions on immigration and the curtailment of the citizenship rights of Catholics. Similar points appeared in the platform of the American Protective Association in the 1890s (Lipset and Raab, 1978, pp. 79–82), and the first revival of the Ku Klux Klan in the 1920s was more concerned with Catholics than with blacks: 'there was a general feeling that the election of every additional Catholic to public office would hasten the time when our government would be turned over to a foreign Pope' (Louks, 1936, p. 106).

These nativist movements were not particularly successful. They rose rapidly in periods when the major parties were weak and collapsed as abruptly when their more obviously popular measures were taken over and presented in more moderate form by the major parties. Although there remained a subtle but enduring anti-Catholicism which, for example, prevented Al Smith winning the presidency in

1928, and which was only buried with the election of J. F. Kennedy in 1960, by and large American national life has managed to operate a separation of church and state, of religion and politics. At nation-state level there has remained a considerable amount of 'God talk' and what Bellah (1967) and others have called 'civil religion' but the need for this religion to offend nobody meant that it had so little content as to have few behavioural consequences. However, each religio-ethnic group was able to maintain its own religious culture at town, county, and, in some cases, state level (Lipset, 1964).

FUNDAMENTALISM, ISOLATION AND PRESSURE FROM THE CENTRE

'Fundamentalism' is a religious and cultural movement which takes its name from a series of pamphlets published between 1910 and 1912 (Marsden, 1980; see also the genealogy of fundamentalism in Caplan, this volume, Chapter 8) which articulated a reaction to two powerful tendencies in the major Protestant denominations. The first was the rationalising of the faith. Liberal theology and the 'higher criticism' school of Biblical studies were working together to reduce the supernatural and miraculous elements of Christianity in order to appeal to what was taken to be the mind of the modern scientific world. The second and related trend was the replacement of a concern with personal salvation and righteousness by a desire to improve the social and political world. Evangelical Protestants believed that if individuals were 'saved', the world inadvertently improved. The 'social gospel' preachers stood this on its head to argue that the improvement of the social world would cause people to become better and, for those who still used the language of conversion, would increase receptivity to the gospel.

The fundamentalists were those who refused to accept the new thinking. They continued to insist that the Bible was the word of God, that miracles really happened, that unless one had experienced religious conversion one was destined for an actual hell, and so on. In the first stage of the reaction there were fundamentalists in all the denominations (although there were proportionally fewer in those denominations – Episcopalian, Presbyterian and Congregationalist – which recruited primarily from the upper classes). As it became clear that the majority of Protestants would not be diverted from their apostate ways, the fundamentalists withdrew to form their own conservative Protestant denominations.

They did not stop at church formation. They built schools, colleges and even a liberal arts university. They produced their own papers and magazines. They built radio stations and when the technology presented itself, they were quick to appreciate the potential of television. They made programmes and paid companies to air them. Finally they created their own networks.

In sociological terms, fundamentalists were working to create social institutions which would permit them to reproduce their own culture sheltered from modernising influences. The problem was that such boundary maintenance activity depended on a weak (or benign) federal government which would permit the regions (and pockets of fundamentalists more centrally located) to go their own way. Although it was clearly the intention of the drafters of the Constitution that the central government should be subordinate to the states, the whole thrust of modernisation has been towards an active and powerful centre. An early and traumatic example of the centre's unwillingness to permit the peripheries to follow their own interests was the civil war (which actually produced far less change in the South than had been intended). By the 1950s and 1960s it was not the army but the Supreme Court and the Congress which were imposing liberal and cosmopolitan values on the South. Without multiplying examples one can characterise the last hundred years as a period in which regional autonomy has gradually been eroded by federal government intervention on issues ranging from spending on public works and civil rights to the drawing of constituency boundaries.[3] At the same time the distinctiveness of regional culture has been threatened by the growth of national corporations, the population movements caused by four wars, and the gradual concentration of the media. Putting it simply, the 'Bible Belt' has been penetrated by cosmopolitan culture. The South has oil, cheap labour and sun, the heavy industries of the North are in decline, and people are moving into the South.

If the gradual ending of the isolation which was an important part of the success of fundamentalism is one source of concern to fundamentalists, another is the increasing 'permissiveness' of the culture from which they can no longer remain isolated. Although it is fashionable for liberals to characterise the NCR as 'extremists', it is worth remembering that the world they wish to recreate was the world of most Americans as little as thirty years ago. Where once two-thirds of the states' legislatures were willing to vote for prohibition, there is now talk of legalising marijuana. Where once divorce brought considerable social stigma, there are now single parent, lesbian and male homosexual 'families'. In what was once 'one nation under God', public prayer is no longer permitted in public schools.

EXPLAINING SOCIAL MOVEMENTS

There is not space here for a comprehensive review of competing explanations for social movements such as the NCR. My main interest in this chapter is in examining the problems of *sustaining* involvement in the NCR, rather than explaining the genesis of the movement, but I do want very briefly to consider two common, and to my mind flawed, analyses. The first, exemplified by Gusfield's account of the temperance movement, is the 'status defence' model. It supposes that rural and small town Anglo-Saxon Protestants engaged in symbolic crusades (so-called by the followers of this mode of explanation to set them apart from 'real', that is, economic or political crusades) in order to defend, not their culture, but their status (Gusfield, 1963). Unable to do anything about what really bothered them – their loss of status and power to the cities and the Catholics and other low status groups who inhabited them – they directed their protests against what they saw as the erosion of their distinctive culture. The main problems with this argument are that (a) it is rarely demonstrated that the supporters of such movements do share a common status, and (b) no thought is given to the problem of justifying the rejection of the actors' own accounts of their motivation and the replacement of such accounts by those of the sociologist.[4]

A solution to the problem of moral reformers not sharing a common status which they could be presented as defending is to argue that they are driven by common *inconsistencies* of status.

> The status inconsistency perspective can be traced to Lenski's ... proposal that individuals who have discrepant or inconsistent ranks on status dimensions, e.g. high educational achievement and low occupational attainment, may be subject to discontent and stress that is reduced by compensatory attitudes or mitigating behaviors.
>
> (Simpson, 1985, p. 56)

But like the status defence account, the inconsistency theory has been consistently failed by the evidence. The amount of action which can be explained by inconsistencies between dimensions of status is almost always *less* than the amount which can be explained by any particular status dimension on its own. Higher education and a high status occupation are generally correlated with liberal attitudes; less education and lower occupational status are linked with conservatism. Extensive use of statistical techniques, the sophistication of which is well beyond the quality of the original survey data, has so far either failed to produce results or has produced contradictory ones: Zurcher *et al.* (1971) believe that status inconsistency produces anti-pornography crusaders while Simpson claims that inconsistency 'intensifies liberal rather than conservative responses' (1985, p. 160).

My reading of the research is that beliefs are caused by culture. The best predictor of support for NCR positions is conservative Protestantism. The NCR is a movement of *cultural* defence (Wallis, 1979, pp. 92–104). To return to the brief observations about regionalism, the potential for a new Christian right movement was created by the combination of (a) increased encroachment by the cultural and political centre into the regions and (b) increased 'permissiveness' of that centre. Many fundamentalists felt that their way of life was under threat.

THE RISE OF THE MORAL MAJORITY

The constituency may have been there but the creation of the NCR owed a great deal to three conservative strategists who were not themselves fundamentalists.[5] Richard Viguerie, Paul Weyrich and Howard Phillips were professional conservative political organisers who differed from other more traditional conservatives in seeing the potential of a right-wing movement based, not in the first place around the traditional issues of the economy and foreign policy, but on social and moral issues. With their desire to mobilise conservatives irrespective of party affiliation, they readily appreciated the value of the fundamentalist milieu and in 1979 they encouraged Jerry Falwell, a television evangelist from Lynchburg, Virginia, to lead an organisation which they called the Moral Majority. The Moral Majority became one of the best known of a number of overlapping and interlinked organisations, some of which, like Christian Voice, were also specifically 'Christian' while others such as Phyllis Schlafly's Eagle Forum, Stop ERA (the equal rights for women amendment) and Jessie Helms's Congressional Club were more 'secular' in their conservatism. I will not take time here to observe scrupulously the differences between various NCR organisations, but will regard the Moral Majority Inc. as representative of them.[6]

The Moral Majority and other NCR organisations work on a number of fronts. They sensitise conservative Christians to political issues and their need to get involved. America is portrayed as a society which was great while it obeyed God's commands but which is being undermined by godless 'secular humanists' who control Washington, the big corporations and the media. America will become great again when the liberals and atheists are driven out of the Temple. This is the message which Falwell and other right-wing evangelists offer from their television pulpits and their direct mailing computers. The NCR also seeks to promote its views by recruiting pastors to communicate this vision to their congregations. They are invited to rallies where the need for involvement is explained, encouraged to preach from their pulpits on the need for activism, and taught how to take such practical action as organising voter registration. This is vital. In Britain everyone is registered to vote. In America one has to go out of one's way to call at a certain office at certain times of the day. In the South the rules were designed to discourage blacks from voting, but until the late 1970s fundamentalists had a similarly low rate of registration.

Another part of the NCR campaign has been to 'target' liberal candidates in elections and make public their records on votes which can be construed as 'moral' or 'family' issues. Those legislators who have voted the 'wrong' way on school prayer, funding for abortion clinics, the ERA (and other issues such as defence spending, the renegotiation of the Panama canal treaty, gun control and so forth which seem at best tangentially related to NCR interests) are portrayed as being anti-family, anti-America and anti-God.

THE IMPACT OF THE MORAL MAJORITY

It is difficult to assess accurately the impact of the NCR. It is certainly the case that it raised a lot of money and spent it campaigning against liberal candidates and liberal positions, and registered many new voters. It is also the case that four leading liberal senators were defeated in the 1980 elections but, as Lipset and Raab (1981) have shown, the swing against these Democrats was the same as the swing against the Democratic Party in states where the NCR was not active in targeting and, particularly in the case of George McGovern in South Dakota, the liberals in question were well known to be out of step with their constituents before the NCR made them targets. According to Johnson & Tamney's survey of Middletown 'the Christian right had virtually no influence at all' on how people were going to vote in the 1980 Presidential election (1982, p. 128). On the other hand, Miller and Wattenberg (1984), pp. 300–12) claimed a strong connection between religious fundamentalism and having voted for Reagan. The question of impact is complex. It may well be that NCR organisations have had no discernible impact on voting behaviour and yet have still had considerable influence in giving a new confidence and respectability to conservative social and moral positions.[7] My own feeling is that analysts have been far too willing to take at face-value the claims made by the NCR. We know that Falwell has previously exaggerated the audience for his 'Old Time Gospel Hour' television show (Hadden and Swann, 1981, p. 47). Apart from the odd quaint 'traveller's tale', the fundamentalists of the Bible Belt had been ignored by the media since the 1950s. When the cosmopolitan journalists 'rediscovered' fundamentalism, they over-reacted. It will be some time before the detailed research necessary to make balanced judgements is complete.

WHAT DOES THE MORAL MAJORITY WANT?

> Moral Majority Inc. is made up of millions of Americans, including ministers, priests and rabbis, who are deeply concerned about the moral decline of our nation, and who are sick and tired of the way many amoral and secular humanists and other liberals are destroying the traditional family and moral values on which our nation was built. (Moral Majority brochure, c. 1983).

The aspirations of the Moral Majority can readily be listed, although it is sometimes difficult to draw the line between specifically NCR desires and the ambitions of other conservatives. Moral Majoritarians are against abortion and pro-traditional family, by which they mean that, while they would not deny basic civil rights to homosexuals, they do not accept homosexuality as a legitimate alternative 'life-style'. They want to maintain the traditional sexual division of labour and oppose the ERA. They want public prayer back in public schools and they want changes in the tax laws to make it less expensive for parents to send their children to private Christian schools. They want school books to be vetted so they do not promote 'secular humanism' and they want the Genesis story of the Old Testament to be taught as a plausible alternative to evolution as an account of the origins of life. In addition, the Moral Majority shares the secular conservatives' desire for heavy defence spending, an aggressive foreign policy, the unrestricted right to own guns, a curbing of trade unions, the dismantling of business legislation, a reduction in welfare spending, and an end to 'affirmative action' programmes for ethnic minorities; in brief, either 'less' government or a more conservative government.

Falwell denies that the Moral Majority is a 'political' organisation. Given that it and other NCR organisations support and denounce candidates in elections, this claim can be dismissed, although the fact that it is made shows one of the problems the NCR has in legitimating its action in a society in which religion and politics are supposed to remain separate. Falwell also denies that the Moral Majority is a religious organisation.[8] It is certainly the case that its aims, although generated by a particular religious culture, are promoted as if they could be isolated from the base. By 'religious' Falwell means 'pertaining to salvational knowledge' and it is his great hope that the Moral Majority is not a religious organisation for, if it were, it would be restricted to the population of Baptist fundamentalists. For reasons which I will make clear in a moment, the NCR needs to transcend any particular denominational identity.

To date, the grassroots support for NCR activity is still predominantly southern Baptist fundamentalist. This does not mean that it rests on the congregations of the Southern Baptist Convention, many of which are quite liberal. Although some Southern Baptist pastors and more of their members are supporters of the NCR, the strongest support for the movement comes from those Baptists loosely grouped in a number of self-consciously 'fundamentalist' associations. A survey of reactions to the Moral Majority in a northern city showed that more than a third of the 'ardent supporters' had been raised in the South and a similar proportion were some variety of Baptist (Buell, 1983, p. 22). By 1980 there were substantial Moral Majority chapters in 18 states and most of these were in the South or South-West.

Although the leaders of NCR organisations emphasise their support from Jews and Catholics, their desire for a broad-based movement is not reflected in the membership. In a survey of Moral Majority support in the Dallas–Fort Worth area, only 10 of 110 Catholics were positive towards the movement and 74 per cent of the Jews were hostile (Shupe and Stacey, 1982, p. 41). This narrow denominational base is not surprising. The 'holy roller' gospel shows were a key element in the mobilisation of support. Moral Majority Inc. was launched with funds raised by an appeal mailed to all those viewers who had given funds to Falwell's Old Time Gospel Hour and many of the organisation's cadres were recruited through Falwell's contacts in the Baptist Bible Fellowship and the Southwide Baptist Fellowship. In 1984 these two associations were joined by the World Baptist Fellowship and the General Association of Regular Baptist Churches in an Easter convention in Washington which pressed the government for more conservative moral legislation.[9]

There are considerable obstacles to non-Protestant conservatives becoming involved. Catholics share the NCR position on abortion and tax relief for Christian schools but they have not forgotten that some NCR activists were, and perhaps still are, members of the initially anti-Catholic Ku Klux Klan, or that at the end of the last century fundamentalists were vocal opponents of separate Catholic schools. Conservative Jews are in a similar position. However acceptable the present NCR leadership's positions on Zionism, American fundamentalists and right-wing political activists have a history of anti-semitism. This sort of problem is even more pressing in the case of black Baptists who are conservative in theology, morals and on many social and political attitudes and hence who should be natural recruits for the NCR, but who are conscious of the racist pasts of many of the people associated with NCR organisations. Senators Thurmond and Helms, while never as openly obstructive as Governor George Wallace, did nothing to promote civil rights. Helms's proposed solution to the school prayer controversy is to permit individual states to make their own decisions. At a press conference in 1983 when he was promoting this notion he used the phrase 'states rights': the old code for the Southern states' resistance to civil rights legislation. Black Baptists, who would be happy to have public prayer in schools, are unwilling to work to achieve that goal in alliance with conservative whites they suspect of being at heart racist.

But even without these specific fears, the NCR has limited appeal to anyone outside the WASP world because its arcadia – the one nation under God which was blessed – is white and Protestant. There are no Catholics, Jews or blacks in NCR mythology.

THE LIMITS OF REGIONALISM

One might wonder why the fundamentalists want to recruit Catholics and Jews. The answer is that without such support, they are powerless beyond the boundaries of their own regions. Furthermore the things which concern the NCR are fundamental issues of a sort which will normally have to be judged by the Supreme Court and Congress. Thus, even when they can command a majority in their own states and counties, the fundamentalists can be over-ruled. Unless they choose to retire, the members of the Supreme Court are appointed, by the President, for life. Hence the importance of the Presidency for setting the tone for a generation of legal decisions. Of course, the judges are not oblivious to public opinion but it is really only such major shifts as can be recognised in, for example, the passage of successful legislation in the federal (as opposed to the states') legislature, which would lead the Supreme Court to consider a significant change in its position on any of the issues which concern the NCR. Essentially, the fundamentalists can only effect the changes they desire if they are politically successful at federal level and that requires that they form alliances with other conservative groups.

Such a strategy requires a number of attitudes and it is the implications of these for sustaining commitment which I wish to explore.

The NCR needs to *compartmentalise* and keep separate religion and the moral crusades which the religion has produced. Although fundamentalists are opposed to abortion on religious grounds, they must be prepared to work with those who share their dislike for abortion but who do not share their religion. While this sort of compartmentalisation is typical of modern society it goes against the grain of fundamentalism which refuses to accept that religion can be kept in a box marked 'family' and 'Sunday'. While the leaders of the NCR seem to be able to compartmentalise, other fundamentalists such as those associated with Bob Jones University have been highly critical of those who, as they see it, preach morality without preaching the gospel. Bob Jones III went so far as to describe Falwell as 'the biggest threat to Christianity to come down the pike in a long time' (1980, p. 1).

Successful compartmentalisation is a threat to the commitment of grassroots supporters because they have been recruited to the movement through their religious ideology which, in order to make the movement effective, they are now supposed to lay to one side. The failure of the fundamentalists successfully to compartmentalise is an obstacle to the participation in the movement of conservative Catholics, Jews, Mormons and others, because on those occasions when the barriers break down, they are reminded of what the fundamentalists really think of them. For example, doubt is cast on Falwell's performance as leader of an organisation which claims to represent 'our shared Judeo-Christian tradition' when it is made known that in his Moral Majority manifesto he said 'If a person is not a Christian, he is inherently a failure' (1979, p. 62). The chairman of the New York state Moral Majority said: 'I love Jewish people deeply. God has given them talents He has not given others. They are His chosen people. Jews have a God-given ability to make money, almost a supernatural ability to make money ... They control the media, they control this city...' (quoted in Bouchier, 1982, p. 88).

The theologically orthodox position for fundamentalists was given by Bailey Smith, then President of the Southern Baptist Convention: 'It's interesting at great political rallies how you have a Protestant to pray, a Catholic to pray and then you have a Jew to pray. With all due respect to these dear people, my friends, God Almighty does not hear the prayer of a Jew' (quoted in Bouchier, 1982, p. 89). In order to work in alliance with other religious conservatives, the fundamentalists who form the vast bulk of the rank-and-file NCR must compartmentalise religion and politics. That is, they must accept the very social psychology which fundamentalism exists to oppose.

The problems of working with 'secular' conservatives can be described under the heading of *accommodation*. The NCR leadership has been embarrassed a number of times by their more enthusiastic supporters. Falwell disowned one chapter of the Moral Majority for picketing a bakery which allegedly produced 'sexually explicit' gingerbread men. Accommodation to the prevailing norms will increase secular conservative support but it will cause the grassroots to doubt the movement's orthodoxy. Individuals are already leaving, and a California chapter of the Moral Majority has seceded because the national organisation was becoming too 'liberal' (Lienesch, 1982, p. 418).

If religion and politics require different criteria for judging the acceptability of others and a difference in willingness to mute distinctive features of one's ideology in order to succeed, they are also distinguished by different notions about the *certainty of knowledge* and about *time-scales*.

Generally speaking, religion is about certainty. It is about knowing how to attain salvation and until the relatively recent rise of liberal versions of Christianity and Islam (and with the possible exception of the more philosophical forms of Buddhism) it has been about dogma. Fundamentalists are perfectly traditional in their belief that they have full assurance of being saved. In contrast, American politics are about fudging and compromise. Successful politicians are not dogmatic, even if they may be willing temporarily to appear committed to a dogma which looks like a vote winner. The American system with its balances and checks has been designed for inertia and most politicians are happiest when doing nothing because to do something will offend some group of voters or other. Without a strong party policy to blame for their actions, most American politicians are loath to be too closely identified with particular ideologies and positions. The result is considerable tension between the grassroots fundamentalists with their dogmatism and the more pragmatic, politically minded activists (especially those who work in the lobbies in Washington), and, for the fundamentalists, disappointment with the lack of clear commitment, even from those politicians who are supposed to be on their side.

One has similar differences of expectations in regard to time-scales. Fundamentalists have been mobilised by a combination of dramatic threats and promises. Unless America is turned around now, it will suffer God's wrath. If Christians get involved and 'we can get God back into the classrooms', as one NCR activist put the school prayer issue, 'then we can see an end to drug-taking and violence and teenage pregnancies and all that illiteracy. We will see an end to crime and my wife will be able to go downtown shopping in the evenings again'. Religious believers can think in these terms because they believe in an active creator God who can, if he wishes, change people and worlds. Experienced politicians know that not only does it take a long time to produce any significant change in public policy, but it takes even longer for policy change to produce effects, and then usually not the ones which were anticipated. Although it is a gross over-simplification, the point can be briefly made by contrasting the spheres of religion and politics as being characterised by, respectively, optimism and realism. The failure of many grassroots Moral Majoritarians to appreciate this has led to many becoming dissatisfied with six years of Reagan who, after all, was 'their President', and eight years of active campaigning which have produced no obvious change.

Compartmentalisation, accommodation and conflicting expectations are especially problematic because of the fragile nature of fundamentalists' commitment to politics. In contrast to the Protestants of Ulster or South Africa, who have a long history of involvement in political and ethnic conflict and whose religious ideology is a vital part of the dominant political ideologies, American fundamentalists have alternated between periods of pietistic retreat from the world and active involvement. It is not so long ago that Falwell himself preached against pastors being active in politics.[10] The novelty and precariousness of most fundamentalists' involvement in politics suggests that failure to 'turn America round' will send them back to their verandas, back into pietistic retreat, and will make the Bob Jones University position of preaching revival and leaving God to do the social and political work increasingly popular.

'WE WERE USED; JUST VOTE-FODDER FOR THE POLITICIANS'

Fundamentalists have not been slow to notice that their legislative agenda has not to date been shortened by success. The 1983 bill 'to strengthen the American family and to promote the virtues of family life through education, tax assistance and related measures', introduced in the House by Congressman Hansen and in the Senate by Paul Laxalt, covered such a diverse range of measures that it was bound to fail to pass the scrutiny of the House Committees on Armed Services, Education and Labor, the Judiciary and Ways and Means, and it did not make it to the floor of the House. But even narrower bills – such as those to permit school prayer – have failed, largely because conservative politicians could not unite behind a common measure. While Reagan made a lot of pro-NCR noises, saying that he thought the Genesis account should be presented in schools, that prayer should be permitted, and that he believed in the Apocalypse, he has so far failed to use his considerable personal influence to force conservative politicians to unite behind NCR legislation. This is in sharp contrast to his ability to make progress on conservative economic, foreign policy and defence initiatives. The conclusion that many grassroots fundamentalists are coming to is that their support was solicited by secular conservatives and that having delivered their funds and their votes, they have been neglected in favour of better established conservative interest groups.

CONCLUSION: RELIGIOUS POLITICS IN SECULAR SOCIETIES

I have argued that the NCR in America faces motivational problems of essentially two sorts: those which explain why groups other than

Protestant fundamentalists have been less than enthusiastic in their support, and those which suggest that many members of its core constituency will have trouble sustaining their involvement in their moral crusade. This second point is, for the moment, largely a prediction, although as early as 1983 I found enough signs of discontent among grassroots Moral Majoritarians in Virginia and South Carolina to feel confident that the next few years will produce evidence of declining membership and funding. I have presented the above argument in such a way as to make it clear that these problems are a natural result of the difficulties of engaging in religious politics in a pluralistic and secular society. Elsewhere I have discussed Protestant politics in Ulster and South Africa and offered a comparative analysis of Protestant politics in a variety of social and political contexts (Wallis and Bruce 1985; 1986). I will not repeat the details of those comparisons here but confine myself to some general concluding observations about religious politics in pluralistic settings. Leaving aside the Machiavellian interest of those secular conservatives who encouraged the creation of various NCR organisations, the NCR came into being largely because grassroots fundamentalists felt that their culture and life-styles were being threatened by an increasingly hostile and interventionist centre. They could either go further into sectarian retreat, modelling themselves after, for example, the Amish or the Doukhobors, and further isolate themselves from the modern world, or they could choose to fight back.[11] Fighting back brings with it the problem that in order to have any impact where it matters, in the centre, they must adopt some of the attitudes and practices of the very secular cosmopolitan culture which they wish to repel. In order to resist the incursions of the modern rational world, fundamentalists must act and think like members of that world.

Notes

The research which informs this analysis was funded by the Nuffield Foundation. I would like to record my gratitude to the Foundation and to the The Queen's University of Belfast which gave me sabbatical leave and permitted me to spend two months in 1983 in Virginia and South Carolina. I would also like to thank Professor Roy Wallis of the Queen's University for his comments on this and other related papers. As will be seen from the bibliography, we have collaborated on a number of related publications and his advice has played a major part in my thinking on religion and politics.

1. For reasons that should become clear I do not regard the common recourse to 'God talk' in American public life as evidence of serious religiosity. In order to accommodate the diverse religious traditions of the American people, the 'civil religion' has to be almost completely devoid of specific content. Like the 'established' status of the Church of England, unchallenged because it is irrelevant, the religious elements of public rhetoric are not to be equated with those religions which actually play a major part in patterns of action and world-views.

2. The ways in which the *structure* of the American political system permits well-organised minorities to achieve considerable local power and influence – and hence prompts moral crusades which intervene directly in electoral politics – are discussed in detail by Wallis and Bruce (1986, ch. 11).

3. Trivial as it may seem, central control over constituency boundaries is crucial because 'gerrymandering' has long been used by dominant groups as a technique for devaluing the votes of minorities. Since the extension of the franchise to blacks, there has been a running battle between the local Southern white elites and the federal government with the former doing everything possible to undermine the spirit of civil rights legislation. Gerrymandering has effectively been ended by a Supreme Court judgement on the maximum permitted variations in the size of constituencies.

4. Both the general problems of reductionist explanations in social science, and the weaknesses of these particular theories are discussed at length by Wallis and Bruce (1986, ch 2).

5. For general accounts of the rise of the NCR see Peele (1984), Crawford (1980) and Liebman and Wuthnow (1983).

6. Details of various NCR and 'new right' organisations are given in note 5 above and in Bouchier (1982). The reader with a serious interest in the links between various right-wing organisations and the previous careers of right-wing activists should locate copies of *Group Research Report*, which is published by Group Research Inc, 419 New Jersey Avenue SE, Washington DC 20003.

7. It is also the case that, for reasons discussed by Wallis and Bruce (1986, ch. 11), NCR groups have been most successful at the local level of school boards and county administration.

8. This ambiguity reflects both the abstract problems of defining and justifying 'moral crusades' which result from religious ideologies in a largely secular society, and the practical problems of maintaining tax deductible charity status.

9. The histories of these various groups are given by Melton (1978). Although membership data is always suspect, it might be useful to give some idea of the size of the various constituencies. The American population numbers around 224 million. Of those, about 197 million are Christian and 60 million are 'affiliated Protestants'. Of these some 59 million are 'evangelicals'. Perhaps 30 million of these people could be accurately described as 'fundamentalists' of whom the largest single block would be the fundamentalist wing (between two-thirds and three-quarters) of the Southern Baptist Convention which had a total of

14.2 million members in 1970 (Barrett, 1982). The four fundamentalist Baptist associations which arranged the Baptist Fundamentalism '84 rally are small in comparison, with perhaps 2.5 million members altogether, but it should be remembered that members of conservative churches tend to be more active and more committed than members of less conservative churches. If one takes Baptist fundamentalists as Falwell's natural constituency, one can see that he has a considerable base, which is strengthened by it being concentrated in particular states, but which is not sufficiently strong to support a viable political movement outside the South and South West.

10. In 1965, Falwell preached a sermon called 'Ministers and Marchers' in which he argued that 'Nowhere are we commissioned to reform the externals ... our only purpose on this earth is to know Christ and to make Him known' (in Fitzgerald, 1981, p. 63). He now regards this, the position taken by the fundamentalists connected with Bob Jones's University, as false prophecy.

11. It is important to note that fundamentalists and evangelicals are not hostile to modernity generally but only to particular elements which are seen as threats to their religious culture. Ironically, it is the fundamentalists who have been fastest to use new technologies in the promotion of their message. They do not reject the material rewards of advanced capitalism. It is really only a fairly narrow range of beliefs and activities which they would reject as 'worldliness'. I have argued elsewhere (Bruce, 1984, Ch. 8) that evangelicals and fundamentalists are profoundly rationalistic in their world-view and, although disturbed by particular scientific theories and propositions, are quite 'at home' with science. It would be a mistake to see fundamentalists as archaic.

References

Barrett, D. B. (1982), *World Christian encyclopaedia: a comparative study of churches and religions in the modern world, A. D. 1900–2000* (Nairobi: Oxford University Press).

Bellah, R. N. (1967), 'Civil religion in America', *Daedalus*, 96, pp. 1–21.

Bouchier, D. (1982), *Liberty and justice for some: defending a free society from the radical right's holy war on democracy* (Washington: People For the American Way).

Bruce, S. (1984), *Firm in the faith: the survival of conservative Protestantism* (Aldershot: Gower).

Buell, E. H. (1983), *An army that meets every Sunday? Popular support for the Moral Majority in 1980.* Paper presented at Midwest Pol. Sci. Assoc., Chicago.

Carroll, P. N. and D. W. Noble (1982), *The free and the unfree: a new history of the United States* (Harmondsworth: Penguin).

Crawford, A. (1980), *Thunder on the right: the new right and the politics of resentment* (New York: Pantheon).

Falwell, J. (1979), *Listen America!* (New York: Doubleday).

Fitzgerald, F. (1981), 'A disciplined charging army', *New Yorker*, 18 May.

Gusfield, J. (1963), *Symbolic crusade: status politics and the American temperance movement* (Urbana, Ill.: University of Illinois Press).
Hadden, J. K. and C. E. Swann (1981), *Prime-time preachers: the rising power of televangelism* (Reading, Mass.: Addison-Wesley).
Johnson, S. D. and J. B. Tamney (1982), 'The Christian right and the 1980 presidential election', *J. Sci. Stud. Rel.*, 21, pp. 123–31.
Jones, B., III (1980) *The Moral Majority* (Greenville, S. C.: Bob Jones University Press).
Jones, M. A. (1960) *American Immigration* (Chicago: University of Chicago Press).
Liebman, R. C. and R. Wuthnow (1983), *The new Christian right: mobilisation and legitimation* (Chicago: Aldine).
Lienesch, M. (1982), 'Rightwing religion: Christian conservatism as a political movement', *Pol. Sci. Qtly.*, 37, pp. 403–25.
Lipset, S. M. (1964), 'Religion and politics in the American past and present', in R. Lee and M. Marty (eds), *Religion and Social Conflict* (New York: Oxford University Press.
Lipset, S. M. and E. Raab (1978), *The politics of unreason: right-wing extremism in America, 1790–1977* (Chicago: University of Chicago Press).
—— (1981), 'Evangelicals and the elections', *Commentary*, 71, pp. 25–31.
Louks, E. H. (1936), *The Ku Klux Klan in Pennsylvania: a study in nativism* (New York: Telegraph Press).
Marsden, G. (1980), *Fundamentalism and American culture: the shaping of twentieth-century evangelicalism* (London: Oxford University Press).
Melton, J. G. (1978), *The encyclopaedia of American religions*, 2 vols (Wilmington, N. C.: McGrath Publishing).
Miller, A. H. and M. P. Wattenberg (1984), 'Politics from the pulpit: religiosity and the 1980 elections', *Pub. Opinion. Qtly.*, 48, pp. 302–17.
Peele, G. (1984), *Revival and reaction: the right in contemporary America* (Oxford: Clarendon Press).
Shupe, A. and W. Stacey. (1982), *Born-again politics: what social surveys really show* (New York: Edwin Mellen Press).
Simpson, J. H. (1985), 'Status inconsistency and moral issues', *J. Sci. Stud. Rel.*, 24, pp. 155–62.
Wallis, R. (1979), *Salvation and protest: studies of social and religious movements* (London: Frances Pinter).
Wallis, R. and S. Bruce (1985), 'A comparative analysis of conservative Protestant politics', *Social Compass*, 32 (2–3), pp. 145–61.
—— (1986), *Sociological theory, religion and collective action* (Belfast: The Queen's University of Belfast).
Zurcher, L. A., R. G. Kirkpatrick, R. G. Cushing and C. K. Bowman (1971), 'The anti-pornography campaign: a symbolic crusade', *Social Problems*, 19 (2), pp. 217–38.

10 Fundamentalism and Modernity: the Restoration Movement in Britain

Andrew Walker

INTRODUCTION

Fundamentalism is a slippery concept. It seems to me axiomatic that a folk-term that emerges from within a given sub culture and in a particular historical situation, and then becomes sanctioned by extended usage through mass media and by social scientists, is unlikely to have any great precision or explanatory power. Too often sociologists, for example, have plucked a word from natural language that has gained numerous idiomatic uses, and have then attempted to hack it into shape (in the name of theorising) on their Procustean beds. The 94 sociological definitions of 'community' (Hillery, 1955, pp. 111–23) remains a salutary lesson for all would-be investigators of the social world.

Concerning fundamentalism *per se* our problem lies in whether to use the term at all and if so how to disentangle it from its Protestant origins, and separate its prescriptive elements from its descriptive components.

Whether the term itself was in fact coined in 1920 by the editor of a prominent Baptist paper (Caplan in this volume, Chapter 8) or slightly earlier, as Bruce (in this volume, Chapter 9) suggests, there is no doubt that by the mid-1920s it was a self-advertising label by many Christians who wore it like a badge of pride. To be fundamentalist was a way of opposing biblical and historical criticism as pioneered by the Ritschl school of theology and as exemplified in the early twentieth century by Schweitzer's *The Quest of the Historical Jesus* (1910).

The proud epithet, 'fundamentalist', arose within Protestant evangelicalism, but it was primarily championed by the Nonconformists (notably the Baptists and Methodists) and the newer sects (notably the Christian Brethren, the Assemblies of God, and the Elim

Foursquare Gospel Church). In no sense was fundamentalism a term that was adopted by the historic churches (with the exception for a short while of the Calvinist Evangelical wing of the Church of England).

Indeed it was as much the fact that fundamentalism was identified with various sects and working-class enthusiasms – and in particular Holiness spiritualities – that helps explain why 'respectable' Protestantism soon distanced itself from this neo-orthodoxy. Earlier sociologists, not least Niebuhr, came to identify fundamentalism with the poor and disinherited, and saw its biblical literalism as concomitant with the uneducated masses. Even today many sociologists and historians tend to see fundamentalist religion in terms of social class and theories of economic and social deprivation (for example, Anderson, 1980).

Ecclesiastical and academic reaction to Protestant fundmentalism has led to a gradual redefining of the term by followers themselves since the Second World War. In Britain, for example, whilst fundamentalism is firmly established in sociological argot, it is no longer the proud boast of Nonconformist and sectarian churches. Neither the Baptists, Brethren, or Salvationists use the term. Increasingly, Pentecostalists are abandoning it. The Elim Evangel, for example, has dropped the word 'fundamentalist' from its title page. Leaders of the new British religious movement, Restorationism, which I have recently investigated (Walker, 1985a), see fundamentalism as a label imposed upon them by opponents and reject it 'because of its negative connotations'.

Furthermore, the 'symbolic universe' of Baptists and Methodists has shifted in the last thirty years. Methodists have become increasingly liberal in their theology, and social concern has largely replaced the earlier doctrines of salvation and sanctification. The Baptist Union is now an alliance of low churchmen and evangelicals. Many of them reject the term 'conservative evangelical' as well as 'fundamentalist'. In short, fundamentalism may or may not be a useful category or tool of analysis, but it is no longer an accurate description of religious self-identification as it was sixty years ago.

In some respects academics failed to distinguish the tenets of fundamentalism from its social origins. Originally it was a form of a self-identified *Weltanschauung* by religious minorities, but was appropriated and translated into an analytical concept by disinterested (in the scientific sense) outsiders. I can say this with some confidence because the fundamentalist reaction against modernism was shared by many others who never adopted this label; neither were they so labelled by their opponents.

This holds true for many Catholics, Anglo-Catholics, and Reformed Protestants in Presbyterian and Congregational churches. The most significant figure in Protestant theology in the 1930s and 1940s was Karl Barth, who almost single-handedly held back the tide of modernism. His counter reformation (not the truth of his propositions) can be said to have been defeated when the forces of theological liberalism overwhelmed his dogmatics in the form of Bultmann's demythologising and further scientific exegetical studies.

Significantly, however, Barth was rejected by the self-styled fundamentalists who saw his work as too intellectual and denying the inerrancy principle of scripture. (No doubt many of them also disliked his socialism.)

In the 1940s and 1950s the work of C. S. Lewis stands out like Chesterton's before him as a romantic resistance to modernity. The fact that we feel unease in attaching the notion of fundamentalist to these men highlights, I believe, just how entrenched our thinking has become when we try and think of fundamentalism outside constricting boundaries of working-class sects and/or closed ideologies. This symposium, if nothing else, has attempted to tease out and flex the generic properties of fundamentalism by the rigours of reformulation and empirical example. The work demonstrated here shows that we have come a long way from the self-advertising fundamentalism of Protestant Nonconformity.

Personally, however, I think that we have also demonstrated the inadequacies of fundamentalism as a unifying paradigm that can encapsulate the many phenomena under investigation. I suspect that anthropologists and sociologists as a whole have paid insufficient attention to the social etymology of fundamentalism and its particular Protestant origins. Basically, I agree with Jonathan Webber (in this volume, Chapter 5) that what we are trying to address in this symposium – in my view, the central phenomenon of interest – is modernity understood in MacIntyre's (1981) and Berger's (1980) sense – and strategies of resistance to it.

In some respects, perhaps more than any other 'fundamentalist' group examined in this volume, Restorationists belong to the classic mould. They clearly stem from Protestant fundamentalism and they also exhibit many of the features normally associated with sectarianism. However, they can also be seen as a sociologically sensible resistance movement to modernity, and in this chapter I want to try and balance these two aspects of this new religious movement. If I am right about the centrality of modernity to this debate then it follows that the modernity-resistance model allows us not only to investigate Anglo-Catholicism and Eastern Orthodoxy and neo-orthodoxies from non-Christian religions, but also such strange 'fundamentalists' as Germaine Greer (1984) and Schumacher's circle (Kumar, 1980).

I do not want to be seen as dismissing Barr's seminal work out of hand. But his fundamentalist continuum (1977, p. 187) strikes me as a spectrum that bursts apart fundamentalism as a unifying construct. It is another way of saying that core components fit empirical examples, more or less. In this respect Nancy and Richard Tapper (in this volume, Chapter 3) not only offer us the usefulness of Barr's work, but lend weight to the argument that it does not form a coherent whole.

So, for example, the core component of 'exclusivity' fits Peculiar Baptists, Exclusive Brethren, some Islamic Sects, and Shakers. But it is not a major feature of charismatic groups (Caplan, in this volume, Chapter 8). Nor does it usefully apply to the rise of the New Religious Political Right (NRPR) (Bruce in this volume, Chapter 9).

The oppositional character of fundamentalism (Barr, 1977, p. 208) does seem to be a generic or universal feature of many new religious movements, but not in the sense that committed believers will always constitute a minority. Certainly the NRPR in North America are not a minority in Barr's sense.

Looking at the major features of Barr's Protestant fundamentalism, there arise a number of serious problems. Inerrancy (Barr, 1977, p. 47) may have been the central dogma of those neo-orthodox who opposed modernism in the 1920s. It may also be the case that we can usefully extend inerrancy to include forms of Islam and Marxism. But many charismatics reject it, and so too do some conservative evangelicals (Winter, 1980).

Furthermore, whilst Barr is correct in isolating eschatology and ahistoricity as major components of Protestant fundamentalism (which can also be applied out of its original context) he fails to see that 'reason and rationality' (1977, pp. 12–13) in modern Protestant fundamentalism is increasingly being subsumed under the emphasis on the supernatural and the miraculous. Indeed the phenomenal rise of worldwide neo-Pentecostalism[1] is essentially a religion of emotionalism, experientialism, and supernaturalism; it is not an explosion of interest in apologetical and propositional theology.

Protestant fundamentalism is undergoing mutation. Steve Bruce (in this volume, Chapter 9) shows what happens when a traditionally isolated fundamentalism gains real political muscle and steps into the political and secular arena. In Britain, whilst there is no direct equivalent to the NRPR, there has been the emergence of a kind of fundamentalism akin to the old 1920s model yet disguised in middle-class form. This formation both flatters to deceive and yet offers interesting methods of fundamentalist adaptation. This new fundamentalism is probably the fastest growing religious phenomenon in Britain[2] – which may come as news to many readers – and will be described and analysed in the rest of this chapter.

THE RESTORATIONIST MOVEMENT

The Restorationist movement in Great Britain is part of that broader classification known as the 'house church movement'. As I have shown elsewhere, however (Walker, 1985a, pp. 17–20) the so-called house church movement is a hopeless misnomer. It is an inappropriate label that has been attached to churches in houses within existing denominations, and also a number of competing extra-denominational religious structures (see Thurman, 1982). To compound the confusion, what began outside the denominations as churches in homes have now become full-blown churches with house groups attached.

A number of these churches are entirely independent, and others cohere together in small and declining sectarian movements. The most significant of these are the Chard churches, and the fellowships of Pastor 'Wally' North. By far the most controversial, well-organised, and largest of these many 'house churches' are two groups that originally formed one movement that began in the early 1970s. I call both groups Restorationism, and divide them into Restoration One and Restoration Two (R1 and R2 for short).[3] These groups cannot yet be described as stable or established sects; schism and realignment have so far been an endemic feature of their existence. Nevertheless, I believe that the evidence is overwhelming that these groups, which number some 30 000 to 40 000 members,[4] are the largest indigenous Christian sectarian formation to emerge in Britain since the Pentecostal churches of Elim and the Assemblies of God were firmly established in the 1920s.

Before attempting to show the social and religious context which gave birth to Restorationists, I want first to examine their beliefs and identify the theological matrices in which they are situated. In doing this I want also to show that Restorationists do not perceive themselves as sectarian or fundamentalist.

Restorationism is a qualitative understanding by church members of the work of the Holy Spirit. They believe that the original Church of the New Testament soon became corrupt through apostate doctrines and non-biblical ecclesiastical structures. Denominationalism is a work of Satan, and not in God's original plan for His Church. The power of the Holy Spirit was withdrawn (becoming the *deus absconditus*) and the Church fell into decay.

The Restorationists wish to return to, or restore, the New Testament pattern (as they understand it) of the early Church. Church recovery began, they believe, with the Reformation and was then accelerated under the holiness spiritualities of Methodism and classical Pentecostalism. However, these movements failed to unite the Church, and they perpetuated the sin of divisiveness because of a failure to adopt God's own government and plan for the rule of His Church. For Restorationists, then, ecclesiology is a central concern. In order for genuine revivals of the Spirit of God to go beyond revivalism and become a true restoration of the early Church, there has to be both Holy Ghost power and the rule of God's spiritual government.

This government, Restorationist teach, is based on an interpretation of holy orders outlined in St Paul's epistle to the Ephesians, Chapter four. Verses eleven and twelve are the key texts:

> And these were his gifts: some to be apostles, some prophets, some evangelists, some pastors and teachers, to equip God's people for work in his service, to the building up of the body of Christ.   (New English Bible)

From this leadership list Restorationists deduct that the Church should be run by divinely appointed apostles, prophets, and elders. Furthermore, they hold to a doctrine of 'shepherding' or radical discipleship whereby church members submit themselves to their accepted overseers and spiritual counsellors. Whilst discipleship practices are not logically entailed by apostleship doctrines, Restorationists tend to link the two together.

The belief in apostleship as both a theological and an organisational principle, when married to paternalistic social relationships and a rejection of existing denominations, gives Restorationism its cutting edge, and distinguishes it ideologically from classical Pentecostalism and evangelicalism. To say that this distinguishes it also highlights how similar it is in all other respects to well-established Protestant evangelical sects.

The majority of Restorationist teachings are taken from Pentecostalism. The 'born again' experience is seen as the initiation into the Church, and believers' baptism by total immersion is followed as a sign of Christian commitment. Restorationist eschatology is a development of the adventism of Brethrenism and early Pentecostalism. The doctrine of the 'baptism of the Holy Spirit with signs following' is the same as traditionalist Pentecostalism in North America and Europe.

If Restorationists tend to focus more on demonology than their classicial Pentecostalist counterparts, this reflects a growing tendency in the neo-Pentecostalism of the Charismatic Renewal movement (with which Restorationism is often confused).

Restorationists believe that they are living in the last days, and that they are in the vanguard of God's Church. They believe also that the Church – as defined by Restorationist principles – will grow to gigantic proportions. Starting as an alternative to the secular society, the Restoration kingdom – kingdom is a key principle for them (see Walker, 1985a) – will eventaully become a 'mountain'[5] to fill the whole earth. When the kingdom is built on the charismatic guidelines of Restorationism, Christ the king will return to claim his inheritence. The kingdom is not only a spiritual concept, it is the place – the communities – where God's reign is acknowledged and his rules obeyed.

This strong authoritarian note, of what I prefer to see as a theocratic or charismatic apostolate, is reflected in the structures of the Restorationist Kingdom. Children submit to parents, wives to husbands, all to elders, elders to apostles, and apostles to each other. This 'covering',[6] as it is called, is not to be understood purely in traditional religious terms. To be covered means that you submit your whole life – religious, social, and economic – to your elders and apostles. Members of the kingdom can not be part-time members. Commitment is total, and the idea of nominal Christianity is abhorrent to Restorationists.

The majority of Restorationists are biblical literalists, hold to a belief in the inerrancy of scripture, are scornful of denominations, and tend towards social exclusivism. All this plus their 'triumphalism' (as their opponents see it) seems like an obvious recipe for fundamentalism and sectarianism. Their belief that they live in the 'end-time' and their very ahistorical sense of the Church – 'there was the New Testament Church and now there's us' – confirms this suspicion.

Personally, I am convinced that for now[7] Restorationism fits Bryan Wilson's sectarian category of 'restored churches' (see Wilson, 1970, p. 207). This is so because restored churches act separately to and in competition with existing religious agencies but in the name of universality, and with a search for comprehensiveness that more resembles Troeltsch's notion of church than sect.

In other words, because of their behaviour and activities (and some aspects of their theology) restored churches can be classified as sects even though they see themselves as churches, or 'the Church', and seek to bring all men and women to it. Restorationists themselves vigorously deny the sectarian tag. So too did the two historical sects that Wilson cites as 'restoration churches': the Catholic Apostolic Church and the Christian Brethren (ibid.).

In this paper I cannot go into the close relationship between the earlier nineteenth-century restorationism and its present manifestation, but it is worth noting that Restorationists follow the church order and charismatic apostolate of the Catholic Apostolic Church and the evangelicalism, aggressive baptismal doctrines, anti-sacramentalism, and notion of universality of the Brethren. To be exact, the apostolic doctrines of Restorationists resemble those of the Catholic Apostolic Church, but they are interpreted in exactly the same way as they are by a small Pentecostalist sect, known as the Apostolic church, that was established at Penygroes in South Wales before the First World War.

Only the shepherding doctrines, which in practice are intertwined with the charismatic apostolate, can be said to be new doctrines in Restorationist theology. They originate in the 1960s from the teachings of Juan Carlos Ortiz, an Argentinian, and his North American counterparts known as 'The Fort Lauderdale Five'. The seriousness of commitment and the notion of 'covenanted relationships' which such teachings entail, evokes the Puritanism of the sixteenth century when all Christians were exhorted to be saints. A phrase that aptly captures Restorationists is 'Pentecostal Puritans'; they have all the fire and excitement of their Pentecostal counterparts, but with a level of commitment and totalitarian control not common in such sects.

It is the totalitarian control that has caught the media's eye in Britain and led to charges of 'brain-washing cult' and 'pyramid structure'. Whilst there have been numerous horror stories of aggressive and rough-shod behaviour by leaders, it would be more accurate to describe Restorationism as benevolent paternalism rather than outright totalitarianism (see Walker, 1985a, ch. 13). Feminists (and misogynists) would be interested to know that Restorationism is primarily patriarchal, and all leaders are men.

Restorationism appeared to erupt on the British religious scene with the suddenness and mysteriousness of early morning mushrooms. By the late 1970s people started noticing that house churches were everywhere, and almost before their eyes this mycelial structure had taken root in virtually every part of the country. Within a short time, what I call the R1 branch of Restorationism could attract about 8000 people to its annual presidential event at the Great Yorkshire Showground. The Dales Bible Week, as it was called, was matched by a similar – though smaller – event on the South Downs. The other branch of Restorationism, R2, was holding its own residential 'Festival' week at the Staffordshire showground by 1983; over 4000 people were resident in that year.

Many Restorationist communities in England contain several hundred persons. In Cobham in Surrey, Gerald Coates's (R2) community numbers over 400. Terry Virgo, apostle in R1, heads over forty churches with his 'headquarters' in Hove, Sussex, holding meetings every week for 500 people. In Bradford, R1's Bryn Jones's leading church has some 500 people. Several other Restorationist churches can boast 200–300 members.

In June 1985, Bryn Jones became Britain's first 'electronic evangelist' as he beamed the kingdom 'end-time' message around Europe via satellite. The 'Harvestime' organisation, which is a commercial enterprise that supports Jones's apostolic team, has an annual turnover of about three-quarters of a million pounds. At just two 'special offerings' taken in Wales and Yorkshire in 1985, the Bradford group in R1 raised £300 000.

And so the question arises, where did this movement come from and how can we account for its great success in just ten years? What makes this question so compelling is that against the grain of most charismatic movements, Restorationism is primarily middle-class, boasting a fair sprinkling of the intelligensia. It attracts a very high proportion of young families and a nearly equal balance of men and women.

In order to undestand how Restorationism hit the religious world with such vigour and surprise, we need to see it against yet another form of 'fundamentalism' – or reaction to modernity – the Charismatic Renewal movement (see Walker, 1984). That this is part of a worldwide movement is attested to by its appearance in India (Caplan, in this volume, Chapter 8). In Britain, it was this Renewal (as it is usually indexed) that unwittingly shielded the new sectarianism from public view, and also gave it its momentum.

A nascent yet unformed Restorationism had begun as early as the late 1950s. The pioneers, who were mainly from a Christian Brethren background, had become Pentecostalists but refused to align themselves with the classical sects. When the Renewal movement began in the early 1960s, these independent itinerant Pentecostalists at first supported it. However, their 'outsider' status left them out in the cold as far as leadership was concerned.

By the late 1960s, the Renewal movement was firmly ensconced in both Anglicanism and Catholicism. The little no-mans-land of independent churches and communities that had been pioneered by such men as David Lillie, Denis Clarke, Campbell MacAlpine, and Arthur Wallis[8] were not so much swept aside as buried beneath the surge of the Renewal. As the wave of neo-Pentecostalism engulfed whole sections of British churches, slowly, quietly, and virtually unseen, the 'house churches' began to emerge.

Few noticed that as the house churches became partly absorbed into the Renewal – borrowing their liturgical mannerisms and singing their new songs – a new and distinctive Pentecostal movement was on the rise.

The Renewal in America and Britain in the 1960s was partly religious counter-culture, and partly the self-expressionism of hedonism. Like the hippy drug-culture, Renewalism was initially anarchic, and championed non-rational reality as the touchstone of authentic experience. But just as the hippies gave way to yippies, and serious political concern and social action replaced flowers and songs, so too did the Renewal movement attempt to move on from free-wheeling liturgies, singing in tongues, and charismatic happenings, to a more theological and social expression of charismata.

This moving-on was not to the taste of the still small and unorganised house churches. Most of the people in these groups were lower middle-class and from evangelical yet sectarian backgrounds. They did not always approve of the style of liberal ecumenism of Renewal leaders. Nor did they feel happy with those who practised infant baptism and seemed luke-warm concerning the inerrancy of scripture. A number of Catholic Renewalists were neither evangelical nor conservative in their theology or politics. Would the revival disappear, wondered many of the charismatics who became increasingly restless on the sectarian fringes of the Renewal?

By 1970, in the Leprosy Mission hall, a group of leaders from the new (and still unformed) house churches began to meet, and they became known as the London Brothers. Their work, and their self-understanding, was given a significant boost by a political event. In 1971, Peter Hill, himself a member of a house church, organised what Malcolm Muggeridge called the 'Festival of Light'. This massive demonstration against the 'permissive society', and pornography in particular, attracted the house church people in droves. Many charismatics kept away from the 'Festival' because they were wary of its right-wing political support, but the house church members came in great numbers, and began to realise just how many of them there were. Two leading apostles in R2, John Noble and Gerald Coates, insist that the 1971 demonstrations were a major stepping stone to the emergence of Restorationism (Walker, 1985a, pp. 51–3).

By the early 1970s the optimism of the 1960s had turned sour for religious and secular groups alike. There was a growing interest in the occult, and the successful return of the devil in such films as *The Exorcist* gave the charismatics – emerging from their anarchic phase – the sense that the world was irredeemably evil. The house church Pentecostalists, with their roots (unlike many mainline charismatics) in evangelical adventism, saw violence and sex as the marks of Satan's kingdom. What were the holy signs of God's kingdom, they began to ask?

It is unfashionable in anthropological and sociological circles to overstress the importance of charismatic personalities. This is sensible if we want to see charismatic authority as the truly social phenomenon Weber identified (Weber, 1964). Nevertheless, given the optimum conditions, and the openly expressed needs and fears of perturbed people, it is remarkable how often powerful leaders present themselves at the right time. This is what happened to the house churches in 1971. Shortly after the Festival of Light, under the urgency of an outbreak of adventist enthusiasm, prophets and visionaries, who could discern the signs of the 'end-time', took over the leadership of the house churches. These men saw themselves as apostles and God's delegates in a new, glorious, restored Church. Their self-selection was confirmed by inner conviction, and the outer signs of prophecy. Known orginally as the 'Magnificent Seven', and later augmented to the 'Fabulous Fourteen',[9] it was this oligarchy that gathered together the scattered house churches and took them forward into an organised and successful religious movement.

By 1974 the principles of Restorationism were almost complete, and for a time there was a generic Restorationist organisation under the leadeship of the fourteen. The fact that this organisation divided in 1976 to form what I have called R1 and R2 does not detract from the success of the movements. They have continued to attract many disaffected Renewalists from the mainline churches; many of these people are middle-class, and include amongst their numbers significant defections from the Baptist Union, Evangelical Free Baptist churches, and the Christian Brethren.[10]

The fact that I have sought to understand Restorationism in relation to Renewalism should alert us to the possibility that taken together these movements are both a modern and middle-class mode of fundamentalism. Exclusivity, however, has not been a major feature of the Renewal, and R2 increasingly shows signs of abandoning it. The principle of inerrancy has not only been weak in the Renewal, but leaders in R2 have themselves been debating the issue, and show some signs of relinquishing it.

As resistance movements to modernity, the Renewal and Restorationism would seem to share two similar characteristics, which I will call the need for certainty, and a search for catholicity. Restorationism, the most radical of the two movements, adds a further dimension missing in Renewalism. This aspect of resistance I will term 'a call to community'.

Protestant fundamentalism arose in the 1920s as a response to Darwinian and historical criticism. Renewalism and Restorationism have been a reaction to liberalism in the churches begun by the publication of *Honest to God* (Robinson, 1963) and brought to a head by the debate concerning the incarnation and resurrection of Christ (See Hick *et al.*, 1977). But Restorationism in particular has also been a resistance to the social and moral changes wrought by the 'permissiveness' of the 1960s.

The problem of neo-Pentecostalism is that instead of standing against social and religious disorder by falling back on rationalism and apologetical defence of scriptures, it has swum with the tide of the 1960s mood of authentic experience and the primary acceptance of non-rational reality over propositional and credal truths. Certainty, in short, resided in supernaturalism. The sombre mood of the 1970s and 1980s has reawakened millenialism and the need to return to the scriptures 'to test all things'. In this respect the developments of Restorationism more closely resemble the fundamentalism of the 1920s than Renewalism.

Both Renewalism and Restorationism share a desire for catholicity: the return of the Spirit is seen as necessary for the whole Church. Unfortunately, for Renewalists, not all their fellow denominationalists see things this way, and therefore neo-Pentecostalism has been resisted and contained within the existing mainline structures. Anxious not to create a new sectarianism, Renewalists have opted to form grassroots interdenominational organisations: they meet in retreats, conventions, and conferences. It could be argued, of course, that this impressive interdenominationalism is a barrier to true ecumenism, and may be a sectarian implant in the heart of the historic churches.[11]

The Restorationists, as we have seen throughout this paper, have rejected reformism, and have burst out of the periphery of the mainline churches and other sectarian groups to try and build simply 'the Church'. Their search for catholicity, which is quite genuine and was a major motivation of the whole movement, was doomed to failure. Indeed, the tragedy of Restorationism is that it is predicated upon contradictory goals: not only a desire for catholicity, but also a search for purity and certainty. The second goal traps and frustrates the catholicism leading to goal displacement. Like the Christian Brethren before them, Restorationist catholicism turns out to be in practice the establishment of a voluntaristic and separatist movement.

Nevertheless, Restorationism has tapped a latent desire of Christians unreached by the Renewal movement. It offers not only (greater) certainty than the Renewal and an illusive catholicity: it creates community. No wonder that R1 and R2 are replete with young isolated nuclear families from the lower-middle and middle classes. In Cobham, for example, such young families form the dominant group. Restorationism offers nuclear families extended members, as the charismatics move next door to each other. And communities emerge (paradoxically) by association as kingdom people take over whole streets, and share their lives together in relative isolation from the world. Crèches, doctors, insurance agents, skilled workers – a virtual service industry – are available to all members of the kingdom.

The communities promote camaraderie and a real sense of identity and belonging. Unlike many evangelical circles, divorcees are welcomed and able to remarry. Such a communal structure will only have a minority appeal in Western culture where the myth of total autonomy and individualism is so strong. Nevertheless, as long as apostleship and the concomitant discipling methods continue as a form of paternal benevolence most Restorationists seem willing to cope and anxious to serve the leaders. An endemic problem of Restorationist discipling is that benevolence is never guaranteed (see Walker, 1985, a, ch. 13).

CONCLUSION

If we wish to be worldly wise (and weary) no doubt we could simply say that Restorationism, and perhaps even the Renewal, is mere fundamentalism. It certainly makes as much sense to label Restorationism as 'fundamentalist' as it does Sikh revivalism (Dietrich in this volume, Chapter 6). But then Dietrich faces the same problem as myself: she wants to say something about the nature of religious revival in the contemporary world in a way which 'fundamentalism' will not let her.

For, whilst I could clearly make out a good case that Restorationism loops back to the classical fundamentalism of the 1920s, I think it of greater significance that we should look at the sociological sensibility of Restoration's resistance to modernity. It may be true that social scientists have overplayed the secularisation thesis, but clearly while implicit religiosity abounds, institutional religion in the West seems unlikely to halt its decline. It is not the sects that are really under threat from the disengagement of broad churches from the arenas of political, economic, technological, and social life; it is the churches themselves.

Ever since Weber and Troeltsch saw the universal and comprehensive churches embracing the world, it could be argued with equal force that we have witnessed the world embracing the churches. The sacred and profane have become confusingly intertwined; theologians have adopted the secular tools of critical analysis, liturgy has become theatre, and a once anthropomorphic yet holy God has become simply *anthropos* (see Cupitt, 1979). The fragmentation of the sacred world of Catholicism and early Reformism into a myriad of relative truths hardly seems a recipe for long-term survival in modernity.

The great historical and national churches of Christendom were created and established in organically functioning communities. Their 'cultural embeddedness' can no longer be assured in the social and geographical mobility of industrial society. Sects, which are themselves a feature of modernity, see what a policy of open arms has done to the churches as they surrender to modernity. As sects
b10

seek to resist the merciless pressures of secularisation and secular ideologies they opt to shut out the world, ignore it, or re-affirm it in order to transfigure it.

The New Religious Political Right in North America is having to face the consequences of adapting the theological certainties of traditional fundamentalism to the vagaries of *realpolitik*. They would like to re-create the world as sect, but without the discipline of Islam and its purer vision, they seem to be fumbling like the Founding Fathers towards a new Jerusalem that is as safe and dull as a New England town.

For Restorationists in Britain, hovering between a pre-sectarian institutionalism and the establishment of a first generational sect, their vision of filling the whole world with the restored kingdom of God looks an even less likely bet than the establishment of 'that old time religion' as the Puritan theocracy of the United States of America. But they are already too secure simply to blow away, and they will adapt their sectarian responses to modernity as circumstances dictate.

Perhaps the central question sociologists of religion and anthropologists should be asking is not 'will Restorationism and other new sects survive modernity?' The question is: will the churches?

Notes

1. At the World Council of Churches' Consultation on the Renewal at Bossey in Switzerland, March 1980, most authorities were agreed that neo-Pentecostalism had affected between two and four million people.
2. According to the BBC's Radio 4 documentary 'Front Room Gospel', broadcast on 23 March 1984.
3. R2 did not come out of R1, as I incorrectly stated in my article 'From Revival To Restoration' (Walker, 1985b). I wrote this paper in 1983, but proofs never arrived from the publisher to allow for corrections.
4. Numbers are notoriously difficult to estimate, but my earlier guesses of 70 000 to 100 000 were certainly too large.
5. The 'mountain' is the stone that smashed the image in Daniel's Old Testament vision (Daniel 2:44). Restorationists interpret this as the Church.
6. 'Covering' means watching over, or protecting, and Restorationists take the term from the story of Japheth who covered Noah's nakedness (shame): Genesis 9:20–27.
7. The 'for now' is crucial, for, as I argued recently in a paper at All Souls College, Oxford, restorationist sects are essentially one-generational.

8. Only Arthur Wallis has survived in Restorationism from this group. He has never become an apostle.
9. Restorationists may be Pentecostal Puritans, but they are quite capable of self-deprecation and satire.
10. Working-class members have also joined from Elim and the Assemblies of God.
11. It remains to be seen whether the Renewal has a long-term future within the mainline churches. 'Moving on with God' so often, in practice, means moving out of the institutional churches.

References

Anderson, R. M. (1980), *Vision Of the Disinherited* (Oxford University Press).

Barr, J. (1977), *Fundamentalism* (London: SCM Press).

Berger, P. (1980), *The Heretical Imperative: Contemporary possibilities of religious affirmation* (London: Collins).

Cupitt, D. (1979), *The Debate About Christ* (London: SCM Press).

Hick, J. *et al.* (1977), *The Myth of God Incarnate* (London: SCM Press).

Hillery, G. A. (1955), 'Definitions of community: areas of agreement', *Rural Sociology*, 20, pp. 111–23.

Greer, G. (1984), *Sex And Destiny* (London: Secker & Warburg).

Kumar, S. (ed.) (1980), *The Schumacher Lectures* (London: Bloud & Briggs).

MacIntyre, A. (1981), *After Virture: a study in moral theory* (London: Duckworth).

Robinson, J. (1963), *Honest to God* (London: SCM Press).

Schweitzer, A. (1910), *The Quest of the Historical Jesus: A Critical Study of its Progress from Reimarus to Wrede* (London: A. & C. Black).

Thurman, J. (1982) *New Wine Skins: a study of the house church movement* (Frankfurt: Verlag Peter Long).

Walker, A. (1984), 'Pentecostal Power: Charismatic Renewal Movements and the Politics of Pentecostal Experience', in E. Barker, (ed.) *Of Gods and Men* (Macon, Ga.: Mercer University Press).

—— (1985a), *Restoring the Kingdom: the Radical Christianity of the House Church Movement* (London: Hodder & Stoughton).

—— (1985b), 'From Revival to Restoration', *Social Compass*, 32, pp. 261–71.

Weber, M. (1964), *The Theory of Social and Economic Organisation* (ed. T. Parsons; New York: Free Press).

Wilson, B. (1970), *Religious Sects* (London: World University Library).

Winter, D. (1980), *But This I can Believe* (London: Hodder & Stoughton).

Author Index

211

Subject Index

214